Heretic's Heart

Also by Margot Adler

*Drawing Down the Moon: Witches, Druids, Goddess-Worshippers,
and Other Pagans in America Today*

MARGOT ADLER

HERETIC'S

A Journey Through Spirit & Revolution

HEART

Beacon Press

Boston

BEACON PRESS
25 Beacon Street
Boston, Massachusetts 02108-2892

Beacon Press books
are published under the auspices of
the Unitarian Universalist Association of Congregations.

02 01 00 99 98 97   8 7 6 5 4 3 2 1

Text design by Christopher Kuntze
Composition by Wilsted & Taylor Publishing Services

Library of Congress Cataloging-in-Publication Data
Adler, Margot.
    Heretic's heart : a journey through spirit and revolution / Margot Adler.
        p. cm.
    Includes bibliographical references.
    ISBN 0-8070-7098-x (cloth)
        1. Adler, Margot.   2. Radio journalists—United States—Biography.   3. Women and religion.   4. Spiritual life.   5. Nineteen sixties.   6. Popular culture—United States—History—20th century.
    I. Title.
PN4874.A29H47   1997
070.9'2—dc21   96-53538

And if you ask me where I learned
To live so recklessly,
My skin, my bones, my heretic heart
Are my authority.

—Catherine Madsen, "The Heretic Heart"

Contents

Introduction

I am watching a commentator on Public Television discuss the case of a former terrorist from the 1960s who has turned herself in. The pundit tells me that the sixties were a time of darkness. Although I have heard statements like his before, I still find myself startled by his words, since I, and many of the thousands who participated in the events of that era, continue to describe them as luminous.

"Why can no one write successfully about this period?" so many of us continue to wail. "Why do we let the history we have experienced be so easily rewritten?" Over the years various autobiographical accounts have appeared, usually by men of a certain fame. They are usually sad and occasionally embarrassing; heavy on sex and drugs, with politics kept to a minimum; told with the supposed voice of experience and an odd absence of doubt, as if their authors once were lost but now truly know where they are going. But if these writers were painters you would say that their present canvases are much smaller now. And if they were starship captains you would say they had given up the search for new worlds.

I look back on the 1960s differently. Although I was part of many of the defining political events of the period—as a civil rights worker in Mississippi, as a student activist in the Berkeley Free Speech Movement, and as an American sugarcane cutter who went to Cuba with the Venceremos Brigade—by position and gender I was never considered a part of the dominant story. Accounts of the sixties by women are rare and our vision is somewhat different.

Further, for many of us politics and ideas meant more than sex, drugs, or rock and roll. Like most people that age at the time—although so few admit it even now—I was pretty inept at sex and only did it comfortably when I was alone. As for drugs, I smoked "grass" with the rest, but I was too scared to take LSD in my teens, or even in my twenties, and when I finally tried it in my thirties, the 1960s were long gone and the 1970s were giving their last gasp. As for rock and roll, when I was offered a ticket to Woodstock I turned it down. Just a commercial rock concert, I thought, perhaps a bit too smugly. I rejected much of the sixties' counterculture as decadent, but I also believed that the drugs, the sex, and the rock and roll were but the outer trappings of a rich world of ideas. I still believe this.

One of those ideas was simple. As stated every week on *Star Trek*, it was that the world is infinitely varied and that variety is to be cherished; that there are an infinite number of ways to live, to love, to create structures of society and government and community; that change is the only constant and if there is a "prime directive," it is to respect difference, to let others choose their own path in freedom, and to assume that there are always more possibilities than one can conceive.

This book is partly about the 1960s as a quest for that ideal, the 1960s I experienced. We believed that anything was possible and that everything was open to reexamination. That ecstatic sense of possibility, a feeling that is so hard to come by today, was borne out by reality; sweeping changes were happening every day, brought about by concerted human action.

But the 1960s were also about a struggle between different notions of authority: between individual and group authority, between received wisdom and intuition, between the knowledge that comes from one's own skin and bones and heart, and knowledge that comes from the ecstasy of community effort. It was also about a struggle between politics and spirit that continues to this day.

I spent most of the 1960s desperately trying to be a cadre— a revolutionary communist or socialist footsoldier, totally dedicated to the battle to change the world. I failed as a cadre, and that's part of the story. My own life today, as a journalist somewhat uncomfortably in the mainstream, and as a priestess of the old religion of nature, is an attempt to bridge two different worlds that are often at odds.

So this book is also the story of a journey, even an initiatory one. Starting with a childhood of enormous freedom, lonely daydreams, and the mysterious spiritual gifts of wild nature, it moves through an adolescence of turbulent politics and revolution, and circles back to spirit, nature, and mystery at the end.

My account of this journey starts in the 1950s, partly because the decade of the 1960s was the rebellious child of the 1950s and partly because these conflicting notions of freedom, autonomy, and community, of spirit and politics, were formed for me in that period.

The tired joke about the 1960s is "If you remember it you weren't there." But a friend of mine observes with amusement that I didn't need a good memory, I had rent control.

I have lived in the same sprawling old apartment on Manhattan's Upper West Side for forty years. In our culture hardly anyone keeps their possessions in the same place for that amount of time. I have several cartons of documents and letters from my parents' lives, much of it dating from World War II; I have every letter I ever wrote my mother, starting in the 1950s, and every letter she wrote me. And then there are two hundred pages of letters between me—a Berkeley radical in 1967—and an American soldier in Vietnam. The original impetus for this memoir came from people who had heard some of these war letters read aloud.

Living in the same place year after year, I never went through the inevitable paring down that almost everyone in my generation of mobile professionals has done and continues to do with each move. My own journals and letters from friends sat in cartons for decades; I just never got organized enough to throw them away. And while I am in terror at the hubris of anyone under sixty committing even a portion of their life to the relative eternity of the written word, I also realize how rare it is, in an age when the phone call has replaced the letter, to have so many documents from an era that has suffered from such poisonous revisionism. Much of my journey was already on paper before I sat down to write about it.

Of course, saying that doesn't mean that my memory is not still flawed, fickle, selective, and often faulty. Sorting through diaries and letters was a humbling experience. Although I had clear recollections and often a letter or a photograph would bring back a flood of pictures and memories, a few of my most vivid recollections turned out to be questionable. Reading these letters and journals has been exhilarating and disturbing; it has brought home to me how distorted certain stories may be, how apocryphal others. For example, in order to evoke some remembrances of childhood, I returned to my grammar school to find my favorite novels. Some were lost, some were exactly as I remember them, and others were two different stories tacked together in my mind. Another example: letters from a boyfriend I had remembered as a mere sexual predator revealed a nineteen-year-old who was an exquisite writer, with an astonishingly honest and poetic nature.

But the letters and journals do confirm what I best remember. For all the limitations of my generation—our unconscious actions, our unexamined ideas, our often silly phrases—we were alive to the deepest spiritual values. We believed that exploration was lifelong, that one's life work had to be honorable, creative, and transformative. We seldom thought about consumption, or the eventual need to live the good life, issues which obsess the current generation of adolescents. We believed that nothing was fixed, either in human nature or in society, and so we experimented endlessly.

We had a multitude of failures and successes. To echo the words of Ms. Frizzle, the science teacher in the wonderful series of children's books and TV shows: "We took chances. We got messy. We looked for connections." If *Heretic's Heart* can show one fraction of the ecstasy we felt in our work and play it will have succeeded.

"It's Only Once Around the Merry-Go-Round"

CHAPTER 1

M Y MOTHER, Freyda, has been dead for twenty-five years, but her exuberant energy was so intense that she still receives mail. A skeptic might say that it's the persistence of junk mail in our society that is remarkable, that explains why civil rights groups are still asking her for donations and banks are still offering her credit cards. But as I recently began to go through personal and family documents—journals and letters dating from the 1930s to the 1960s that I'd kept over the years—I came to realize that much of my life has been animated by my mother's persistent spirit, and that she, more than anyone, has a claim on setting and naming the parameters of my political and spiritual journey.

My mother died in January of 1970. She was sixty-one. She had been a heavy smoker who quit too late in life (actually, one of her friends recently hinted to me that she never really quit). Her illness was diagnosed just months after the end of a bitter New York teachers' strike in which my mother, in deep turmoil, had crossed a picket line for the first time in her life—that of her own union—to support a group of black parents. Her illness also happened at a time when she was truly happy and in love, perhaps for the first time. Just a year before her diagnosis, she confided to me that she had finally experienced "going over the rainbow." I always wondered if a small voice inside her said that she came from a suffering people and had no right to such happiness. She developed lung cancer which quickly metastasized to her brain and then her liver. The end was a lingering, unpleasant death that she only partly comprehended.

In the late 1960s, most patients with cancer were not told the truth of their situation. In my mother's case, many doctors, including a psychiatrist, decided that she did not really want to know. Their policy of disguising the truth was taken to such an extreme that when my mother asked to see her medical records, one of her doctors served up a phony piece of official-looking paper that said her tumor was benign. "B-e-n-i-g-n," she told all of her friends, "is the most beautiful word in the English language." And then she could never understand why she wasn't getting better.

Among those of my parents' generation, illness and death were rarely discussed. When I was a teenager my father waited a full week to inform me that my grandmother had died, not wanting to "ruin my vacation." And when my aunt went into the hospital some years later for cancer, I was told "it was a heart problem."

Most of my mother's friends also accepted the wisdom of the time, believing that she either did not want to know or in fact knew everything on some deeper level. At the time I felt intuitively that this policy was hellish, that my mother, a woman who planned so well for everything, would have despised such paternalism. She would have desired the truth in order to prepare for the end of her life with dignity. But I did not feel I could fight the combined judgment of seven male doctors single-handedly. I acquiesced. And I raged, silently, confused that I, a mere twenty-three-year-old, *knew*, while the most powerful figure in my life was kept from the truth, infantalized. I knew I would never again take a doctor's statement at face value and all institutional documents would remain suspect. For several years after my mother died I would take a longer route to avoid the hospital that had deceived her. And when my mother told me, several months after she'd been told her tumor was benign, "I feel like I am in a dark tunnel, and I can't see the end," I did not find myself reassured that my own silence was right.

What a character my mother was, even in illness. "How strange," my mother wrote to a friend (who had also just had a serious brush with death) only days after she was shown that piece of paper with the big lie written on it, "that both of us at the last lap of our full lives should be reborn! But perhaps this gift is only given to people capable of dying many times.... I am O.K. I was scared shitless.... But even in death fantasies I remained the manipulator, so I wondered how I could get my friends in the Juilliard Quartet back from tour to play Schubert's *Death of the Maiden* for my funeral." Four months later she had a seizure; the cancer had entered her brain and she became a shell of her former self for the last three months of her life.

While she never got the Juilliard Quartet to play for her funeral, she left a packet of explicit instructions for funeral arrangements, and even a request that the minister of the Judson Memorial Church in Greenwich Village, a man known for his radical innovations in both drama and politics, give the service. In her letter she said that although her roots were Jewish, she and this minister had talked seriously and philosophically about the end of life.

The memorial service took place on February 4, 1970. It was crowded, and although the service couldn't take place in the space she actually requested—"perhaps an open airy school rooftop"—it did have some of the flavor of joy in life that she insisted on daily. There were students she had taught thirty, forty years ago. There were old friends, but also people she had affected who simply read the obituary in the *New York Times* and came. Knowing how much my mother had defied convention in her life, we asked her mourners to contribute to the defense fund of the Chicago Eight, the activists who were on trial as a result of their leadership of the demonstrations at the 1968 Democratic Convention, rather than sending flowers. Instead, of course, most people gave money in her memory to their favorite charities like the American Cancer Society, as well as to a few groups that my mother would have probably spit on, had she still had the breath to let spit fly.

"When I think of Freyda Adler," the playwright Saul Levitt said, reading his eulogy during the memorial service,

I think of certain streets in Brooklyn, long dark mean streets and of struggling people ... frantic and worried—complex difficult people.
This is the world she came out of.
She grew out of it carrying with her a burden of fears and anxieties.
She had a preoccupation with herself, like that of a drowning person needing to stay above water, and this feeling was in her all her life.
I say all this about Freyda to begin with because it makes all the more remarkable her gift of response to others. She could be summoned out of her preoccupations—summoned out of her drowning feelings. You had to call out:
"Freyda, listen ..."
"Oh, I wasn't listening."
"Then listen."
And she listened....
Imagine that. To feel panicked and frightened about oneself—and yet have the capacity to be called out of such fears ... to have a capacity to respond.
She acted through her life for causes or for this or that per-

son or for children.... Her gift of response went wider—to
the struggle for quality education—for neighborhood control
of schools—for civil rights. But essentially her response was to
the people involved in such struggles....

It seemed that she lived in a great personal democracy. Who
else was equal among equals with so many people on all levels
of life? I know of no one who was more unselfconsciously
responsive to direct human exchange.

And within this great range of people there was a smaller
private circle—those with whom she was almost literally
constantly in touch—those to whom she said goodnight
every night—tucking them in for the night and being tucked
in herself. These were friends for thirty or more years.

I say for myself Freyda had a successful life. By which I
mean she fought back against a difficult personal heritage and
held all her life to the certainty that human exchange was primary and the rest secondary. This is what the young people
are trying to say. In some future this will seem very normal.

At the close of her life Freyda Adler had the feelings of a
young person—an enthusiastic vulnerable young person. This
is how, I believe, we all see her. Even now.

Freyda was born on Sixth Street and Avenue C, on the Lower
East Side. Her original name was Freda Pasternack. Her
mother, Rebecca Margot, never learned to read. Her father,
Moritz, was also uneducated, but he taught himself to read
and write in Yiddish. Both parents came to the United States
at the turn of the century, in steerage, and both were dead
before I was born. Freyda used to say that her father spent his
first night in the United States on a New York City park
bench. According to the story, after Moritz arrived he went
to see his brother, who had come to America earlier and had
become a successful businessman. This brother threw Moritz out on the street. That's how he ended up on the bench.

I was never told much about my maternal grandfather, except that he committed suicide in 1937, six months after his

wife died of an illness; that he left a note that said simply, "Pay so and so the five dollars I owe him"; and, perhaps most unusual, that he died by throwing himself off the sixteenth floor of the Flatiron Building on 23rd Street, the building where his more affluent brother worked. Telling this story, my mother always said that after his death she sold the family house in Brooklyn and gave most of the money away, even handing some of it out in the street. While this always seemed hard to believe, the suicide took place in the middle of the Depression, and, knowing my mother, it just might have happened that way.

But one day I was looking through my mother's papers after her death and there, in my mother's own hand, translated from the Yiddish, was her father's suicide note—a note filled with much more pain than the stories I had been told. Moritz wrote:

That I wasn't worthy of more—all my enemies will laugh and be happy. I won't see them, but, children, don't be angry with me, for alone I can't live, and I can't stand it, as I did until now. I am sad enough at taking such a step. My wife doesn't leave my thoughts for one second. I don't sleep and I can't eat. I am very lonely and nothing can save me. The more I think, the more thoughts I get. I am not writing right because my thoughts aren't right.... [then a digression about a woman he was seeing, perhaps a mistress] ... Why did I keep her? I couldn't help myself because one can't be alone everywhere. I broke down. I am no philanderer with women.... I have two children, very good ones, but I feel that I was unworthy to them—I am paying for that.

I have taken nothing from anyone.... I am afraid of people. ... I have enough money to live but I am full of woe because my wife is away from me and can't bear how my dear child Willie suffers. I have tried various ways not to be lonely, but it didn't succeed.

Will: I have 50 cases of eggs in Northern Market, five cases of Lucky's in Jersey City.

I have no more patience. This is the last writing. Good bye. I am a fool. I cannot help it.

I want to be near my wife—not to forget. Call up Eckman and tell him he should excuse me.

Reflecting on this letter, I realize that Moritz never mentioned his daughter, my mother, by name. Of course, his was a world in which boys were more valued, even though Freyda would make a successful life for herself and her brother would not.

My mother did not tell me much about her parents. I do know that, growing up as a first-generation American in a home where English was a second language, she did what so many other children of immigrants did to survive—she ran as fast and as far away as she could from the culture that oppressed her, only to return, years later, to pick up the few pieces of her Jewish roots that still nourished and sustained her, mainly a certain sensibility, a way of looking at the world, and a sense of identity, as well as a group of intimate, loving Jewish friends.

Of her relatives, she only expressed abiding love for two— her Aunt Gertie, an old radical and union organizer in the garment industry, and her brother Bill, a man who had music and comedy in his blood but who had put his love and talent aside to enter the grocery business just like his father. At one point Bill was hospitalized for many years with severe depression. When he got out, near the end of his life, he finally followed the joy of his heart, and was a volunteer comedian at hospitals and old-age homes.

The picture my mother painted of her childhood was bleak. "My brother was given the fifty-cent Hebrew teacher," she said, "but since I was a girl, I was only given the twenty-five-cent Hebrew teacher, the one where you learned to pronounce the words but not to understand the meaning." I knew that she was drawn to the theater at an early age. At seven, she said, she saw the great Yiddish actor Jacob Adler perform King Lear, and, returning home, acted out all the parts, to the delight of her family. There is a faded picture— now more than seventy years old—of her acting in a school play. She is radiant. I knew that her brother had been offered money toward a college education, which he rejected, and that my mother wanted it desperately, but it was not offered to her.

At the age of eighteen my mother left home. She worked in a candy factory and a five-and-dime, to put herself through Maxwell Training School for teachers. She also worked as a "skip tracer," tracking down people who didn't pay their bills. She met and married a violinist named Manual Compinsky, but the marriage didn't last long. Unlike many of her friends, as a teacher in the public schools she was gainfully employed throughout the Depression.

"I remember when I first met her," said my mother's friend Dena Levitt, a film editor. "She was passing herself off with this incredible story that she was half Jewish and half French. I never believed it." And, determined to escape a background that seemed to be nothing but a source of oppression, she did change her last name from its original, Pasternack, to Compinsky (the short-lived marriage) and finally to Nacque. I knew she had mingled with bohemians in the Village during the 1930s, and had associated with poets, writers, and theater people. I knew that she had gone for therapy with Fritz Perls, the founder of Gestalt therapy, and that she had refused to go to bed with him when he sat her on his lap and told her that by doing so she would solve her problems with her own father. When she told me about this she simply laughed it off; although she was fairly vulnerable in some ways, she was pretty tough in others.

Many of the stories of her adventures functioned as allegories. They either described how the world worked or were humorous escapades with a moral: spunk and chutzpah will always outfox the authorities. For example, while working in the candy factory she was admonished to stop chewing gum. But instead of complying she gave a defiant speech in her own defense, which so surprised the floor supervisor that her jaw dropped and her own gum fell out of her mouth.

And then there was the time my mother—this gum-chewing working-class kid with the New York accent—was invited to an elegant ball by a real count. She looked so much like Greta Garbo in some early photos that I could well imagine her being led around the dance floor by royalty. On being introduced to Duchess So-and-so and Viscount So-and-so she was so amazed and so sure it must be a joke, she said, that at the next introduction she gave a winning smile, put her hand inside her jacket, and said, "How do you do. I'm Napoleon."

Of course, growing up with such a woman for a mother was not always easy. She was a dominating presence, with an intense energy, and endlessly stimulating. While she was at home with physical affection and a wide range of emotions, and was so absolutely and totally unconditional in her love that it sometimes still takes my breath away, she could also be remote and lost in a world of her own. And for two crucial years of my childhood she was exactly that drowning person of whom Saul Levitt spoke—invisible, asleep, deeply depressed, diving down so far that she almost went under. She even attempted suicide after her marriage to my father collapsed.

But mostly she was exciting and embarrassing, just like Auntie Mame. In fact, Freyda carried herself in the same theatrical manner as Rosalind Russell did in the title role in the film, used her voice almost as dramatically, and dressed with equal flair, although she never possessed the funds Auntie Mame did.

My mother believed not only that life should be lived with zest, but also that American citizens had inalienable rights, including the right to get the appropriate money due one, by an insurance company for example, even if it meant lying a little. "These shoes cost thirty dollars," I remember her telling an insurance agent who had come to inspect a leak and some water damage. I squirmed inside, since they were my blue silk graduation shoes and I knew they had cost seven dollars. "You have to do this," my mother told me patiently. "They only give you a portion of the money anyway, and this way, what you get may come nearer to the damage you actually suffered." I was mortified.

My mother also believed that an American citizen had the right to call the president of a company if, for example, a department store wasn't giving the proper service which all citizens deserved. I remember, as a twelve-year-old, standing with my mother in either Bloomingdale's or Lord and Taylor, as she tried to complain about a coat that was torn. "Always go to the top," was her motto. And it was appallingly effective. Soon the manager had come to the floor and I had hidden myself behind a rack of clothes, determined not to be seen and certainly not to be associated in any way with this crazy, demented woman who was too loud and too demanding, and, God help us, was getting everything fixed exactly as she wanted it. To this day, I squirm when anyone at my table in a restaurant calls the waiter and sends back their food. And my husband tells me that I have an irritating tendency to always side with the merchant whenever he tries to bargain.

Another of my mother's mottoes was "Always go to the source." She was a natural reporter. In 1943 she told her students to look up the original pre-Disney version of Bambi.

She was elated when her students preferred the German original by Felix Salton, a sad story, without "that dopey love stuff." Still another motto: "Always act like you belong." This is one of her lessons I've really tried to live by. Once, at the age of twenty, while selling housewares in Bloomingdale's, I wandered by chance into the executive Christmas party. I ate and drank with the rest, just assuming that it was a party for all employees. Later the manager of my department, who had seen me, told me I wasn't supposed to be there. He laughed, amazed that I had just walked in and started stuffing myself with pastries. But of course, that is the very deep secret my mother taught me; if *you* act as if you belong, everyone else will think you do.

And perhaps the best motto of all: "It's only once around the merry-go-round." So do it now. Live life to the hilt. And she generally did. Of course, that motto carries with it a great restlessness—that was part of her too.

Some of my mother's greatest performances took place before I was born, and during my childhood they had achieved the status of legends. In the summer she would become very tan, so dark she could be "taken for black." I would have loved to have been a fly on the wall the day that she walked into a Miami Beach hat shop and heard the proprietors talking about her in Yiddish, assuming she could not understand. They thought that she was a "*shvartze*" whom they could cheat, and she played along until the very end, when she confronted them—I am sure in her most theatrical tones—in Yiddish, of course, the language she had grown up speaking at home.

Looking back at my mother's life, I realize she had an amazing assortment of friends. She lived a truly unsegregated life. She wandered among people of all races—artists and theater people, teachers and writers, doctors and law-

yers, the poor and unemployed—with absolutely no difficulty. She was one of the only white people I have ever met
who actually lived in a universe of true equality. I've always
thought that her secret might be that she grew up in a poor
white family and the most educated family on her block had
been that of the black doctor, or so she said. Whatever the
reason, she had absolutely no white guilt. She could laugh
and be truly relaxed with people of all races and ethnic
groups, and they with her, and, more amazingly, she could
tell people of all races that they were assholes when, in her
view, she felt they were, and they could return the favor and
remain close friends.

She seemed to make friends all over the world, and no matter what the exterior, she could tell if a person was a phony or
had a heart of gold. One day around 1960, an actor appeared at
our door, totally stoned out of his head on some psychedelic
or other. I remember him sitting in the living room, spinning
out delusions. I was fourteen and I remember thinking,
"This guy looks like Jesus Christ, and I think he *believes* he's
Jesus Christ!" And there was my mother carrying on a very
lovely conversation with him, as if it was the most normal
thing in the world, and the next thing I knew, he was painting
my mother's desk with Christlike figures. A few months later
we were keeping a hundred of his books for him. He had
been arrested with a kilo of marijuana and spent the next
three years in jail. But unfailingly my mother knew character. He paid his debt, made a life for himself, and today he
runs a business, has a family, and seems as sane as daylight.

In 1960 Freyda decided to take in a boarder, to help pay the
rent. He was a young, struggling actor who later became a
director and, still later, a professor of theater. He was openly
gay, and many of my mother's friends harped, "Aren't you
worried about having such an influence in your home with
your young daughter?" To which my mother very sensibly

replied, "I'd be much more worried if he were heterosexual." It was a sentiment that was remarkably radical for the times.

My mother's capacity for creating interesting groups, coffee klatches, and lox-and-bagel brunches out of nowhere left me deeply envious. Unlike myself, an only child who spent much of my adolescent years in a world of daydreams, she seemed to make deep friends with the greatest ease. I envied most of all the deep intimacy she had with her six or seven closest friends, the people she, as Saul Levitt put it, "tucked in every night." There was a closeness, an ease, a depth of soul that layered all their conversations. And even when I was in Berkeley, and heavily involved in the most tumultuous events of the sixties, I secretly believed that my life was not a quarter as interesting, nor my daily encounters as rich, as those my mother was having back home in New York.

But when I was living at home, my mother's flamboyance was often simply distressing. I will take to my grave her performance at visitors' day at Camp Tree Tops, when I was twelve. She came with her hair in curlers under a yellow plastic shower cap. Mortified, I longed for some of those gray, shadowy, and blissfully unnoticeable parents that were tagging along beside some of the other kids. Many years later I would come across eight sheets of paper, hidden in her files, from a therapy group she once took part in as part of a master's degree program. Each of the other members of the group had evaluated her qualities: She had a tendency to come on strong, they said, to talk too much, to talk on and on, to dominate the conversation, to push others to her point of view, to be naive, over-enthusiastic, aggressive, egoistic, to try to impress, to come on phony. But she was also, they said, humorous, warm, open, sophisticated, generous, considerate, stimulating, self-questioning, open-minded—a person with great sensitivity and depth.

If my mother's flamboyance was painful to me, even more

so were her looks. Freyda had been an extraordinary beauty. Some of the photographs taken in her twenties and thirties were movie-star quality. She was thin, with thick, dark, startling eyebrows and high cheekbones, and she was never unfashionably dressed, even when she looked beat and bohemian. As an overweight teenager I felt there was no possibility of ever living up to her beauty, and I never tried.

One day in 1963 I helped my mother into a taxi as she grimaced in pain with a gallbladder attack. Her face was drawn and pale as we hurried to the hospital. As we walked to the cab, a man whistled. "See, Mom, they're whistling for you," I said bitterly. Reflecting on this moment years later, I realized that my mother was fifty-five years old at the time, and that the man was probably whistling at me—but I could not even conceive of it at the time. By the end of high school I had learned that sexual unattractiveness was the key to being accepted as a strong, intellectual woman, as well as the best way to avoid being sexual prey. So I wore dark, shapeless clothes and refused to wear makeup, while I watched in amazement as my mother pasted on false eyelashes and shaped them carefully, bought custom-blended makeup, and never forgot to dab herself with a few drops of Joy or Chanel No. 5.

But more than her looks, I wanted the magical aura that surrounded her, that pulled fascinating people into her web, that transformed the most ordinary walk down the street into an encounter with mystery, and usually resulted in friendship. Once Freyda walked into a beauty parlor in Prague, and by the time she walked out the hairdresser had pressed a pendant into her hand, a necklace she had worn as a child in a concentration camp: so profound was their short encounter.

"Please tell me your secret," I wrote to my mother in 1963. I was seventeen and spending a month in France, living with a family that had taken in a bunch of foreign students. I was feeling outcast; the family served us meals but kept themselves apart from us. As for the other students, they were even more conservative than most Americans I knew. My mother was constantly sending me the names of interesting artists and writers and left-wing intellectuals in Paris that I should call up, but I never did. I even felt embarrassed asking for *L'Humanité* at the newsstand, since I never saw anyone else asking for it. I desperately wanted to charge boldly out into the world, but I constantly held back.

"How does it work? How do you meet all those people," I asked.

It *is* magic! I guess it is your vivacious personality. What is your glorious secret? I guess one thing is your beauty ... but, God, it's frustrating! You walk down a street and a hundred fascinating people fall into your lap. When I walk down the street absolutely nothing happens. I'm sure you would have made the most exciting and stimulating, intellectual summer out of my opportunity to stay in Tours. I try, but it just doesn't work. I always find out only at the end what I've missed ...

How little I thought of myself then. It wasn't until many years after my mother died that I understood that she had bequeathed me her energy, her optimism and her joy, and even her sense of adventure. Within months of my mother's death I realized that her passing was my own liberation, since I had always lived in the shadow of this vibrant personality. But it would take me many years to claim my own place. Later I regretted deeply that my mother never had the chance to see that her only daughter had made a good life for herself and had taken to heart many of her best lessons. Only recently did I throw out the last of her clothes, a few items of which I had clung to for decades, dreaming of a different, thinner me. And it was only when I began to look at her letters and papers that I saw her with new eyes. I saw, for the first time, her weaknesses and vulnerabilities, and I felt a great sadness that she had missed some of the great convulsive changes of our era, like the second wave of feminism. I realized the limits that had been placed on her own liberation, how much she and her woman friends had given up of their dreams and goals and creativity during the 1950s, and how little they had asked for in relationships. Of her most intimate group, all but one was divorced.

Rummaging through my mother's papers is like discovering a hundred treasures, buried insights, a complex of dates that suddenly hang together meaningfully and cast light on a story I once thought I knew.

The first pile comes from the 1940s. My father was an army psychiatrist during the war, and my parents were stationed all over the Southwest. Freyda had given up her teaching position in the New York public schools and became an announcer and reporter with an Okmulgie, Oklahoma, radio station. She even wrote a women's news show. There, among her papers, is a eulogy for FDR from April 1945. "The friend of all mankind," she wrote, "friend to the persecuted Catholic, Jew, the dark skinned ..." What she didn't say was that he was the man she cried for as she had never cried when her own father committed suicide.

And there, the faded newspaper article she wrote, "I Passed For Colored in a Jim Crow Car."

Freyda had taken a train from Los Angeles to Oklahoma just days before civilian travel was curtailed during the war. The trains were crowded, two and three people in a seat, people crammed in the aisles and sitting on their baggage. By mistake her luggage was transferred to a car that, once the train entered the South, would become a Jim Crow car, a car for Negroes only. Looking to find her luggage, she tried to enter this car, but a conductor said, "You can't go in there." When his back was turned she slipped by him, a metaphor for her whole life—she simply never took no for an answer. Finding her luggage in the car, and the car almost empty, she sat down.

She asked the occupants if they minded if she sat with them, said that she was from the North and hated Jim Crow, and the occupants said, "If you don't mind, we'd be glad to have you." The conductor came through, punched her ticket and said nothing. But they were in New Mexico, where there was no Jim Crow.

After the train crossed into Texas, there was a sudden jolt and people screamed. Three coaches had derailed and were tilted toward the edge of a deep ravine. There was a five-hour wait before an emergency engine could pick up the passengers. Freyda, experienced with children, helped the families sing songs and play games, and all distrust melted. "The children who had regarded me suspiciously as 'the white lady' now laughed and sang with me." There was lots of humor, with many in the car saying things like "It sure 'nuff serves those white crackers right," "It was the work of a just Lord that caused the accident two hour after the Jim Crow car was put on," and "Funny, there was no accident before that."

When the train got going again, the conductor came in and stared at Freyda. He said, "Do you belong here?" and she said, "I do." "Lady, are you colored?" he asked. "I don't know." "Are you white?" "I don't know. I think I am a mixture." "Lady, what are you?" "I don't know, sir. What am I?" Freyda wrote that after one conductor left, puzzled, he would be replaced twenty minutes later by conductor no. 2 and the questions would begin again: "Lady, do you belong here?" "Yes, these are my people. I belong here." "Lady, do you belong with these people?" "These are my people. If they belong here, so do I." "Lady," he'd say, "Perhaps you don't know, but this is Jim Crow territory, and if you don't belong here, you'd better come back into the other cars. It's against the law, you know." "I know, sir, but these *are* my people."

"After three or four of these interviews had taken place I began to enjoy myself," she wrote. "Between these scenes the passengers would laugh and joke about it, but when a conductor came in, their faces would be an impenetrable mask." When she finally arrived in Oklahoma, a porter insisted on taking her bag, but when she offered him a tip it was refused. "That's okay," he said. "You're my people."

The story she told was true. Tucked away in my mother's papers were letters she had received from the people on the train, blacks from Pittsburgh and Chicago who told of family troubles and wrote asking for her picture.

Through these and many other stories and sources, I slowly pieced together my mother's history of passionate commitment to integration. Another of her articles, "Don't Call 'Em Mister," tells another story of the South during the war years. Some local Democratic politicians asked Freyda to speak on behalf of Roosevelt to blacks and mixed audiences in Oklahoma. People said she could electrify a crowd. Her speeches became known through the Negro church and community grapevine, and groups all over Oklahoma began to ask for her. After the first rally, a white state senator came up to her and said, "I sure like the way you slung it to those niggers. You sounded as if you meant it." Later he told her, "Don't you believe anything these niggers tell you. Ah know you are from the North, but there is one thing you cain't do down here, don't ever call 'em 'mister.' We sure 'nuff need the vote, but there's not a white man in this state that would 'mister' any one of them jigs. A nigger will knife you in the back every time you're not looking."

In the same pile of papers, I found a small piece of yellowing notebook paper filled with typed words under the name Lotti. Was Lotti a friend? A coworker? A housekeeper?

The white man doesn't hate us, he's just plain afraid. If he
really hated us, he wouldn't trust us with his food—we could
poison it. He wouldn't trust us with his children, his babies,
we could harm them. He trust us all right. It's his own white
brother that he doesn't trust. All this talk of hate'n doesn't fool
us, he just talk hate to scare us. As long as he can believe he
hates us, and we are scared, he can keep us down. It would be
bad, if we all woke up as I did (too late tho) and realized he's
just plain scared that if we got the breaks we'd jump right in
there in his territory.

And then these words, written twenty years before the civil rights movement would bring thousands of white students to the South:

Sure it's good to have you, but it's like a feather. We need
strength here. You'll leave. How you going to build up
strength for us who must remain. Sure you show us another
way, but it doesn't mean much unless you remained here, and
made your bread and butter, and then see if you'd help us.
Only those who stay here can really help. Then you could give
strength to the good white folks who're afraid. Then maybe
we could do something.

In the end, my mother became a radical integrationist. She combined work in the arts, the theater, communication, and urban affairs. In the 1960s she ran a program to bring theater to more than 300,000 children, many of them living in the slums. But by the end of her life she was pessimistic, believing that both North and South were filled with hypocrites. "I realized as early as 1943," she wrote, "that the power structure didn't care." And when she returned to work in the New York City school system, also during the 1960s, she wrote that the demand for separatism and "black schools" was a "just punishment for the hypocrisy inherent in the feeble attempts at integration in all large urban centers."

As an administrator for a school integration experiment, she found that both black parents, forced to bus their children with no adult supervision, and white parents, who found their school's population increased by half with no new facilities, were rightly upset. Teachers and administrators had no official help from the New York City Board of Education when struggling to make the plan work. In 1968 she wrote, "People may talk as if they have a commitment to integration, but in reality they are subsidizing segregated education. If white resistance cannot be overthrown, and only decentralized black schools will do the job, then so be it." Describing herself as a member of a white minority group brought up in a multiracial environment, she said sadly that while she understood separatism, she could not support it, for to do so would deprive children of the rich diversity she had been privileged to experience.

Her experience had led her to understand—much earlier than most—that there was as much racism in the North as in the South. When she was called the equivalent of a "nigger lover," but in more polite language, during the teachers' strike of 1969, she wrote, "I learned long ago ... that we are all corruptible, and being Jewish, black or Anglo-Saxon is no guarantee against catching the racist virus. There were German Jews during Hitler who would have accepted Hitler's persecution of the vulgar, uncouth, Eastern, Polish Jews, provided that he realized that the German Jews were a different breed." As for the angry language of blacks, she wrote, "The blacks being less middle class haven't yet learned to mask their racism in white, hypocritical clichés." And as for herself, she said, "I have fought racism in any form. The real enemy in our society is the years of poverty and racism woven into the warp and woof of American life."

In my mother's papers are letters and more letters. Dense, handwritten letters from friends and neatly typed replies from famous people that she had written to, to protest or to congratulate them about something or other. Letters from Robert Kennedy and Benjamin Spock and Eugene McCarthy, and from an assortment of senators and representatives and other government officials that she had written to about this issue or that, as well as educators, actors, heads of museums. All the cards and letters I had ever written her, dating back to the 1950s. And a plain white envelope with the words "Kurt and Freyda, love letters." Inside, scrawled in her handwriting on a torn slip of yellow lined paper: "In the beginning / how could we ever have ruined such beauty! But *we* did!" The "we" is underlined. "I've left these for Margot so she will always know she came from 2 parents who once loved beautifully." Inside is nothing so grand as love letters, but little notes of endearment, holiday cards, birthday and anniversary greetings, little slips of paper attached to presents—and notes from my father, with endearing nicknames in them and occasional confessions of love.

There are also documents from the drowning period, several years that are so painful I have almost blacked them out—the years after my parents separated. My mother had discovered that my father was having a relationship with another woman, and gave him an ultimatum she was not ready to hold to: Give her up or leave. I remember my father moving into a nearby hotel, watching him slowly and in much too orderly a fashion stand inside the bedroom closet and fold up dozens of his ties, one by one, as I, a child of eleven, screamed bitterly.

My mother was, in fact, totally unprepared for an abrupt end of twenty years of marriage, and she dove into a deep depression, often sleeping until noon each day. In 1959 she spent several months at a sanitarium, which just postponed the day of reckoning. After she came home, her attempt at suicide was both a cry for help and a thinly disguised, even theatrical, attempt to reach my father. She swallowed a bottle of pills and then, she said, she saw the open door to my room where I lay sleeping and she telephoned for help. After they pumped out her stomach they gave her shock treatments. When she first awoke in the hospital after the suicide attempt, Freyda claimed, her brother's wife, my aunt Lil, was sitting by the side of her bed. Lil was a woman of difficult temperament and I had always assumed they were never very close. "My first words," said Freyda, "were 'Does he know?' And Lil slapped me across the face and said, 'He doesn't give a good goddamn!' That was the moment," said my mother, "that I began to get well."

Throughout my mother's illness I shuttled back and forth between parents. I felt a great silence around me. My father had remarried and lived only six blocks away, and life seemed more normal there. True, it was a bit grayer and less emotional, but my father and his wife, Tanya, got up early in the morning, sat down at the breakfast table, drank orange juice, and did the *New York Times* crossword puzzle. I reveled in this normalcy. At least here I had parents who were actually awake.

I blocked out most of the memories of my mother's depression and escaped to school just as graduation loomed, plunging me forward into four years of high school. Despite its "fame," the High School of Music and Art seemed rather dreary, rigid, and friendless. As for my mother's illness, I remember a body sleeping, lying under the covers, and a feeling of deep restlessness within as I waited for an awakening. Hers? My own? One day, at the age of fourteen, I went walking as the snow fell, blanketing the city. "I stand in your silence," I wrote, where the hushed world sleeps, loving that unreality.... You are a silence of peace, not like others I have known, where silence covers despair.... Your cover is a quiet one, sleep's cover is a turmoil, where the despairing sleeps to forget.... Forgetful sleep, let me never be a part of you!"

On the day I turned thirteen, my mother wrote me this:

The last few years have not been easy for you darling—you stood by and watched your mommy in great pain and it must have been very difficult and painful for you—sometimes not even understanding what it was all about—like a wounded mother deer trying to explain to a baby fawn how the hurt came about. But that is only poetic license—for people are not fawns—they have the gift of words and can explain their feelings much better (sometimes only—it's true) than animals. What did come through to you darling is that no matter what the grownups suffered and it did affect you, they always loved you and always tried to do what they thought was best for you. I know I made many mistakes my precious girl, but this too was part of my growing up, and the search for ways to be a better mother and therefore a better person.... Life sometimes is quite painful darling, often even ugly for people in their ignorance do cruel things to each other, but for the most part, take it from your old mommy, it is full of beauty and much joy. It is this capacity for living richly and fully in many moods and with many colors—it is this gift I give to you my darling on your 13th birthday—for of course you already have it!!!

Did I really have this capacity for living richly and soulfully? I certainly did not believe it. On the day that my mother got out of the hospital I did what was both a powerful step toward survival and the cruelest act I have ever committed: I told my mother I did not want to live with her, that I wanted to be with a normal family, like the one six blocks away at my father's home. I told her I didn't want to live with someone who was depressed and sleeping away her life.

My mother, in turn, did the strongest and sanest thing she

had ever done in her life. "You're my only daughter, honey," she said, "and you're living with me." Each house had its flaws, and for a while I ran back and forth, deeply torn, despite my parents' often unsuccessful attempts to refrain from using me as a political football, but eventually my mother did pull her life together.

Decades later, people ask why I am not more furious with my mother for attempting suicide and therefore for deserting me. They ask me why I'm not more angry at her for being so large a presence and making me feel so much in her shadow. But, like many divorced parents, my mother ended up as friend and confidant as much as mother. I certainly knew things about her that children seldom know about their parents, talked with her as a girlfriend for hours at a time and shared secrets with her that many of my other friends did not know. My mother was the one person to whom I could show all my feelings, so that we could fight and love and laugh on a huge scale. I could express fear, anger, and joy without ever feeling that I was being judged. Once, during the height of my teenage rebellion, we argued so forcefully that she threw a fork at me—it whizzed past my ear—the only act of physical violence from her that I remember. I, in a rage equally strong, picked up a chair, held it over my head, and for an instant seriously threatened her with it. But at the core, despite her failings, I had no doubt that I was totally loved. While I felt judged by others and by the world, I never felt that my mother's love was dependent on any action, achievement, emotion, or state of being. It was simply eternal. If anything, I felt a bit guilty that I didn't deserve such unconditional love, that I did not have the same kind of love within myself, to give to any other human being.
 {   But I still might have grown to hate her, to resent her vitality and beauty, had I not gained something else: a sense of deep optimism and joy, of always seeing the glass half full,

never half empty, of believing that life must be lived to the utmost or it will pass you by. My mother believed that luxuries were lovely to have, but that you should never put money ahead of doing work that is interesting; a life rich in friendship and adventure was always better than a secure one. My mother believed that friends were sacred, and that good conversation was usually more exciting than sex; she believed that the work you do should be chosen for love, and for its value to the world, or, as with art, because it gives people a new vision. Finally, she believed that every day could be a new adventure, and that if you looked at the world as an adventurous person, unusual events would more likely fall into your lap. My mother would never have said, in the fashion of the new age, ("You create your own reality," although she often did so. Instead she would have said, ("Shit happens; oppression is real. But if you treat the world like a joyous adventure you can surf over the shit and oppression with relative ease and be open to the constant opportunities for joy.")

It was not until years after my mother's death that I began to understand her ability to live life fully. I was in Carville, Louisiana, at the last remaining leprosarium in the United States. Leprosy is now called Hansen's disease and it is treatable. But the people who came down with it in the thirties and forties and fifties were isolated, quarantined, and stigmatized. Some of the graves in the cemetery at Carville have no names on them because families were afraid that their houses would be burned if people found out that any of their relatives had leprosy. Some of the people who were quarantined in Carville are still living there because they were separated from their families, imprisoned with no livelihood. But today these former inmates can come and go, no longer confined, because the disease is no longer contagious if treated.

In the 1980s I went to Carville to do a story for National

Public Radio, and while I was interviewing the old-timers with Hansen's disease, I met a man in his sixties who had come there as a teenager. He was a former guitar player and singer who had lost three fingers because of the disease. He still sang beautifully. At the end of our interview this man said, "You know, I have lived my whole life here. For many years I was imprisoned. I no longer can play the guitar. I have lost three fingers. But today I am happy." His face was serene; his body language was relaxed. He was smiling. And I found myself stunned to realize that he was not lying; he was filled with joy about life. He showed me the newspaper he edited, his songs, and the chickens that were running around the garden. I realized that he had made a decision to be happy— to find sustenance in his work, his singing, his friendships. Later I realized that this was my mother's deep, Zen-like lesson to me. Despite depression, shock treatments, a difficult childhood, two unsuccessful marriages, and lung cancer just at the point when she was finally living the life she desired, she experienced joy daily.

Many years after her death, I came across a collection of condolence letters. Most were the obvious kind, sympathetic notes from people who had never met her and wrote what was expected. But a director of children's theater wrote, "Whenever she addressed a large body of people, she would send out an electric charge that could unsettle or inspire." My City and Country grammar school principal wrote most strangely, "I really cannot do more than try to imagine a relationship so close and intense as yours has been—my family was always so distant and uninvolved." And then a card that said it best: "Alive, alive, she was so alive. She knew what it meant to be alive."

An Alien in America

ON A SHELF in my bookcase stands an album of 78-rpm records that my father, Kurt, brought back from East Germany in 1951. Most are scratched or cracked, occasionally even a chunk of a record is missing. Their labels bear the names of some of Bach's most famous motets and cantatas. But the labels are fake. And the records contain intellectual contraband—communist songs by Hans Eisler and Bertolt Brecht, some quite beautiful—camouflaged so that no questions would be asked when my parents went through customs on their return to the United States. Those records have come to symbolize for me the anticommunist hysteria of the McCarthy period, that spiritual winter when truth often needed to be hidden. They have also come to symbolize something central in my father's character—conventional on the surface, even a bit stuffy, yet radical underneath, with a certain secretiveness that made him keep much of his life to himself—something that is true to this day.

Back in 1951 I was five years old, and my parents and I were living in an apartment on the Upper West Side of Manhattan, overlooking Central Park. By then my father, who was the only son of Alfred Adler, of "Freud, Adler, and Jung" fame, had put his wild youth behind him and become a psychiatrist just like his father. (Interestingly, my father didn't settle down until his own father died, in 1937.) The second youngest child of four, my father was born in 1905 into a world of educated and assimilated Austrian Jews. He had nannies and went to elite schools, but detested their authoritarianism; he was thrown out of one school at the age of seven, after he told a classmate the truth about where babies come from.

As a young man he was apparently charming, and he spent so much of his time at the Herrenhof Café (where he won quite a bit of money at cards) that he used the café's address for receiving his mail. He earned a Ph.D. in physics at the University of Vienna, and, like his father, was also very musical. As a child, he sang in the Vienna Philharmonic Chorus under Bruno Walter, and as an adult he played the recorder superbly, even into his seventies. He later became friends with one of Brecht's musical collaborators, Hans Eisler. (I still possess, folded up among my mother's papers, Hans Eisler's telegram when I was born: "We are delighted about Margot Susanna's avant-garde spirit. Started to compose Cantata. Great love to you and the new Easter Rabbit from Uncle Hans and Aunt Lou.")

Perhaps not surprisingly for the son of a world-famous psychiatrist, Kurt's politics picked up where his father's social democratic leanings left off. At one point, he even belonged to a communist youth group in Vienna, and all his life he dreamed of achieving a synthesis of his father's psychological theories with the theories of Karl Marx, a goal he never fully achieved.

My father recalls that he always felt close to his father. One summer the teenage Karl Popper, who later became a great philosopher of science, came to Alfred Adler complaining about having a worm in his head. My grandfather told Popper that there was nothing really wrong with him and asked my father to spend a day hanging out with Popper. "What happened to the worm?" I asked. "It went away," replied my father.

The abrupt termination of a great tale about himself is typical of my father's style. He has always been very taciturn about the particulars of his past. Is it modesty—this is, after all, a man who has devoted his life to furthering his father's ideas about psychotherapy—or is it something more? To tell the truth, for years I suspected that my father led a secret life, since there were so many blanks. For example, during the 1920s he was briefly married and then divorced, but apart from that bare fact, that's all I know. My father would often tell a story about his childhood where the punch line was "... and my father said to me, 'never trust authority.'" That story, along with his admiration for Stalin (he didn't dispose of his edition of the collected works of Stalin until the late 1970s), suggests a lot about the contradictions within his character, even if it leaves them largely blank.

Most people think of the 1950s as a golden age, when young girls were supposed to be joyfully obsessed with crinolines, dances, and crew-cut boys driving flashy cars, and everyone liked Ike. But my upbringing was shaped by other forces and left me alienated from the symbols and rituals of the mainstream culture. I not only had a glamorous, charismatic mother to contend with, I was raised by left-wing parents in New York City—one of the few places in America where even during the McCarthy period there were enough communists and socialists to achieve the critical mass for an alternative community, a parallel world complete with schools, clubs, and summer refuges where we felt comfortable, the kind of places that Western Europeans of my generation still take for granted.

As usual in my family, it was my mother who told the story that captures the complexity of my world the best.

"We were riding on a bus in mid-town Manhattan," she

would begin, "and it was just after Gerhart Eisler escaped on
the *Batory* ..." The *Batory* was a Polish ocean liner; Gerhart was
Hans Eisler's brother. A year earlier, in 1948, Hans had been deported from the United States for having joined the Communist Party. Hans had no desire to leave, but he made the best of
it and even went on to write the East German national anthem;
there are many who, having heard the anthem played at hundreds of Olympic ceremonies, might say its journey into oblivion was the only thing worth regretting about the demise of
the German Democratic Republic. (My mother always claimed
that Hans was an artist first and was actually not very political;
he might have joined the Party, she said, but he hadn't done
much about it. When Hans was ordered to leave the United
States, many composers and musicians rushed to his aid, including Leonard Bernstein and Aaron Copland. My mother
helped organize a concert of his music at Town Hall.)

"But you knew Gerhart—his brother, too—" my mother
would gush, continuing the story, "and he gave you a red toy
piano." (Its color is something I've always wondered about.) Although Gerhart and Hans had both come to the United States
as refugees, unlike Hans, Gerhart was a serious communist
who would later have a position in the East German Government. "Anyway, Gerhart had escaped on that ship, and we were
riding on the bus, and there were headlines all over the newspapers: 'Atom bomb spy escapes on Polish ship.'" I have no idea
how "atom bomb spy" got into my memory of the tale, since
there is no reference to Gerhart having any knowledge of
atomic secrets. "And there was this picture, and this headline,
and *you*," my mother would laugh with the amazement of it,
"you looked at somebody's newspaper and the picture, and you
said, absolutely loud and clear, 'Look Mommy, Uncle Gerhart,'
and I grabbed you by the arm and we got off that bus as fast as
we could!"

It wasn't until 1994 that I went to the public library to find out what headline I might have actually seen in May of 1949 as I sat on a bus with my mother. New York City had seven newspapers at the time. Some of them—the *New York Times*, the *Herald Tribune*, and the *New York Post*—were too staid to use such an inflammatory headline. But tabloids like the *Daily Mirror* had the right feel: "Report Eisler, No. 1 Red, Flees." Or, two days later, "Battling Eisler Hauled Off Ship" and "Drag Eisler Ashore."

My mother's action on that May afternoon, rushing me off the bus as quickly as she could, will be understood by anyone who lived through the McCarthy period. Although the Korean War was only a background murmur in my life, and the Army-McCarthy hearings just a phrase, by the time I was ten or eleven I had a sense that the world out there was dangerous, and that I was somehow a stranger in my own country, not because we were Jewish or because I was the granddaughter of a famous psychiatrist, but because we were sympathetic to ideas that others considered alien and subversive. I knew that there were certain questions that you didn't ask people and certain things you didn't say, and yet I was the kind of person who sometimes told the most intimate details to perfect strangers!

The evidence was clear. During the period when my mother was helping to organize the Hans Eisler concert, for example, our phone would occasionally ring, and when my parents answered it they would hear a recording of "The Star Spangled Banner." I knew that some of my parents' friends had lost their jobs, that others had been questioned and brought up before committees. I met many blacklisted playwrights and actors, including Zero Mostel, and I attended parties for Alger Hiss. I knew that you never asked anyone if they were a member of the Communist Party, and I knew that if you were asked such a question you always refused to answer, even if the answer was no, because for reasons that I never really understood when I was young, people who answered that one question before investigative committees had to then answer everything else about *everybody*, including their friends, and if they didn't, they were thrown in jail. I knew that Hans Eisler had been deported and I knew many Eisler songs by heart. I also knew all about those contraband Eisler recordings and their false labels.

And then there was the day that my family had hastily run down to the passport office, even though no trip to Europe was being planned, because a new law was about to go into effect demanding answers to questions that, in my mother's words, "were none of their damn business!"

Because my parents were sympathetic to communism, some of the experiences that would unite Americans most deeply were denied to me. When President Kennedy was shot in Dallas, a day almost every American over the age of forty-five remembers, my family did not mourn. Although I sat glued to the television set for the next three days, numb and in shock, like everyone else, this man was not my family's friend: He was the president who had invaded Cuba and he had, in the view of my family, precipitated the Cuban missile crisis a year earlier. Worst of all, there was the authorities' insistence that Lee Harvey Oswald, accused of Kennedy's murder, was not only a communist but a member of the Fair Play for Cuba Committee. Since everyone in my family supported the Cuban revolution, and had probably even given money to this very same organization, an organization I think my mother had even *joined*, we were all quaking in our shoes for weeks, in fear that we would become targets.

Despite these ties to socialism, there was surprisingly little ideology in my family. Just as in some families art and culture are a substitute for religion, in ours socialism operated as a kind of metaphor for being good, cooperative, and helpful to others.

As early as I could think about things, I knew one was supposed to be generous, and that I tended to be selfish. From the trip to Europe when we brought back the Eisler records there is a picture of me drawn by a German artist/baby-sitter. I am standing in a castle in Germany, holding two beautiful peacock feathers, one in each hand. And underneath the picture, the baby-sitter has written: "Margot: 'Look what I've got! Two peacock feathers and what nice ones they are. But you know, I have thought about it. If there came a poor child—let's say an orphan, and I had four or five feathers, I would give him one. I might even give him one of these two, but then—of course—the uglier one. Or shouldn't I?' " At five I was already excruciatingly sensitive to the notion of rich and poor, and since 1951 was not a time when the homeless were lying about on the street, as they are now, I can only conjecture that the gulf between the poor and the rich had been explained to me early. Later I was told that the only time I was ever slapped was when I brought the word "nigger" home from the playground, something I do not remember.

It was not until 1960, when I was thirteen, a time soon after my parents' divorce, that I finally asked my father what communism and socialism really were, and why people who believed in them were persecuted in America. My father took me into his study and talked to me for over an hour. I felt so adult, so trusted; the minutes seemed to glow with significance. He told me that communism and socialism were originally the same thing, that they sought to bring about a world where people would share things in common, where each would work to the best of his abilities and each would have what he needed. There would be an end to selfishness and greed, and the only remaining problems would be the continuing dilemmas of living and working and loving.

I asked him if he was a communist. He asked me what I

meant by the word. I asked him if he was sympathetic to communism. He said he was. I asked him if he was a member of the Communist Party, and he said it was difficult to answer, but he had never been a member of the Party in the United States. (In truth, he had only been a member of a communist youth group in Austria—perhaps he was making his life seem a bit more dangerous and romantic than it was in fact.) "I hope no one sees this page in my journal," I wrote solemnly, "because, today, people ignore the Bill of Rights."

That same year I began to be interested in politics. My mother's stories of her youth, her experiences in the Depression and campaigning for FDR, her work during World War II, seemed filled with vibrancy. "Why," I wrote in my journal, "was life so exciting then and why is it so dull now?"

The day I joined my first political organization remains vividly etched in memory. I was riding home from school on the subway. A girl was sitting across the aisle and two boys stood in front of her, talking. "You know that feeling?" I wrote in my journal that night, "when you see someone and suddenly, without knowing why, you think to yourself, 'I really want to know those kids.' You know it just by looking at their faces. You know that somehow these kids think the way you do." Oh how I desperately hoped that at least one of them would get out at my stop. I waited and held my breath. I had to say something to them. But what? Of course you could never say what you really felt: "You look so friendly, and happy and relaxed, and so utterly the opposite of what I feel—aloneness! Oh to be in your midst!"

Amazingly, one of the boys did get out at my stop, and as we walked up the steps to the street I managed to ask him the only thing I felt I could ask, what school he went to. But then suddenly I saw someone I knew, Tommy Hurwitz, a boy a year older than me, running toward us. "Hello, Daniel," he said to this absolute stranger. And then, "Hi Margot." And they began to talk politics. Within minutes they had signed me up as a member of a high school peace group, as well as a member of CORE, the Congress of Racial Equality. I soon joined two much more radical groups, the Tom Paine Club, a discussion group, and the FDR Four Freedoms Club, an activist outgrowth of the Tom Paine Club.

One weekend in April, only days before my fourteenth birthday, I participated in my first demonstration—against Woolworth's. Two months earlier, four black students in North Carolina had sat down at a Woolworth lunch counter and had been refused service. Similar sit-ins had quickly spread all over the South and were now encouraging sympathy demonstrations in the North.

I went with my friend Kathleen. There were only about six whites, including us. We walked around in circles shouting, "One, two, three, four. Don't go into Woolworth stores. Five, six, seven, eight. Southern Woolworth segregates." Soon after this I walked twenty miles on a march for peace, and after I entered high school I joined with other students to protest civil defense drills. In these absurd exercises, instituted in the 1950s, we practiced protecting ourselves from an atom bomb blast by crouching under our desks and closing our eyes. I still have an armband with the protest "No CD [civil defense] drills" stamped on the yellowing cloth in black ink.

But while peace and civil rights seemed reasonably clear, communism was confusing. I knew that the world was divided into individualistic and socialistic societies and that most people in the United States thought everything Russia and China were doing was monstrous. But I also knew that good people whose opinions I respected believed exactly the opposite. "There must be a reason," I thought. "Maybe I'm not hearing the whole story." One day I thought hard about the fact that the Soviet Union would refuse to publish certain articles or

books. I also knew that there were books that were so contro-
versial here in the United States that they had been rejected by
every publisher, and my father argued that it was really the
same. But, I thought, wasn't it better to have individual publish-
ers judging books than the government? I knew that there were
communist publications in the United States, yet they were
small and hardly anyone had read them. They were allowed,
but perhaps this was only because they were small and powerless. It was deeply perplexing.

I wondered about the Soviet purges, about the millions of
people who had been killed. There was nothing theoretical
about this. I knew that my father's oldest sister, Valentine, had
been killed in Siberia by Stalin, in 1942. My father and my
grandmother never spoke about Stalin in each other's presence. Vali's fate at the hand of Stalin functioned like the ele-
phant in the living room—it was there, hanging over everything, but no one talked about it. To me, my father simply said
that "a revolution is not a party." Yes, millions were killed during the Chinese revolution, he told me, but many more were
killed by starvation before the communists came. "This is no
answer!" I wailed into my journal. I also pondered whether it
was more important to have all your individual liberties or to
give up some of them to gain social advantages.

There was also the Berlin Wall. How could it be justified?
The freedom to go where you wanted seemed to be a basic
right. But in 1962 my father sat me down and said that the
Berlin Wall was really about economics. After the Second
World War, he explained, the German mark was replaced by
occupation money; each sector had its own currency. Eventually the Western sectors changed the value of their curren-
cies, so that four East German marks were worth one West
German mark. Many people were living in the East, where
rent was cheap and medical care was free, and working in

the West, earning the more advantageous West German marks. You could buy something in East Berlin for fifty marks, sell it in the West for fifty West German marks, and then trade that money in for two hundred marks in the East. Corruption was rampant, my father said, and East Germany was suffering severe economic losses and a shortage of workers—that was why the wall was built. It seemed to be part of an answer, but not enough.

And then my father showed me a map. I remember it very well since it was so startling: in my mind, being an American, I had a notion of this place called East Berlin that was locked behind bars, but when I looked at the map I realized that it was West Berlin that was surrounded, that West Berlin was right in the middle of East Germany. I still didn't feel good about the lack of freedom, but I did realize there was something we (Americans) weren't seeing. And looking at it both ways made me feel even more of an outsider.

"I've been having these really weird daydreams," I wrote in my journal that fall, after I had started high school. I had begun imagining myself as a seventeen-year-old girl named Yvonne Zorin. She was the daughter of Vladimir Zorin, a Russian diplomat. She lived in New York, at the Russian mission to the United Nations, on East 68th Street, and in my fantasy she fell in love with an anticommunist conservative. "You can imagine the adventures that arise." I had this daydream over and over for several years; later I changed it to become the daughter of Andrei Gromyko, another Soviet official. In my diary I created drawings of myself as Yvonne Gromyko, and every day as I descended into the subway at 96th Street and emerged at 135th Street and Convent Avenue, and then walked into a park and slowly up the endless steep flights of stone steps to get to the High School of Music and Art, I started another version of this reverie.

As the daughter of communist sympathizers in a land where communists were persecuted, this notion of being a stranger became central to me. It became the pattern of a dozen other daydreams: the persecuted Quaker in Colonial America, the telepath in a land where telepathy is a crime. Some of these characters, the Egyptian slaves and Greek pythias and goddesses, came out of novels I had read; others simply bubbled up from my unconscious. But in each scenario I was persecuted, ostracized, snubbed, and in all of these settings I was never the selfish, angry person that, deep down, I usually thought I was; I remained gentle, calm, generous of spirit. I spoke warmly and kindly, slowly winning the friends I needed to survive.

And it wasn't just politics that made me a "stranger in a strange land." There was the Adler "thing." I was also the only grandchild of Alfred Adler, the founder of individual psychology and one of Freud's earliest and most famous collaborators. The Alfred Adler Consultation Center and Clinic was located in the same apartment building where I lived, and there was an Adlerian therapist living next door. I had mixed feelings about this heritage; I was both proud of it and wary. One day an employee of the clinic told me, playfully, that I was going to become a psychiatrist and have ten children who would follow me in the profession. I vowed at that moment that I would have nothing to do with it, and I managed to go through college without taking a psychology course.

Today Alfred Adler is remembered for the terms "inferiority complex," "lifestyle," "compensate," and "overcompensate." He discovered the importance of birth order, and emphasized the importance of power issues (issues of mastery, really) over sexual ones. At least my parents weren't scrutinizing me for evidence of penis envy, Oedipal drives, or oral fixations (unlike some of my friends, I was blessedly protected from Freudian notions). The only thing that was beaten into my head was the Adlerian notion of "social interest," which, while never clearly defined in my youth, seemed to have something to do with being cooperative and merging your individual desires with the needs of society—rather like socialism.

I never knew my famous grandfather because he died in 1937. However, my grandmother, Raissa, was part of my childhood. (She died when I was in high school.) She was a Russian intellectual, a Menshevik, and later a good friend of the Trotsky family. I later learned that her marriage with my grandfather was often troubled and there were several periods when they lived separately. Given Raissa's intellectual interests, she may have found child rearing tedious. Raissa's children held their father in awe, and didn't speak much about their mother: my dad gave his father's letters to the Library of Congress; he gave his mother's letters to me.

My recollections of Raissa are of an old, white-haired woman who wore dark clothes and black, old-fashioned shoes. She never really mastered English, and I spent many of my visits to her small apartment on West 68th Street trying to learn Russian, which never got very far. While she was happy to see me, she seemed emotionally distant and her life remained a mystery. During most family visits, my father and his two sisters, Alexandra (Ali) and Cornelia (Nelly), would speak to Grandma in German, which my father had resisted teaching me, perhaps because of lingering feelings about Nazism and the war. Raissa seemed lonely and only really at home with her books. She never talked with me about her past, but she had gone to school in Switzerland and had studied biology and the natural sciences. (When she was a girl, universities in Russia were closed to women.) My father told me that during the mid-1890s she returned to her homeland and smuggled the works of Marx—then illegal in Russia—back into that country. Later, after she had moved to Austria, she was close friends with Trotsky and his second wife, and was an active member of the Austrian Communist Party, until she was thrown out for her Trotskyist sympathies.

My father tells two stories about the Trotskys. The first dates from the summer of 1911 or 1912. The Adler family had rented a summer house outside of Vienna that was built on a hill. My father, then a boy of six or seven, liked to climb up a fence to the porch on the second story. One day, after reaching the porch, he saw the scariest woman he had ever seen, talking with his mother. The woman looked like a witch from a fairy tale. He was so frightened that he fell backwards off the porch and onto the ground. The woman was Mrs. Trotsky. My father also recalls playing soccer in a park with Trotsky and his two children. Soccer was forbidden in the park, but somehow Trotsky persuaded the guard that these very young children kicking a ball around didn't violate the regulations.

Since the Trotsky stories contained relatively little substance or feeling, I treated them lightly. But one day a few years ago, an old family acquaintance said casually, "It's amazing that the Adler family managed to survive. After all, Stalin's henchmen were ruthless in their attempts to get Trotsky and his associates."

My father's oldest sister, Valentine, was also a communist. She moved to Moscow with her husband, a Hungarian journalist. Her links to Trotsky and to Karl Radek, the editor of *Izvestia*, proved fatal. Sometime in 1937 she and her husband were imprisoned. No one knew for sure about Vali's fate until members of the Adler family approached Albert Einstein for help; Einstein was able to learn that Vali died in a gulag, a Soviet labor camp, in 1942. Everyone said that Valentine was Alfred's favorite, and that Vali's imprisonment so agonized him that it led to his heart attack and death while lecturing in Scotland in 1937. Alfred's youngest daughter, my Aunt Nelly, told me that Raissa had written letters to the Soviet authorities pleading for her daughter's freedom, which Nelly thought put Vali in more danger, since Raissa's sympathies for Trotsky must have been known.

The rest of my father's family fared better due to my grandfather's foresight. Adler decided to move to the United States in 1929, and he had managed to move most of the family, including my father, by 1935. My father's sister Alexandra was one of the first women neurologists in Vienna. In the United States she taught at Harvard and Duke, before becoming a psychiatrist. Nelly, the youngest in the family, became an actress in Vienna and had a brief stage career in the United States, but was hampered by her accent. She married, divorced, had no children, and eventually died of cancer. Kurt, my father, outshone by his brilliant older sisters, bore the heavy burden of being Alfred Adler's only son. The father I knew rose early, dressed and shaved speedily, and was always punctual—facts that were at odds with the portrait of him as a youthful bohemian who got up at noon and received his mail in cafés. When I asked him what had changed, he joked that he had never adjusted to the five-hour time difference between Austria and America: "Why, getting up at seven is no different than getting up at noon in Vienna."

My father had grown up in a Viennese family that was so assimilated that he was totally ignorant of Jewish culture. Alfred Adler had converted to Protestantism in 1904, and the Adler children grew up celebrating Christmas in the Austrian fashion, on Christmas Eve, though in a totally secular manner. My father's world, the world of the Austrian intelligentsia, must have seemed liberating, at least initially, to someone like my mother, who felt she had escaped from an oppressive, impoverished, and uneducated Jewish family.

My mother always said that when she met my father, sometime in the 1930s, he had monogrammed underwear—as if that explained everything. He had been brought up by nannies, had gone on summer vacations, and had enjoyed privileges, while she herself was poor and her mother illiterate. Before they met, both my parents had had what is being referred to these days as starter marriages—that is, they'd married early, had no children, and divorced (this in the 1930s, when according to our current myth, divorces didn't happen).

When I came across my parents' marriage certificate, the date—October 1937—startled me. Fascism was exploding in Europe. Freyda's mother had died in June; her father would commit suicide two months later. Valentine was in a Soviet prison; Kurt's father had died suddenly the past spring. Yet no one had ever spoken to me of the possibility that a series of crises might have helped bring these two people together. And today my father no longer remembers how they met.

Growing up in the atheist, semi-Marxist, non-Jewish, Jewish home my parents created, it took me until I was about five to learn the name of our religion, and even then it was only because I finally asked. "We believe," I was told, "in the brotherhood of man." It was a statement that I knew had something to do with people being good and treating each other with respect, but many questions remained. What *was* the brotherhood of man, what did it *feel* like, and did it include *me*? Perhaps, I thought, it was like the word *mensch*, a word that on the surface simply meant a human being, but was tinged by the emotions of my family and friends to mean a real person, a good person, a person who is generous and loving—a progressive, a person that lives according to good values.

And my family did. Although during the middle of my teenage rebellion, and in my own anger at my parents' divorce, I would scream at my father—that he was a hypocrite, that he talked a good Marxist line but my mother had actually done more politically, that he spoke of a beautiful society while making a wreck of his own family—in actual fact, both my parents did live pretty much according to their principles.

And although, given his age and his era, my father had a tendency to expect his wives to cater to him, he preached gender equality before it was fashionable, and he was a talented therapist to a group of well-known feminist writers. His tastes were simple: he had no car, no credit cards, no country house, no assortment of those gismos and gadgets that most baby boomers today expect.

But our religion, the Brotherhood of Man, seemed pretty sterile, despite its high ethics, and I grew up believing that my Catholic friends had a better deal.

Then, in 1951, my mother had an experience of recognition and revelation that brought her back to her Jewish roots. It took place during that same trip to Europe that brought back the Eisler records with their Bach labels. She later told the story with such passion that it seemed almost sacrilegious to question any part of it.

"The family had arrived in Berlin," my mother recounted, "and we were waiting to change planes when a German official came up to us and said, 'Ihre Papiere, bitte!' [Your papers, please!] And suddenly, at that moment, I smelled the fires of Buchenwald in my nostrils." Then we entered the plane and my mother sat down with me next to a very old rabbi with a very long white beard. "You were sitting in my lap," she said to me, "and you began to play with his beard. You stuck out your tongue and began to lick his beard. I asked the rabbi if we were disturbing him, and he said, 'Nein.' Then he leaned over and whispered, 'Sind Sie eine Deutsche?' [German?] and I said, 'Nein.' And then he whispered, 'Sind Sie Jüden?' and I screamed, 'Yes! And what's more I speak Yiddish fluently!' " My mother said she spent the rest of the plane ride conversing in the Yiddish she had spoken as a child.

When we returned to New York my mother told me, "You're Jewish!" To which my father replied, "No she's not!" Both statements were true. My father was so totally assimilated he had not even been circumcised, much less been given two seconds' worth of Jewish education. But my mother said that not only was I Jewish because I was her daughter, but that anyone Hitler considered a Jew *was* a Jew, and therefore she and my father were equally Jewish, even if my father had no idea what being Jewish was about.

Now that my mother, who had once changed her name and invented stories of a partly French origin, had decided she was Jewish, she decided to embrace Jewish culture. So Freyda called up relatives with whom she had almost nothing in common and invited them—perhaps to their great embarrassment—to a party to celebrate her rapprochement with her heritage. To my father, who grew up with no such traditions, my mother's new enthusiasm seemed bizarre. By conviction an atheist, and brought up in an ostensibly Protestant home, Jewish religion and culture had no echo for him.

I have always believed, rightly or wrongly, that the seeds of my parents' disaffection began with that plane trip from Berlin, and in fact, within a year my father (not always the prince of tact) had said within my presence that he *liked* my mother, but he did not love her. Whatever the truth, the question of my Jewishness would forever in the future involve conflict. Was I in the box or outside it? Was I my mother's daughter or my father's? Being Jewish seemed to mean choosing, something I was determined not to do. And in the end, such religious discord, coupled with my clear love of ceremony and classical myths, propelled me toward a very different religious community.

My Secret Gardens

"How I wish that somewhere there existed an island for those that are wise and of good will."   attributed to ALBERT EINSTEIN

K ARL MARX never gave a concrete picture of the ideal socialist society of the future, but from an early age I knew what it looked like with absolute certainty. I knew all about the perfect society, the one my parents spoke about as more humane, more beautiful, and more just, for I had already been there. Utopia was the island where these socialist writers and artists and thinkers were spending their summers, and it was the schools to which they sent their children.

By the end of the 1950s I had already experienced the state that had withered away, a world of freedom and autonomy that most young girls in the 1990s would find inconceivable. Despite the battles my parents' generation experienced during the cold war, their children lived in a protected oasis. In the 1950s I was a barefoot minstrel beholden to no one.

Starting in 1952, when I was six, my family used to go to the island of Martha's Vineyard every summer. We would rent a car, and we would rise before dawn in order to miss the rush-

hour traffic. I would be silent during most of this six-hour journey, sitting alone in the back of the car next to piles of boxes
and luggage, the window opened wide and my head stuck out
as far as possible, wind rushing across my face, hair blowing
and tangling until it was a mess of knots. Even at that early age,
although I did not have the vocabulary to express such a
thought, I understood the ride as an initiatory journey.

First there was the struggle to pack the car, then the first
moments of leaving the city dirt as we drove North. Then Con-
necticut, a three-hour purgatory. After the inevitable traffic
jam in Providence, we would come to the blessed state of Massachusetts. An hour later, we would arrive at the ferry in Woods
Hole that would take us to the promised land.*

As we approached the other shore, a magic event: just before
the return to the car, I would take off my shoes and later stuff
them into a corner of the trunk—it was a matter of pride that
I would not put them on again until two months later, on the
long trip home.

Then came the test and the sacrifice: the days of necessary
pain I would bear each summer to make my feet tough enough
to walk freely everywhere. I stubbed my toes on hot macadam,
scraped patches of melted tar from my heels, removed several
splinters, even once a rusty tack requiring a tetanus shot,
limped over pebbly coastlines, ran as speedily as possible over
torrid sand at midday, and tiptoed lightly over gravel that was
mixed with sharp pieces of clam and scallop shells. But within
two weeks my calluses were thick and hard, and I was able to
walk anywhere. I was once again a free being. Barefoot was a
matter of honor.

Besides walking, we hitchhiked, and in those days, at least

* The quote that serves as the epigraph to this chapter led a Martha's Vineyard woman to create a series of popular tee-shirts and bumper stickers
printed with the phrase "Grace Happens."

"up island" in the more rural part of the Vineyard where we lived, it seemed natural and safe, even for a nine-year-old girl.

Along the roads of Chilmark, there were blueberries and blackberries and huckleberries for the picking, and by Labor Day there were beach plums. My friend Kathleen and I would find secret hideaways and abandoned barns, filled with old furniture, that became clubhouses. We would sweep out the bird droppings and the spider webs and have a place that was ours alone.

At one point my parents were one of a number of families that rented houses on an old estate, called Dunroving. Kathleen lived with her family in the converted windmill; we lived in the former stable. Hundreds of Canadian geese roamed the estate and lived by the pond, and there were box turtles that sometimes grew to enormous size. There was Indian paintbrush by the side of the pond and water lilies within, and huge and glorious dragonflies with green and blue hues that would dart in and out over the water. There were fields of wildflowers: daisies and yarrow and dandelions and purple bachelor buttons and tiger lilies. There were wild roses and Queen Anne's lace and milkweed. I must have mutilated hundreds of daisies and dandelions in futile attempts to make chains and wreaths, and I later harbored a secret fear that if reincarnation was true, I would come back as the swallowtail butterfly I caught and killed with formaldehyde during a thankfully fleeting collector phase.

There were many skills to learn here—how fast and seemingly effortlessly one could run, jumping barefoot from rock to rock, across a line of ancient boulders out onto the Menemsha jetty, avoiding the fishermen who were casting their lines into the sea. There was the art of walking purposefully on one side of the road if you did not want a car to stop, or striding in a more relaxed manner while putting your thumb out casually if you were trying to hitch a ride. We knew all these things by the time we were nine.

My two best friends were Kathleen and Tina. Kathleen was Irish and spunky, with long blond braids. Her father was a famous Shelley scholar and her mother was a teacher who was often drunk. As for Tina, I thought she was truly to be envied because she lived on this magic island all year round, and I pushed away the knowledge that besides my best friend at school, Sarah, Tina was the only person I knew who was really poor. I also pushed aside the one morning I spent in Tina's one-room schoolhouse, where children of many ages were learning the dullest of lessons by rote. Tina's father was a construction worker who spent his days building mock structures on a nearby island called Noman's Land, so that bombers could destroy them testing out their weapons—it was seasonal but steady work during the cold war. Tina's mother, Esther, was a Wampanoag Indian whose people were native to Gay Head. She ran a tiny one-room antique shop located in the only clean room in their house. Their Lobsterville dwelling reminded me of pictures of Appalachia—with broken objects everywhere, and old food and dirty dishes scattered around—except for one special, immaculate room where the antiques were kept: shelves filled with delicate china and crystal, and shoe boxes filled with antique postcards and photographs. It was a room we looked in at and never entered.

Our world was outdoors. We roamed the Menemsha docks, with their old wooden fishing shacks darkened to gray by the salt air. Swordfish tails were nailed to the outsides of the houses and lobster buoys hung by their doors. Or the Lobsterville dunes—white sand with bluish-gray dusty miller, wild roses, bayberry, and ripening beach plum. And there was the rocky shore, where we looked for stones with unbroken circling lines, and flat rocks which we then skipped into the sea. We would dive for sand dollars in the waters, avoid the occasional Portuguese man-of-war, crack open clams and mussels with rocks and eat them raw, pick up horseshoe crabs on the Lobsterville town beach, find starfish, chase sandpipers, and look for the rarest of finds, the unblemished, unbroken whelk.

Occasionally we entered the community, to see movies or go to square dances where we mostly sat on the sidelines and envied the older girls who were routinely asked to dance. In very different ways, Kathleen, Tina, and I were all outsiders. Kathleen says today that she suspects there was a gulf between Wasps and Jews that we didn't even notice at the time. Being Irish, and having a foot in neither camp, she may have seen this more clearly than I. Tina, being half Indian and half Jewish, not to mention poor, was probably even more on the outs than I was. Our refuge was nature.

In 1954, Hurricane Carol hit the island, a storm so tremendous that Poole's fish market in Menemsha was lifted cleanly from one side of the road to the other, while a hundred-foot tidal wave demolished much of the shore, and the best swordfishing vessel in the harbor, the *Aphrodite*, went down to the bottom. The storm seemed vital, alive, exciting, and—how guilty and ashamed I was to admit it—beautiful. I loved it. I remember standing outside, buffeted by driving, windblown droplets, after the worst of the storm had already passed, feeling an ecstasy as I encountered this untamed force. Later we walked to the ocean to see what was left of the spirit of the storm—the frothing black seas of its aftermath. At nine I had no thoughts for the thousands that had evacuated their homes and boarded up their windows. Standing in the wind was an encounter with air as pure essence—like earth or water or fire, one of the four things we return to in the end.

And of those four elements, the one with the most claim to my soul was ocean. One of my most vivid memories is of my parents floating in the sea effortlessly, bobbing about like small boats. We clearly would have all failed the "test of water" given to suspected Witches* by the Inquisitors—the one where you were guilty if you didn't sink. My father had always told me, "Treat the water like a friend, and it will treat you likewise," and so I did. I would lie just beyond the breakers, letting myself be carried by the sea.

Occasionally I would pretend I was a mermaid; I would cross my legs, pretending I had a tail, and do dives and somersaults while I drifted into daydreams. And after a while I would move just a little bit, to the perfect point where the breakers formed, and I would wait for just the right one, letting it carry me, allowing the surf to turn me over and over until I would slide with the last part of the wave onto the sandy shore, and I would rise up again on my feet, flinging my hair back in total joy, ready to dive in and return for the next one and the next after that.

For Kathleen and me, our two months of summer seemed longer and more vivid than our ten months in the city. We had little to do with our parents in this world; we were free and fearless. In one old photograph we are both straddling the windmill pole on Kathleen's summer home. The pole went from the ground to the third floor. It eventually rotted years ago and was pulled down, but in those days we would climb to the top daringly and look down at our world.

I was eleven when my Eden exploded. We had rented a tiny cottage overlooking the Menemsha docks. It was a late-August day in 1957, perhaps 6:30 in the evening, and the sun was getting lower but it still flooded our windows with a golden light. The

---

* The words "Witch," "Pagan," "Neo-Pagan," and "Wicca" are capitalized in this book—just as I capitalize "Christian" and "Jew"—to acknowledge that many present-day Witches and Pagans are practicing *religions* worthy of respect (see my book, *Drawing Down the Moon: Witches, Druids, Goddess-Worshippers, and Other Pagans in America Today,* for further explanation).

fishing boats were returning from their day's work; you could hear the mix of sounds from gulls and sailors. My mother and my father sat me down at the table looking out over the docks and told me what I must have suspected but blocked out for years—that my parents' marriage was loveless and was ending. I remember several years before, at the age of eight, standing on a staircase in the house of a friend while I watched the marriage of her parents disintegrate. I peeked over the banister down into the kitchen, where I saw the mother sobbing. She was holding a large kitchen knife in her hand, and she was trimming the fat off a generous piece of sirloin and stuffing cloves of garlic into the meat as rivers of tears ran down her cheeks. I watched her furtively but fascinated, and I think some part of me already knew that my parents were taking the same route and that the scene I was witnessing would not remain foreign. Now, as I sat overlooking the docks, listening to my parents' words, I felt a sense of doom. It would be many years before I would return to Menemsha.

Thrown out of paradise, I went back to Manhattan, my other island, and the only other haven I knew: school.

If it seems a stretch to imagine a nine-year-old girl hitchhiking barefoot on Martha's Vineyard in reasonable safety, it will seem almost inconceivable that just after I turned nine I began to travel to school by myself on the New York City subways. My mother trained me carefully, over a period of weeks, showing me how to enter the subway and where to change trains. Often I would stand mesmerized in the front car, looking out at the tracks speeding by below. Pushed and pummeled by rush-hour crowds, on one wintry day I found myself tightly pressed into the folds of a woman's luxurious fur coat. I let myself cuddle in the soft fur unobserved. At the Twelfth Street exit, I would climb up the stairs and walk less than a hundred yards to the doors of my school, City and Country. Almost everything that was eventually to dominate my life—music, ancient history, Pagan spirituality—began for me at this tiny Greenwich Village school.

Founded in 1914, the City and Country School is still a vibrant, functioning community, but if you took a tour of the school today, your first impression might well be that everything—the old buildings, the battered furniture, and the classroom materials—have the well-worn look of a child's most loved toys.

When I returned recently to City and Country, to stir the cauldron of memory, and entered classrooms that still looked familiar after some forty years, I found it difficult to navigate the rooms of the six- and seven-year-olds because of the complex block structures—often entire cities—that took up most of the space.

On the second floor was the general store, managed by eager nine-year-olds who took the money, wrote up the sales slips, and kept the supplies in stock. The contents of the shelves did not look much different than they did in 1955, when I was nine: boxes of chalk, reams of paper, crayons, number-two pencils, glue, rubber bands, erasers, staples, paints, pens and brushes, notebooks, lined yellow pads, index cards, binders, rolls of masking tape, large pads of newsprint. Down one flight of stairs was the post office, managed by the eight-year-olds, who sold regular stamps and stamps that they themselves designed for an internal mail system that linked together the school community.

Those special stamps were printed in the print shop, two flights up. As I walked up the stairs my nostrils were assaulted by the wonderful, pungent smell of printer's ink. I entered a room where five eleven-year-olds were working and talking earnestly. The two ancient printing presses must have seemed large, even hulking, to the small people who put their feet on the pedals and turned the wheels; nevertheless, the elevens ran the print shop and created all the school forms, as well as poetry books, individual stationery, and linoleum woodcuts of their own designs.

The gym was on the top floor, a simple room with a polished wood floor and one wall covered with Swedish bars. The pianist would play an assortment of classical selections, and not only would we dance and skip and leap, but often we would hear a piece of music and be told, "You are now under the sea," and we would pretend to be anything from sea creatures to submarines. Sometimes in this "rhythms" class we would act out scenes from periods of history, with only large colored silk scarves for props: a market scene in ancient Egypt, perhaps, or an alchemist's shop in the Middle Ages. Usually these scenes were taken from the historical periods we were studying in the classroom, and often they were later expanded into plays or musicals. The rarest and most precious aspect of this curriculum was that everything was connected.

Although this was the 1950s, we all wore jeans. Both boys and girls played with blocks, and there was no dress-up corner to differentiate us. We played the same games, did the same sports, and only our reading choices differed, although not always. Since all the materials were open-ended, and paint, clay, blocks, and wood could take on any form, gender didn't seem much of an issue, at least for the first ten years of my life.

Caroline Pratt, who founded C & C in 1914, had herself grown up harvesting wheat, baking bread, and milking cows, but she believed the world of the child was growing smaller and smaller. She determined to found a school that would emphasize learning as firsthand experience. When she was growing up, she wrote in her book *I Learn From Children*, no one had to tell us where milk came from, or how butter was made.... No wonder school was a relatively unimportant place—a place where we learned only the mechanical tools, the three R's, and a smattering about things far away and long ago. Our really important learning, the learning how to live in the world into which we were born and how to participate in its work, was right at hand outside the schoolhouse walls.*

But now, she noted, the world was far beyond the grasp of most children.

Pratt wrote that many people who visited her school were shocked at the movement and the sound: "Swirling around the visitor's head, beating against her unaccustomed ears, there was noise, until the walls of the room must bulge with it. Of the twenty souls in the room, only one was quiet— the teacher."

And yet, Pratt pointed out, while City and Country did not look like a typical school, its activities followed a very familiar and complex pattern, one seen everywhere in the world except in the traditional school: "the normal pattern of human activity, adult or child."

And this odd little school, which was situated on a cozy block of four-story houses in Greenwich Village, was my community, my utopia, and the place that remained whole and intact and vibrant, even when my own family fell apart. And in fact, all those jobs we did were secondary to the real magic that took place, for City and Country took as an axiom an idea that has been echoed by a host of philosophers and writers from Marx to Muir to Einstein—that when you try to pick out something by itself, you find it connected to everything else in the universe. And in school that meant that every historical period we studied was reflected in the

* Caroline Pratt, *I Learn From Children* (New York: Cornerstone Library, 1970), 7–8. Subsequent quotes are from pages 13 and 14.

poems and paintings we created, the plays we presented, even in the math and science we were taught, and most certainly in the books we read. We dipped into each period and claimed it as our own.

Of all the rooms, it was the library that was truly our paradise. It was a fairly small room with an old wooden floor painted black. Sunlight poured through two very tall windows. At the center was a long table. Small wicker chairs with frayed red pillows created the outer circle. Today most of the books here are very old and some of my favorites are missing. But this was the room of fantasy and magic for many of us who went here. The seats seemed—to my smaller self—as comfortable as clouds.

City and Country didn't believe in teaching reading until children were seven, and we never saw a textbook. By then we were hungry for books, and most of us learned to read quickly. Once the printed word was easily understood, we were allowed to enter the library. There, for one half-hour period every day, we could read for pleasure. We entered this hushed sanctuary as if under a spell. There we sat, legs crossed, or knees up to our chest, or one leg splayed out, occasionally chewing on bookmarks or pencils, drinking in page after page. Occasionally one of us would raise a hand, asking Bluie, the librarian, for the meaning of a word or phrase. And Bluie, the gatekeeper of this 1950s "Holodeck," would whisper the answers in our ears, and go about her larger purpose—to gently nudge us toward the next and even more exciting journey.

The books that still retain the greatest vividness for me were set in the historical periods we studied—ancient Egypt, ancient Greece, the Middle Ages. They had titles like *The Spartan, The Perilous Seat, Mara, Daughter of the Nile, Luck of Scotland,* and *The Gauntlet.* Others were more famous: *Le Morte d'Arthur, Sir Gawain and the Green Knight,* and T. H. White's *The Goshawk.* But my reading was varied. I identified as much with the baseball pitcher in *The Southpaw* as with Arthur in *The Sword in the Stone.*

I would take books home, walking toward the subway with the pages open, oblivious to the world, developing some kind of sixth sense so that I would only occasionally bump into a passerby as I proceeded down the street or ran down a staircase into a dimly lighted subway passage. In fact I was so used to reading while walking and standing up that the crowded and bumpy subway trains of morning rush hour were no obstacle. I quickly developed the skill of balance, rolling on the balls of my feet, not holding on to anything so as to turn the pages faster, as well as the odd talent of reading upside down, which enabled me to look down at any sitting passenger and devour their newspaper or book.

In our present culture, we have a tendency to believe that "progressive" means "lax"—a school that emphasizes fun, as opposed to a "serious" school wed to academic studies and firm structure. And even when I was growing up, I was told by some that City and Country was the "Auntie Mame" school, the experimental school in Greenwich Village alluded to in the film, where Mame has put her nephew and where the children are found running around naked. But although school was a joyous place for me (in fact I cried when I was sick and my mother would keep me home), City and Country was, just as Caroline Pratt observed, a very serious place, with a complicated structure. The jobs we performed, the trips we went on, and the historical periods we studied were all connected purposefully. If our job was making the school signs when we were ten, it was no accident that this took place in the same year that we studied the development of writing—from Egyptian hieroglyphics to the illuminated manuscripts of the Middle Ages. Egypt entered our poetry, our mathematics, our paintings, and our plays. There were complicated attitudes toward death and the soul, and wonderful, mysterious words to say over and over, like "faience" and "lapis lazuli." When our studies turned to the Middle Ages, we made parchment from animal hides and learned how to bind books and illuminate their pages with gold leaf and colored inks. We read about the pain of serfdom and the romance of falconry. And as a minstrel in a school play I learned my true calling.

I cut my hair to pageboy length and wore a black velvet tunic and green leotards. I strummed a cardboard lute with brown twine for strings. And I sang. That was the one thing that was real. The song came from the fourteenth century and told the story of a falcon:

> My Falcon Fair I loved so dear, that home I brought the
> treasure.
> To rest so soft, to hawk no more, for hunter's cruel pleasure.
>
> He quickly learned to have no fear, and my commandments
> heeding,
> Away he flew, my falcon fair, beyond my window speeding.
>
> He westward flew; I followed fast, but all in vain I sought him.
> I heard his voice; 'twas quickly stilled. A savage eagle caught
> him.
>
> And now I knew 'twere better far to show such kindness never.
> Because I loved my falcon fair, he's lost to me forever.

Although I no longer remember the subject of the play, standing before the court, my pretend lyre in hand, there were two things I knew from that moment on. I wanted to *have* a falcon. I wanted to *be* a minstrel.

My father sat by the side of my bed one night and told me that a falcon wasn't very practical. I knew all about falcons by then, having read T. H. White's *The Goshawk*, as well as many historical fantasies. My father argued the advantages of homing pigeons as pets. He wove tales of how they carried messages from rooftop to rooftop. A falcon with its hood and jesses and love of raw meat was, after all, a bird of prey; not quite congenial in a Manhattan apartment. The homing pigeon was, of course, a ruse. I was finally appeased with two white mice in a cage.

But a *minstrel*—that was different. What could my father say to that, he who had sung with Bruno Walter in the Vienna Philharmonic Chorus? It was already assumed by many that I would become a singer, and I was already singing many of the solos in the school chorus. And yet minstrel is a calling that doesn't exist in our world. We have performers and singers, but our contemporary society doesn't really have a word that captures the spirit of the minstrel of old—bard, song collector, musician—a person that brings others to ecstasy and even action through song.

Then, when I was eleven, Bluie, the librarian, pressed a worn, brown book into my hands and it captured my heart. It was called *Luck of Scotland* by Ivy May Bolton. The heroine was a fifteen-year-old Scottish girl named Constance Clume. She lived in the thirteenth century, in the time of feuding clans and wars with England and a Scottish hero named Robert the Bruce. Being "just a girl," she was forced to stay home and—I remember this sentence so well—"bide by the inglenook," a phrase I have never heard since. But, forced to flee at the arrival of the English army, Constance cut her hair short, dressed herself as a boy, and made her way across the border country with her harp, disguised as a minstrel. She had a beautiful voice and great ability as a harpist, and her songs stirred the souls of the country folk. As she wandered from farmhouse to farmhouse, she discovered that although she was a mere girl, her songs raised courage, created a new fighting spirit; bands of men who were once despondent took heart and found the strength to resist the English and fight with Robert the Bruce for Scotland's independence. When England learned of the new recruits, a price was put on the minstrel's head. Eventually she was captured by the English and her identity was discovered, but she won her freedom through the strength of her music.

In December 1957 a strange and almost mystical event seemed to cement my belief that this one book spoke of my deepest desires and talents. I pressed my parents to buy a copy, and told them during the next holiday season that *Luck of Scotland* was the only gift I wanted. My poor mother went to various bookshops asking in vain, but the book, originally published in 1940, was no longer in print. Being young, I refused to take no for an answer and forced her to search in several stores.

"Just go into that one." I pointed as a window full of books quickly flashed by a bus window. When my mother walked in some days later, she was given the familiar reply. "It's been out of print for years," they said. "*Luck of Scotland?*" A frail, English, male voice came from behind. "Why, my sister wrote that." And several days later, there was the package under the Christmas tree. "To my brother Guy, from your sister Ivy," it said on the flyleaf. "As that particular book had been out of print for some time," Guy Bolton wrote later to my parents, "I suppose I was the only person in New York who could have supplied it. There is something a bit eerie about it, isn't there?" Forget that Ivy Bolton was now living a life far removed from Scottish battles, as a nun in New Jersey, this act of the gods seemed confirmation enough that my road was true.

What was this notion of song that floated in and out of all my years of education, and yet had little to do with the piano lessons I was given as a child, or the musical theory courses I later took in high school? Music, like books, became an integral part of my fantasy life. I would sit at the piano for hours, not practicing, but letting my hands stray through the keys, improvising, while my thoughts returned to far-off ages. I would dream of being historical figures gleaned from books, or new creations that emerged from novels but took on a life of their own, transformed in my head.

My memories of City and Country are infused with songs—folk songs, work songs, holiday songs, rounds, madrigals, songs in African and European languages. By the time I left the school, at the age of fourteen, I knew by heart at least half the songs in the *Fireside Book of Folk Songs*, as well as hundreds of others that were handed out on mimeographed sheets, handwritten in fading purple ink. I remember slipping unnoticed into the music room before graduation and rifling through the file cabinets, taking one copy of each song. I sorted and stapled the sheets together. When I was done, I had thirty-six sea chanteys, twenty-three work songs, forty carols, and fifty-six rounds.

Then there were the political songs, anthems from the French and Russian revolutions, and songs like "Freiheit" and "The Peat Bog Soldiers," which were sung during the Spanish Civil War. Or my anarchist favorite, "Die Gedanken Sind Frei" (Thoughts Are Free):

> *Die Gedanken Sind Frei; my thoughts freely flower.*
> *Die Gedanken Sind Frei; my thoughts give me power.*
> *No tyrant can map them, no hunter can trap them;*
> *No man can deny, Die Gedanken Sind Frei....*

* "Die Gedanken Sind Frei," in *Rise Up Singing* (Bethlehem, Pa.: Sing Out Publications, 1989), 214.

It may seem as if the students at City and Country lived in a permanent state of freedom, but occasionally the world of the 1950s and its fears did intrude. Our music room over-looked a quiet, tree-lined street of three- and four-story brownstones. I remember looking out one lovely spring day when I was eleven and just entering that awful period of pu-berty when girls often become embarrassed by life itself, and when they begin to be utterly convinced that the hordes of daily commuters can peer into their soul and even notice the sweat under their armpits. We began to sing "Meadowlands," the Red Army song ("Meadowlands, Meadowlands / through you heroes now are treading, / Red Army heroes of the Nation, / heroes of the mighty Red Army, / Ah . . ."), and at that very instant, I noticed a woman passing under our win-dow, looking up. For a moment I was paralyzed by fear. "Surely she knows what we're singing," I thought. "Surely she thinks we're communists!" Beyond our protected realm, Mc-Carthyism was thriving. But in fact our selection of songs was deeply eclectic. I may have learned the Red Army song, but I can also still sing by heart "The Bonnie Blue Flag" and several other rebel songs from the American Confederacy.

What was it about singing that led me to feel such joy? As an only and lonely child, I found separation the constant theme of relationship, and music the binder and healer. Al-though I had always been able to put an end to my own feel-ings of estrangement by staring into a bonfire or entering na-ture, song was a doorway into an entirely new world. It was a group creation, a way into a shared state of ecstatic harmony.

But being a minstrel is not like a rock performer or an opera singer. A minstrel needs a community to exist. Not finding it, by the time I was fourteen I decided that I would take the next best choice and be a singer. It was even part of my family tradition. Not only had my father sung in Vienna, but his father had been urged in his youth to give up science for an operatic career. In one letter, Alfred Adler wrote that when he was a child he always had tunes running in his head, that "tunes came to me instead of thought."*

City and Country not only allowed me to float in a river of song, when I was ten years old the school also introduced me to the power of ritual. At 4:00 A.M. on the first of May, 1957, my mother and I set out for school. We took the subway, joining riders who were already beginning their working day. I noticed bakers and painters, their overalls smeared with the white of paint and dough.

Before dawn our class was taken to the country, where we were led to gardens filled with pink and white and purple flowers. As the sky slowly reddened and the sun rose, we picked armfuls of budding branches. When we were laden with more than we could carry, we returned to school. We walked up the stairs, singing medieval May Day carols, our arms filled with blossoms. How simple and unexpected and joyous to give such gifts! Later we danced around the maypole, as we would every year.

Ever since that May morning I have understood that ritual has the power to end our alienation from the earth and from each other. It allows us to enter a world where we are at home with trees and stars and other beings, and even with the carefully hidden and protected parts of ourselves that we sometimes contact in dreams or in art. More gentle, but also more powerful than many a drug, ritual returns us to our always present but often unfelt, connected selves.

City and Country was also where I first met the Pagan gods. I resonated with the wildness of Artemis, her solitary ways in nature, but I also wanted Athena's strength, the wis-

*Phillis Bottome, *Alfred Adler: A Biography* (New York: G. P. Putnam and Sons, 1939), 15.

dom and political savvy of the goddess of a great city. These two goddesses seemed so much more powerful than any of the images of women that surrounded me at home and school. The real women around me were shockingly vulnerable, even if they talked boldly and brazenly at times. I watched my own flamboyant, theatrical, and seemingly invincible mother fall into depression after her divorce. I looked at my mother's friends—all earthy, funny and wise, but they had all sacrificed careers for their husbands and children, and almost all of them were now divorced. The women around my mother were vibrant and original, but most had begun their creative work late in life and never quite lived up to their brilliance.

And so I secretly dreamed I was Athena or Artemis come down to earth, and spent hours creating fantastic adventures. Deep down, in my heretic's heart, I knew that I did not want to worship these goddesses, they were beings I desperately wanted to become.

Looking back at my years at City and Country, it doesn't seem odd to me that I adopted the ancient Greek religion as my own. Mythology and nature were the only real elements of religion I encountered, and they were powerful. I was totally unaware of the religious and ethnic differences that created chasms in the outside world. My friends were Irish, Italian, Jewish, and Chinese, and I never gave it a thought. When I left C & C to enter a large public high school where most of the blacks and Jews and Catholics stuck with their own, I went into shock. Of course I had never had to deal with the outside world's notion of hierarchy, either. In City and Country we called our teachers by their first names, and instead of filling out report cards our teachers would have dinner at our homes twice a year; after we went to bed, our parents and teachers would talk. It was only in our last year before high school that our teachers began to give us grades, so that our entry into the "real world" would be less traumatic.

But City and Country was not perfect. Although many of us read eighty books a year, a few of us never learned spelling or grammar until high school. Not all of us were suited for a school that so emphasized self-motivation. And although City and Country was a nurturing place, it did not shield us from the cruelties common to childhood.

My introduction to these cruelties came at seven, when a new student entered our class. Now a writer of fiction living in Canada, Sarah was brilliant and unusual, and she was poor. Sarah's father had died when she was young and her mother was an alcoholic.

Sarah's relative poverty must have showed. (My mother remembered one snowy day when Sarah came to school with no boots and her feet wrapped in newspapers.) And, as a new kid, she was picked on. Twice a day we would play in the three yards adjacent to the school. In one of the yards there was a swing, a hanging ladder, and a large rubber tire that hung by a rope. Sarah was wearing jeans and a light, green, pullover sweater that accentuated her Irish looks. The sweater was a bit short, and she wore no belt. Sarah was a great climber and she could easily climb on the tire and hang from her feet, her short blond hair grazing the pebbles on the ground and her sweater falling away from her belly, leaving much of her upper body exposed. Suddenly a group of boys were pulling her off the tire, punching her and kicking her and trying to pull off her pants. The teacher was in the adjacent yard, and by the time she arrived a crowd of children had gathered around.

In that instant, I was aware of two things simultaneously. I knew that I should come to her aid and I knew that I was afraid that if I did, the boys might turn on me and I could become the next victim. I understood immediately what was right and courageous. Guilt-ridden, I stood silently by.

I do not like to use the word "patriarchy" lightly, but thinking back on that experience, I know in some way that Sarah was too much of an individual, too much of a tomboy, and that, even in that most iconoclastic and individualistic school, the boys were telling her not to step out of line. For although our teachers stressed independence and explora-tion, this was, after all, the conforming 1950s.

By the time I was twelve I had read Pat Boone's book of advice for teenagers, *Twixt Twelve and Twenty,* and had been ad-vised by as liberated a woman as my mother that I should not eat a meal or drink a coke faster than any boy I dated or else I would be found too threatening. And while our school sought to emphasize freedom and hard work, outside it po-tential was limited and roles were strictly defined. Our own friends were often the prison guards of our soul, smilingly offering us the straitjacket and telling us where to toe the line, showing us what occupations and interests were accept-able and which clothes and which colors were appropriate. Our teachers often lost the fight, and our peers, influenced by the society at large, often won. It still amazes me how easy it was to be terrorized by children of the same age and size, how early I and many of my friends had learned the art of trying to please others, and how unbearably difficult it was to tell someone no. Our culture is full of stories of the emo-tional and sexual abuse adults inflict on children, much of it deep and tragic, but little attention is given to the daily and even more common abuse one receives from one's child-hood peers.

But despite these outside pressures, City and Country re-mained an empowering community that, for the most part, worked. In June 1960, only five months after the decade that would so transform our lives had begun, we graduated. Of our class of twenty, four are published authors, and most of us have successful careers in fields ranging from photography to corporate law, with several teachers, artists, and musicians among the group.

At graduation, our principal, Jean Murray, told us that we had been an unusually creative class and she had no fear that conformity would overwhelm us, "but we wanted to be sure that your hearts and hands and souls and bodies could learn not only skills, but the beginning of wisdom and understanding." She told us that the world was in "a perilous and wondrous state of upheaval, exciting, promising, terrifying, and threatening"; that people were trying to forge a better place for human beings to live; that creative, feeling, intelligent people must throw their weight on the side of beauty, love, and creation and against the powers of despair, destruction, hate, fear, and sterility.

After the speeches ended, we entered for the last time the sacred sanctuary—the library. It had been transformed. A white tablecloth was draped over the central table and formal dishes were set in place. In a scene of unusual elegance we were served a meal of foods that we had chosen by vote. And most surprising of all and yet so fitting, our own teachers were our waiters, the ones who served us our food. It was a reversal of roles that showed us once again the central lesson of the place: that true respect does not have to be tied to inequality.

The Free Speech Movement

CHAPTER 4

IT'S A SUNLIT MORNING in 1964. My mother and I are traveling across the country on our way to Berkeley, and she is slowly coming to terms with the departure of her only child for college. I'm floating in a swimming pool somewhere in the Midwest, saying various syllables over and over, like "Oregon" and "all." I am trying to lose my New York accent; like so many immigrants, I am trying to remake myself.

Living in New York City, I looked upon Berkeley as so many Americans have looked throughout history upon the West— as an escape from everything that defined my past. For me, Berkeley was not only an excellent school, and a place with a rich history of student activism; going to Berkeley meant fleeing New York, my parents, the memories of four depressing high school years during which I had few real friends. Most of all, I was fleeing from myself and from the large one-hundred-and-eighty-pound body that encased me. California, a place I had never seen, seemed a place of open space, infinite possibilities—radicals, surfers, palm trees, the Beach Boys, and not necessarily in that order. I was determined to enter this mythical realm and to claim it as my own.

Looking back, I realize now that I also wanted to free myself

68

from being my mother's daughter. All during her life I felt in the shadow of this beautiful, theatrical, extraordinary woman. Although she never said so, my mother would have far preferred that I go to some fashionable college in the East, preferably Radcliffe, but I knew deep down it would never be. Although no one, including myself, would admit it at the time, I was clearly the kind of applicant that gives college administrators pause. Visibly overweight and wearing dark, oversized tent dresses, with my hair short and shapeless, I was not the type to inspire confidence, despite an energetic, even bubbly nature. And I was absolutely sure every interviewer could see through my outer facade, into the dark, angst-filled, daydream-laden creature below who was secretly spending two or three hours a day living out various historical and science fiction fantasies.

Many years later, having interviewed dozens of young college students as potential baby-sitters, I realize that I was probably exactly the kind of young woman I have occasionally rejected as too depressive or dour, preferring instead those lovely, confident, smiling types with pastel sweaters and circle pins, the ones who seem to know exactly where they are going and do not harbor dangerous dreams. In the end, I was clearly fated to go to a college that was interested only in my grades.

Going to Berkeley was my own attempt—which seemed feeble at the time—to find a rich and interesting life of my own. And it worked: for the next eight years, everywhere I went I found myself mysteriously at the center of extraordinary events.

True, my Berkeley was not the only one. It was a center of bohemianism, yet Ronald Reagan was the governor of the state when I graduated, in 1968, and his signature is on my diploma. Berkeley had the largest number of Nobel laureates and Peace Corps volunteers of any university, but also the largest number of federal contracts for nuclear weapons research.

The 1968 yearbook portrays the conventional Berkeley I did not know: sports teams and glee clubs, cheerleaders, rally clubs, the campus newspaper, the humor magazine, a plethora of honor organizations, bands, theatrical and music groups, but not a single mention of anyone I knew. The student protests are relegated to one or two snapshots. The seven professors who inspired me are neither listed nor photographed. None of my roommates are listed in the index, nor are they to be found in the pages of class photos. All of my friends are missing. I am not there either. It almost seems as if the Berkeley I knew was purposely rubbed out by the official chroniclers of the time, its radical legacy denied. But it is also true that I chose not to have my picture taken for the yearbook (it seemed a silly ritual) and I did not attend my own graduation, something I now regret.

Still, coming to Berkeley in 1964 was like entering a fantasy of what the agora might have been like in ancient Athens (forgetting for the moment that there were slaves in Athens and women were second-class citizens, expected to stay indoors). Much of Berkeley's social life took place outside, and except for the three-month rainy season, the sky seemed eternally blue, the sun was nearly always shining, and the manicured lawns were watered daily. The older structures on the campus, white buildings with Spanish terra-cotta tile roofs, glistened in the sunlight. At times, as dusk approached and the sky darkened into an intense and vibrant blue, the cedars and fir trees were tinged with a golden light and the entire campus seemed bathed in radiance.

The campus buildings were a mix of classical, neoclassical, and beaux-arts structures competing with newer, concrete abominations. The administration building, Sproul Hall, with its four huge Doric columns, looked out on our agora, Sproul Plaza. At noon it often seemed that the entire population of thirty thousand students would pour into the plaza. No stranger to crowds and large city life, I found Berkeley an appropriate size—like a Greek *polis*.

As an only child I had lived alone most of my life, and unlike many students whose thirst for independence is symbolized by the quest for their own apartment, I had no desire to live on my own. What I desperately wanted was company. Living in a boarding house for young women, mostly freshmen, brought the comfort of neighbors and friends—an entry into an instant and easy community I had never had. I privately exulted at this abundance of companionship.

I also secretly enjoyed the most ghastly and shameful aspects of student orientation, watching the cheerleaders and learning the school colors and songs and the silly traditions of the football team. Since my New York high school didn't even have team sports and our senior prom had been canceled for lack of interest, I looked on such things with the fascination of an alien anthropologist or, at the very least, a tourist from another land, which perhaps I was. Even those things that irked radical students the most and were the seeds from which rebellion was already sprouting—the machine-like quality of some of the education, the huge lecture classes with eight hundred students, the small sections led by bored and immature teaching assistants, the inadequate counseling, the invisibility of each person among a student body of almost thirty thousand—those things, at least at the beginning, were liberating. "There is something wonderful about being able to lose oneself in a crowd," I wrote to my mother two weeks after school began. "Knowing that no one knows me . . . there is a beautiful feeling knowing that *I am like a thousand normal people!*"

The part of campus life that quickly became confusing was the dizzying array of choices. "This school is beginning to overwhelm me," I wrote home only a week later.

I want to try everything! But already I wonder if I am taking too much? I guess I am in a weird mood because a girl who lives in this house just had something akin to a nervous breakdown. I hear that this is a common enough occurrence in college ... so it makes you wonder ...

So here's the question. 1. Logically, I should enjoy my work. 2. I should do well enough so that if I want to continue in graduate school it will be possible. 3. I should be able to participate in many of the wonderful outside activities available. 4. I should enjoy myself to the utmost. But somehow, these things do not seem compatible, unless I forget about #2, which I am never able to do. I don't want to complain, but when you are assigned over one weekend 400 pages of reading from Plato, Sophocles, Epic of Gilgamesh, Homer and modern political analysis, it's fair to cry out, 'My God, give me a little time to do this, so that I can go folk dancing or go to a movie.' There are so many choices each night—a party, a meeting, a movie, or realistically, getting some of this damn reading done.

I realize only now, reading these letters from thirty years ago, that my mother's words had method and purpose. Like Auntie Mame, she always tried to entice me away from the predictable, to help me see the larger aspects of life:

October 4th, 1964

Dearest Margot:

Two letters from you! Joy, joy.... They both made me chuckle and hold back a tear or two. The tear not being caused by lonesomeness but by the picture of you weighted down by all those assignments, torn by your newly discovered (finally and thank God) possibilities of having fun, and your sense of guilt at not always plodding away at your assignments.

So at the risk of being a mother which I of course am, and a Jewish one at that, I want to talk out loud about just this point. I have complete trust in your good sense

Margot, so that fun will always be something truly enjoyable and not an extreme attempt to avoid your responsibilities to your work. However the choice you will have
to make is to be a good average student with time to live
life to the hilt, or an A student plodding away at the cost
of missing the real purpose of college which is to make
life More and not Less meaningful. The purpose of all
those wonderful philosophers you are reading is to give
you a sense of values to live by, a way of saying, Yes to
life and not No.

Talking of philosophy, there is something about Zen
that just touches that. The business of so freeing the
mind from facts and pressures so that you have a state
that they call emptying the mind, if I have it right, and I
may very well have only superficially understood it, by
empty it really means being sufficiently open and un-
cluttered so that you are sensitized to receive all the
things around you, be they people, activities or that
highest of reactions to life—the world of art.

All of which, darling, leads me to tell you your biggest
problem is that which plagues imaginative people all
their lives—CHOICES. You will have to decide of three
equally exciting things which one to go to, even if all
three are equally intriguing—after all you only have one
ass. Also you will have to decide that no one but yourself
is pressuring you to be a top student. I only want for your
sake that you just get the necessary grades not to be
kicked out, that's all. I don't give a damn if you get one A.
So my darling sit down and have a good talk with yourself, and know that your mother loves you even if you fail
every goddamn subject—I hope for your sake you don't.
... But if college is pressuring people so they crack, we
had better say the hell with college and look into what is

wrong. The purpose of the humanities is to be able to live
a rich, intellectual and emotional life, to be able to embrace life in all its colors, joys and tragedies, but never to
be so overburdened that one's senses become deadened
and unable to receive the gifts college offers in the first
place.

My mother echoed what many students at Berkeley believed in 1964, but what is very hard for today's students to
fathom in this era of downsizing and burdensome student
debt. The purpose of school was to enlarge oneself, to discover the path to a rewarding and interesting life, to get a
liberal education and ponder the meaning of existence; it
was only secondarily to get a career. Although living well did
not mean having the kinds of material possessions it does today, America was prosperous. Jobs were available and we assumed that we could get them when the time came. Tuition
was low at Berkeley, even for out-of-state students; it was easy
to live cheaply, and students only paid back loans when they
were able. Later, in the 1970s, tuitions would rise, scholar-
ships would be cut, and regulations governing loans would
be tightened, all of which would undercut student activism
and force many to choose money over meaning.

But we were a generation determined to mine experience
for its riches. And my mother, despite her own experiences
during the Depression—experiences which made many
other parents unable to accept their children's seeming aim-
lessness—was eager to hear about our artistic and philo-
sophic journeys.

November, 1964

Dear Mom:

I read *The Stranger*. Absolutely absurd, fascinating. Do

you think life has any meaning? JoAnne (one of my room-mates) and I have decided that it only does on a lower level: in other words, individuals have no meaning at all in the larger universe—we are just ants, or specks of sand, meaningless in the grand scheme of things. However on the lower level, where we make man the center, life has the meaning we give it. Perhaps we live because of an instinct for survival, but once we have decided to live, life can have meaning, and can be as wonderful, and beautiful as possible. But in order to live, we must forget about that upper level where man and life and the earth and Bach and art are all meaningless, because were we to keep our mind on that, it would be too painful.

Dearest Margot:

So you're head deep in the meaning of it all and very much under the influence of the "Existentialists." I think it is wonderful that you are questioning the meaning of it all. And I believe that it is only because we are a tiny speck in the total universe that we can develop true values and say, Yes to life for the short visit we humans are on this planet. How tragic that so many waste it in the jungle of competition and petty shit level concerns.

... Even I, a middle aged woman, still examine the why, and it only makes me go into life more, wanting to extract the most succulent juices from it.... If all we can know is our human condition then this is what is most important, and only by realizing this, and how small we are in the total cosmos do we realize the need for extending our hand to our fellow man who is just as alone as we and needs to extend his hand in our direction as much as we his. So soul search my darling, for when you stop you are sterile and dead.

Within my first weeks at Berkeley I was involved in a buzz of activities in addition to my studies. I had gone to a fraternity party, had sat behind a table for Students for a Democratic Society, had gone to a meeting of the W. E. B. Du Bois Club, had seen films by Eisenstein and Leni Riefenstahl.

In contrast, my "Introduction to Government" course was decidedly at odds with the budding ferment around me. In the early 1960s, most political scientists in the United States—men like Wildavsky, Greenstein, Dahl, Polsby, and McCloskey—believed that American democracy worked only because most Americans were apathetic. Most Americans, we were told in readings for the course, did not care and did not participate in political activities; they placed their dreams and hopes in the private sector instead. The authors argued that this apathy toward the political prevented extremes and promoted stability. (Why, if Americans truly cared about politics, these experts assured us, our country would be as politically unstable as Italy!) When I asked the professor to suggest readings that took a different view, I was told that there were none. Confused and angry, I began to look for other authorities.

Outside the classroom, politics was the breath of life. Standing around the political tables set up in the plaza, students were talking about politics and philosophy, gesturing, shouting each other down. Clusters of students discussed events and ideas for hours. Groups would form and dissipate and form again. Here politics was seen as a life-and-death struggle, and argument was ecstasy. Caring intensely was not only good, but would surely change the world for the better.

While politics bid for my soul, another model, totally at war with the active political life, also beckoned. Gilbert Rose, a teaching assistant in ancient Greek, was enticing me into the classical world. One day Rose put the first three lines of the Odyssey on the blackboard and then, layer by layer as if he were peeling an onion, he uncovered strata of hidden meaning, until we were awed by the mysterious nature of the Greek language in the same way a person is awed when they cut an apple horizontally and see inside, for the first time, the hidden pentagram or star. Rose was a model totally at odds with the image of activism at Berkeley. He would sit in his home, surrounded by walls of books, contentedly poring over ancient Greek texts, while his wife sat at her desk quietly studying Anglo-Saxon. I wondered if they were outside the main energy of our era or if they were investigating the only questions anyone would find interesting a hundred or a thousand years from now.

But while the myths and gods of the past were calling to me, the call of the present was stronger. The Free Speech Movement had just begun when I arrived at Berkeley in the fall of 1964, although it would be another month before there was an organization with that name. Earlier, in the summer, students from Berkeley had organized demonstrations at the Republican National Convention in support of liberal Republican William Scranton and against Barry Goldwater, the convention's ultimate nominee. It's still unclear whether conservatives actually put pressure on the university, or whether the university, worried about its budget and needing to appease its conservative board of regents, simply felt the need to discourage student political activity. Whatever the reason, on September 14, shortly before classes began, a dean notified off-campus organizations that all student political activity was henceforth prohibited on campus.

When I was growing up in the fifties my family possessed two recordings that came to symbolize for me the fight for political freedom. The first was *The Investigator*, a devastating satire about Senator Joseph McCarthy, in which he dies in a plane crash and goes to heaven. After passing through the pearly gates with barely a question asked, he decides that heaven is too lax and convenes a committee of inquisitors, witch-hunters, and hanging judges from across history, to interrogate the population of heaven. One by one he deports every freethinker to hell: Thomas Jefferson, James Joyce, Percy Bysshe Shelley, Wagner, Socrates, Beethoven, John Stuart Mill, and Karl Marx. Each notable has a hearing and says his most stirring words in defense of liberty. As a teenager I would listen to this record and pace around the living room, pretending I was these famous men, mouthing their speeches.

In the end, Joseph McCarthy causes such a mess in the other world that God and Satan both throw up their hands and agree that Joe is ruining both of their realms, so they send him back to earth.

The other recording I listened to over and over was *The Sounds of Protest*, a documentary about the House Un-American Activities Committee Hearings in 1960, in San Francisco, and the protests against them. Three thousand people picketed the committee's hearings at City Hall. With few exceptions, only those friendly to the committee were allowed inside, and demonstrations outside became tense. On May 13, 1960, suddenly, without warning, police used fire hoses on the demonstrators and dragged them down the stairs, the spines of the protesters bumping on every slippery step. I was mesmerized as I listened to the speeches of those who were subpoenaed by HUAC. They argued that they were unable to confront their accusers, that they were being defamed and pilloried not for what they had done, but simply for what they believed. The speakers were stirring and coura-geous: "If you think I am going to cooperate with this collection of Judases, with these men who sit there in violation of the U.S. Constitution. If you think I am going to cooperate in any way, you are insane."* Even more mesmerizing were the civil rights songs of the students and their chants and screams as police turned on the hoses and the students linked arms and were dragged down the stairs. Sixty-four people were arrested; more than thirty of them were Berkeley students.

Having already taken part in many political activities in New York City, I thought the right to political advocacy seemed obvious, and I was soon handing out leaflets, attending rallies, and sitting behind tables filled with political literature—activities that were forbidden under the new campus regulations.

In the beginning, the Free Speech Movement focused exclusively on campus free speech, but eventually it went much further: it demanded that students be treated like citizens, subject to regulation only by the courts. I embraced that goal since I had become enraged at California's paternalism within days of my arrival. (When my mother and I tried to enter a San Francisco cabaret to see a show we were told that since drinks were available and the drinking age was twenty-one I was too young to attend, even though a parent was accompanying me. I was livid. In those days the drinking age in New York was eighteen, and I was accustomed to being treated as an adult.)

Later, the Free Speech Movement also mounted a blistering critique of the university as a "knowledge factory" turning out corporate drones for industry. In 1964, with a student body of nearly thirty thousand, resources at Berkeley were strained; it was easy for students to feel they were being

* *The Sounds of Protest*, LP record produced by the political organization SLATE, 1960.

pressed out like so many pieces of sausage. And this idea of
the university as a factory that would train bureaucrats, engineers, and politicians to keep the establishment going
seemed the absolute antithesis of any real quest for knowledge. (It still does.) Twenty years later, Michael Rossman, one
of the theoreticians of the FSM, would bring an audience of
Berkeley students to hysterical laughter by framing the FSM
critique this way: "We were being prepped to run the society
for the students at Harvard and Yale, who were being
prepped to *own* it."

But even if the student argument made intellectual sense
to me, I felt anything but alienated. I was out on my own. I
floated through my first semester, did well in everything,
and even defended the large lecture format in letters home.
"Are your classes as formidable as everyone I meet thinks?"
queried my ever-vigilant mother, who worried about "classes
of five hundred and more where you are fortunate if you get
a glimpse of your professor once during the semester." "Remember," she advised me, "it will be the intimate connections and contacts with stimulating people on the faculty
through whom the important part of your academic life will
have real meaning. I'd hate for you to be swallowed up in a
mass of bigness and impersonalness."

I was quick to reassure her. "It's really a myth about how
terrible these large lecture classes are," I wrote home. "If you
have a really great professor his classes will be stimulating,
no matter how many students are in the class." I felt a new
sense of freedom and an almost Edenic sense of bliss, and it
was a bit hard to see myself as the soulless IBM card depicted
in FSM leaflets.

The Free Speech Movement was also deeply influenced by
the civil rights movement. In the early 1960s, Berkeley students had begun to picket local Kress and Woolworth stores
in protest of their discriminatory hiring practices, in actions

very similar to the protests I had joined in New York during high school. By 1964, students were joining civil rights protests at Lucky supermarkets, Mel's Drive-in, and the Sheraton Palace Hotel, and many of these businesses subsequently changed their practices.

Then came the Mississippi Summer Project of 1964, in which almost a thousand students went south to register black voters and set up "Freedom Schools" to teach the history of the struggle for civil rights. The death of three civil rights workers brought the world's attention to Mississippi. Between thirty and sixty students from Berkeley traveled to that state that summer, and they returned to the campus, according to Mario Savio, the Free Speech Movement's most eloquent speaker, as different people. When Savio himself returned to Berkeley from the South he said that civil rights was not only the most interesting thing that was going on in America, it was the most "unsullied" thing.*

For the students and former students who would lead the FSM, their civil rights work provided a sense of morality, purpose, meaning, and community. They returned from Mississippi, and from work in the Bay Area, with a belief that confrontation often succeeds in bringing about needed change. They also brought with them skills they'd gained— experience in civil disobedience and knowledge of how to confront recalcitrant authorities.

By September 28, the ban on political activity had become so divisive that all classes stopped at 11:00 A.M. for an address to all students by President Clark Kerr and Chancellor Edward Strong. Chancellor Strong was introducing new student officers and giving his views on the controversy—words that seemed turgid and bland. All the while, about four hundred

*David Lance Goines, *The Free Speech Movement* (Berkeley, Calif.: Ten Speed Press, 1993), 93–94.

students paraded through the aisles carrying signs: "Vote for X (Censored)" and "Ban the Ban." To many of us in the audience, the protesters, unlike the speakers, seemed to radiate life.

On September 30, five students were cited by campus police for sitting at "illegal" tables. After being told to come to the dean's office, they entered the administration building, Sproul Hall, surrounded by three hundred supporters, an event which developed into the first FSM sit-in. The five students, along with three other leaders of the protests, were suspended.

The next day the protesters determined to test the rules again. Jack Weinberg brought a huge door onto the campus, to create a table for the civil rights organization CORE. The demonstrators set up their tables right in front of Sproul Hall. Weinberg was told he was violating university regulations, and just as lunchtime crowds began to gather he began to give a passionate speech about the "knowledge factory" but was arrested before he finished. Using a tactic from civil rights demonstrations in the South, he went limp and was carried to a police car. Students, now gathering in the hundreds, soon to be thousands, spontaneously began to shout "Sit down!" and soon hundreds were sitting down in front of and behind the police car. (Weinberg would sit in that surrounded police car for some thirty-six hours.)

Like many students, I wandered over to Sproul Plaza for the noon rally and arrived just after the arrest took place. It was extraordinary to see this police car immobile, surrounded by a growing crowd. As time passed, students, faculty, clergy, and members of the community began to climb on top of the car to make speeches to the throng, while underneath, Jack Weinberg, this intense-looking young man with dark tousled hair and a dark mustache, his brow furrowed, his eyes blazing, sat calmly next to a policeman, seemingly even relaxed, arms crossed, leaning out the window of his makeshift prison, listening to the speeches along with the rest of us.

As a freshman in my first semester, I felt too timid to make a speech, although I thought of several as I listened; I felt excited by the growing sense of community among the protesters. It seemed ridiculous that Weinberg had been arrested for sitting behind a table covered with civil rights literature, something I had been doing myself just days before. It seemed easy and appropriate to sit down on the ground with the other students. I felt almost no fear, perhaps because the police car, usually such a powerful symbol of authority, seemed tiny and helpless in the face of our growing numbers.

As we sat around the car, blocking its movement, preventing this arrest from occurring, I felt a sense of exhilaration. But there were moments of fear and terror as we wondered what action the authorities would take. Most of the protesters had never participated in any political demonstration before. Many cried or laughed, or were uncertain what to do. We had turned the world upside down, stopped the machinery of the state. There was a feeling of instant community and internal power. We had no name for the power that we felt. Years later, spiritual feminists would call it "evoking power-from-within."

At the height of the demonstration some three thousand people gathered in the plaza. Ministers called for peace, fraternity boys threw rotten eggs, and the students sitting around the car sang, talked, and passed out food and cigarettes. I remember that after many hours someone finally gave Jack Weinberg a coke bottle to pee in.

Bettina Aptheker, in a book on the student rebellion, writes that while the demonstration was motivated by principle, something more than a principle was needed to "evoke such a display of courage."

There was a shared, if not yet articulated sentiment that the authority of the university itself had to be challenged; that many things about it were wrong: that the world stood on its head; that everything was upside down and inside out; and that somehow, somebody, everybody had to straighten it out before we all died for no plausible reason—just as we all seemed to be living for no plausible purpose. There is no other way to explain the presence of that quaking, still joyful, mass of people, clinging to each other.*

The moment was what the author (and Witch) Starhawk would call magic: "the art of liberation, the act that releases the mysteries, that ruptures the fabric of our beliefs and lets us look into the heart of deep space where dwell the immeasurable, life-generating powers."† It was unplanned and spontaneous, and the thousands of students who sat around this symbol of external authority, of the state, could not help but be affected and could not help but begin to think that their cause was more than a simple fight for free speech, that it encompassed a battle to change the nature of power and authority.

In the end, with almost a thousand police amassed on the campus and protesters negotiating with the administration, an agreement was worked out. Students would end the demonstration; Weinberg would be booked and released and the university would not press charges. The cases of the suspended students would go before the student conduct committee of the Academic Senate, and a committee of students, faculty, and administration, including leaders of the demonstration, would meet to discuss all aspects of political behavior on the campus and make recommendations to the administration.

* Bettina Aptheker, *The Academic Rebellion in the United States* (Secaucus, N.J.: The Citadel Press, 1972), 157–58.
† Starhawk, *Truth or Dare* (San Francisco: Harper & Row, 1987), 6.

Perhaps it was an oversight, perhaps it was a trick, but there *was* no student conduct committee of the Academic Senate; instead, the cases were brought before a committee appointed by the chancellor, which was unacceptable to the student protesters and fueled our paranoia. Negotiations and rallies resumed. It was at this point that the Free Speech Movement adopted its name and really began to organize, creating a steering committee, an executive committee with representatives from all interested campus political groups, and various centers for press, communication, work, and legal affairs. The FSM published a newsletter, and it put out two different recordings (including a very funny Christmas spoof, "Free Speech Carols") as well as more serious papers attacking the university's paternalistic ideology, arguing that students were citizens and that political expression on campus could only be governed by the United States Constitution and the courts.

Negotiations with the administration had been lengthy and nonproductive and students were debating whether to engage in new confrontations. The FSM steering committee, led by civil rights organizers, took the more radical position, but although the steering committee made many of the day-to-day decisions, most issues had to be brought before the larger executive committee. A group of moderates led by a leader of the Young Democrats tried to pack an executive committee meeting with a half dozen inactive organizations, so that the moderate position—a vote against renewed civil disobedience—would win out.

"I am now on the Executive Committee of the Free Speech Movement," I wrote home. I was representing a college civil liberties organization that didn't seem to do much of anything, and that I had never heard of. I had been asked to represent this group by a leader of the Young Democrats. When

I had been invited to represent this group it had felt wonderful, but I soon realized that I was being used. When I realized that I was siding with the radicals over the issue of renewed protests but had been placed on the executive committee in order to support the moderate position, I left before the vote.

On Monday, November 9, the FSM and eight other off-campus organizations set up tables in front of the main steps of Sproul Hall. Seventy-five people, including me, had their names taken by various administration officials. On November 10, we all received letters and were asked to appear at the dean's office.

"Don't Worry, Mom," I wrote in mid-November,

it looks as though everything will be fine. I still don't know what will exactly happen to us, but it looks as if it will be nothing more than a reprimand or social probation which is no more than a warning. I met with one of the deans and she was a lovely woman. She asked me no questions about my FSM involvement and only wanted to know if there were any individual circumstances that made my case different from the rest—in other words was I unwillingly involved. I said, "no." She asked me how I was doing in school, how I liked "Cal" and even said that if I was aware of the responsibilities I was taking, then "more power to you." Some of the other deans had intimidated students.

Anyway, the past week has been terribly exciting. We have constantly set up tables and the administration has done nothing. How many can they cite, after all? There have been rumors about police, but so far nothing.

Eventually the seventy-five cited students were sent letters of formal reprimand. We were warned that future violations would subject us to more serious discipline.

On November 20 there was a large march of several thousand students. Everyone wore dresses or suits and ties. Looking at a picture of that demonstration, like looking at early pictures of the Beatles, reminds me how positively "straight" we looked, even at Berkeley, at the end of 1964. The styles that would give the decade its "look" were still a few years away. We would not have recognized ourselves a mere four years later.

Soon after this, the University of California Board of Regents passed resolutions that students be required to obey state and community laws, and that political activities would be permitted in certain campus facilities, as long as they were legal. Four days later the administration announced new rules allowing organizations to get permits and set up tables. Students could solicit donations and advocate political action. Many believed the university had given as much as it could, and that the FSM was dead, having won a partial victory. But the movement, led by its civil rights activists, now understood that its primary demand was that only the courts of law could judge the content of speech and impose punishment. Achieving that goal seemed as elusive as ever.

The Free Speech Movement was at war with a notion that was central to the thinking of many of Berkeley's faculty, and even some of its students, that the university was a place outside of space and time, with different rules from those of the society at large. Many university administrators couldn't honestly understand why students would want to give up the loving hand of paternalistic parents for the colder, harder justice of the outside world. English professor Charles Muscatine has said that the FSM revolutionized the idea of what a university was by overturning the medieval notion that the university was a special place, an ivory tower insulated from the rest of the world: "What the students achieved ... [was] a redefinition of the campus as the polis, or civic home of the students.... They forced that idea upon us, and it turned out to be right."*

By November the university had agreed to all of the FSM's

* Goines, *The Free Speech Movement*, 188.

demands except one: control of the decisions that affected our lives. There was a new notion of politics in the air—it wasn't about voting or political parties, but, in the words of the *Port Huron Statement* of the Students for a Democratic Society (SDS), politics was all "those social decisions determining the quality and direction of ... life."* But this idea was subtle and difficult; it was not an idea that thousands would go to jail for. I am convinced—and so are many others—that the movement would have died, or have been doomed as a weak minority effort if, at the end of November, the administration hadn't made a huge mistake.

On November 27 and 28, out of the blue, four students— Mario Savio, Art Goldberg, Brian Turner, and Jackie Goldberg—received letters from the administration. They were ordered to attend hearings before an administrative committee for illegal activities back in October, when thousands had surrounded the police car. When these letters became public, almost every student involved in the FSM felt personally betrayed. And when the movement demanded these charges be dropped, arguing that only the courts could regulate the content of speech and that this demand be met by noon on December 2, the stage was set for the extraordinary events that followed.

At a huge demonstration in front of Sproul Hall, thousands of students heard Mario Savio, the charismatic spokesperson of the Free Speech Movement, give his famous "operation of the machine" speech. I found his words so powerful that thirty years later I still have most of them committed to memory:

We have an autocracy which runs this university. It's managed. We asked the following: if President Kerr actually tried to get

---

* Students for a Democratic Society, *Port Huron Statement*, second printing, December 1964, p. 7.

something more liberal out of the Regents in his telephone conversation, why didn't he make some public statement to that effect? And the answer we received—from a well-meaning liberal—was the following: he said, "Would you ever imagine the manager of a firm making a statement publicly in opposition to his board of directors?" That's the answer! I ask you to consider: if this is a firm, and if the Board of Regents are the board of directors, and if President Kerr in fact is the manager, then I'll tell you something: the faculty are a bunch of employees, and we're the raw material! But we're a bunch of raw materials that don't mean to have any process upon us, don't mean to be made into any product, don't mean to end up being bought by some clients of the University; be they the government, be they industry, be they organized labor, be they anyone! We're human beings!

There is a time when the operation of the machine becomes so odious, makes you so sick at heart, that you can't take part; you can't even tacitly take part, and you've got to put your bodies upon the gears and upon the wheels, upon the levers, upon all the apparatus and you've got to make it stop. And you've got to indicate to the people who run it, to the people who own it, that unless you're free, the machine will be prevented from working at all!*

How strange to think of these words today, when the idea of the university as handmaiden to industry and government is once again unquestioned. But as I stood in the plaza, hearing those words, they came to symbolize for me the life of freedom and joy and mystery I was seeking and I found myself moved to tears.

December 2nd, 1964, 9 P.M.

Dear Mom:

This is a really incredible situation. I am sitting on the floor of Sproul Hall—the administration building. You

* Goines, *The Free Speech Movement*, 361.

may remember, it's the place I slept in on September 30th. Well, here I am again.

... I can't draw it, but it's one of those Greek style buildings, with white columns and three big windows in front. On each window is a big letter: FSM, so it looks like the building is really ours.

Four students were threatened with further disciplinary action, and received letters threatening expulsion. We are sitting-in in protest of that, and what started as a demand for free speech and advocacy has changed to include the whole meaning of education. There is anger at being only an IBM card, anger at the bureaucracy, at the money going to technology. The main issue remains that students should have to abide only by the laws of the government and the US Constitution in matters of civil liberties—they should not need to abide by special regulations.

This afternoon, there was an inspired rally where all the FSM leaders spoke, and Joan Baez sang. Everyone called for a tremendous sit-in, and then Joan Baez and Mario Savio led about 2000 people into Sproul Hall. Charles Powell, the president of the student government, made a feeble statement which was hissed down, telling people to have faith in the administration.

We went into Sproul Hall, and all the employees left. At 7 P.M., the police asked us to leave, but we refused. We were given instructions in non-violent civil disobedience, how to go limp when arrested. Then a truly extraordinary evening began.

We sang songs. There were rooms available for studying. There was a Chanukah service and folk dancing. In another room, they showed the Charlie Chaplin film, *The Rink*. Professors and teaching assistants created "Freedom Schools," gave classes in non-violence, political science, mathematics, Spanish, and the history of the civil rights movement in the Bay Area. There's been more singing and speeches. Joan Baez is still here. Food and drink are being passed around. We may be here a long time. If we are still here by tomorrow morning, there may be a strike by students and teaching assistants.

The press is here in droves: newspapers, LIFE, NBC, ABC, KPIX. A reporter saw me reading Thucydides and wrote it down. I swear it is the most stimulating experience I've ever had. It's a pretty mixed group. There are even three Goldwater Republicans here who write for the conservative journal *Man and State*, although the tendency is definitely toward the left.

December 3rd, 6:45 a.m.

Things look quite different at 6:45 a.m. For one thing, I am tired. At 11 P.M., Mario Savio spoke and said it looked as if Clark Kerr was going to stall us out—that is, not bring the police, and that we would have to stay a long time. So at 11:30, after more singing, a bunch of us went to sleep until 2 a.m., when I awoke to hear a complete change in the situation. We were sleeping near the telephone the FSM was using, so we heard all the important news. It seems the Alameda County Sheriff and police will come soon and arrest us. So we were given more instructions in non-violence, and all of us on the first floor went to the second and third and fourth. Then Chancellor Strong came, along with the Chief of Police, and gave us five minutes to leave the building, before being arrested. By five a.m., they had only arrested thirty people, but by now they have arrested about seventy-five, including all of those on the fourth floor. There are about

1000 of us altogether. Some people even managed to be hoisted up into the building on ropes, so we have thirty-five new people.

Here's what we have heard: Students for a Democratic Society—remember that's the organization I belonged to—has promised sympathy demonstrations on 100 campuses. Governor Brown plans to come to Berkeley today. Many reporters are still here. Many employees are not going to work, there is a picket line in front of the Student Union and many people will not cross. The Teamsters Union has refused to cross the picket line and therefore the University is without food in the cafeterias. A strike has been moved up to today at noon. Many faculty are with us, including the entire math department which is the most radical department. They have started arresting people on the third floor. We are on the second floor. Dawn has come. Nothing like this has happened, I guess, since the thirties. The people here are really marvelous, and hopefully comprise the future. A great number of students seem vitally concerned with education, a true and meaningful education. And of course, this is an educational experience in itself.

12:10 P.M.

I feel sick—inside and out. I feel depressed and ashamed of my society, afraid, sick and weird—a feeling of half not feeling anything and half wanting to cry on someone's shoulder. I am sitting with fifty other girls in an Oakland police station. The arrests began on the second floor. Now you must understand that there were two police forces involved—the Berkeley police, and the Oakland police. The Berkeley police were quite civil, even kind at times, and, as policemen go, understanding. The Oakland cops were brutal. They ran up and grabbed

Jack Weinberg who was speaking over a microphone and dragged him down the stairs. For each arrest, an officer came up, asked us to leave, gave us a number, photographed us and asked if we would walk. We went limp and they (the Berkeley police) dragged us rather nicely to the elevator. The boys got dragged down the stairs. When we got to the basement, we refused to walk, and the Oakland police dragged us horribly. This guy twists my arm back in a hammer lock, and forces me up, so I have to give in and walk. Then came the most Kafka-esque part—you get fingerprinted, photographed against a wall, and searched, they even undid my bra. Then we waited, singing freedom songs, until we were marched with our photos, a group of twelve, into a paddy wagon where, still singing, we were taken to a police station in Oakland where we are sitting, talking, singing, and studying.

But the worst thing we saw was the brutality before our arrest. One boy was clubbed, several were treated brutally. One girl was dragged and thrown crying into the police wagon. The worst moments were when the police went after the PA system. The first time they got Jack Weinberg; the second time, they tried to get Steve Weissman, but he slipped outside and escaped down a rope. At that moment the place went into bedlam, and two or three students threw boxes and books, fortunately they didn't hit anyone and they were told to stop.

I feel weird and scared. Even though I believe in what I did, I still have that weird feeling of being stamped for life, always having a police record next to my name. Of course I am in good company, but still ... I will write again when I know more about the future—bail, charges, etc.

2 P.M.

I'm still in this room, only 23 of us are left. We have
heard that at least 600 were arrested and there are rumors that the Santa Rita jail can't hold us and we will be
put in navy barracks.

9:45 P.M. San Leandro Armory
Finally at about 4 P.M. we were put into this bus with
barred windows. We were in that 20 by 20 room—a shift-
ing population of 20–55. But our group stayed longest.
The facilities were deplorable. There was no toilet paper.
We finally got some. There was one toilet which was
open and in full view. We sat on the floor. By 4 P.M.,
people who hadn't eaten since last night were starved.
Then, for the first time, even though I had only been arrested for several hours, I realized what lack of physical
freedom means: the fact that I could not go out that
door—that I was completely at their power and mercy,
that my world had become 20' by 20', and it was packed
with others—no room to move. I tried reading Thucydides, but I just couldn't concentrate. I was nervous and
had no outlet, not even the usual escape—food. Many of
the people around me were smoking, but I had no way
to calm myself. And worst of all, I had my period, and it
had leaked and there was no way to change, and nothing
to do.

So finally we were taken in this barred bus to the armory—it seems the jails were overcrowded—so they
created a jail here. We were finally given some tepid tea
and a cold cut sandwich at 5 P.M. More people have arrived, but our knowledge of what is going on at the University is limited. Until a half an hour ago we had no contact. Now, after we have been booked for the second

time, we can use the phone. My fingerprints will go to the FBI. I guess when the thought gets depressing one can always remember that conversation between Thoreau and Emerson when Thoreau was in jail: Emerson: "What are you doing in there?" Thoreau: "What are you doing out there?" So now we are trying to go to sleep on the floor of the Armory with some thin blankets.

It's 10:15 P.M., and I only had one and a half hours sleep on the floor last night. I will try to sleep until we go to Santa Rita and get our mug shots.

December 4th, 12:45 A.M.—Santa Rita

Nine of us were awakened. We got packed into a car to drive to the Santa Rita jail. I felt sicker than ever, woke up cold, shivering with spasms of cold tiredness. I had only slept an hour and the blanket was thin and the air freezing. We walked out into the cold air and a shivering fit really hit me. I just couldn't stop shaking. We were packed into a police barred car, very tight, which was good because it warmed us and we joked about such things as, "misery is a stone cold floor" and talked about "The Brig" and "Mario, Mario my Savio," until laughter threw off the cold and we were heated by each other's bodies and by the car itself. We arrived at Santa Rita and filed in to be mugged. Funny, I always associated the word "mugging" with the antithesis of police—something that happens in Central Park, for example, but they seem to use it for those pictures, you know, those front and side shots with the numbers below, that make you look like a criminal no matter what. I figured out why. They don't let you smile, and by then we were all so miserable looking anyway. So then we were put in some kind of cell, then taken to another regular room, although it was locked, and now there are rumors that we will get out soon, or that we won't get out soon and will have cold showers. But now it seems we may get out.

December 5th

Eventually we were released and taken in a bus to the gates of Santa Rita; there, a faculty-student carpool was waiting to pick us up. These supporters had raised our bail, and were now driving us home. I finally got home at 2:30 A.M. and managed to get five hours of sleep.

I couldn't sleep well, nor do I seem able to study effectively. I keep thinking about the past few days. Last night I was terribly depressed. Everything I had been thinking about the two levels of existence—how at the higher level we are ants in a meaningless universe—seemed true. At the moment, I feel so insignificant. It seems as if the truth will never conquer and that it was of no consequence that there were 800 of us and that the majority of the faculty supported us. The press still shouts, "communist," and there are calls for the FSM to be investigated by a committee like HUAC.

Sometimes I think that I could become an anarchist, if law means the action of the police. Jail affected me. The loss of physical freedom was a shock. The frisking was humiliating; the fingerprinting feels weird. It all has the feel of forever. You feel trapped and powerless. The police have the power to do anything they want to you for 48 hours—after that they must book you. You have practically no rights, and after a while, the police seem to be an evil power, because by this time you no longer associate them with law and order, but with hitting nonviolent students, wrenching, throwing, dragging people down stairs, and you realize that they have the backing of the society and you have nothing but your convictions.

The feelings I experienced inside Sproul Hall and later, in jail, were a complex mix: an ecstasy of community bonding and collective power, followed by a sense of total powerlessness. There were moments where all potential and possibility opened, and moments of utter futility, when a thousand students seemed nothing more than a thousand grains of sand. A few years later, when I would enter the imposing court buildings in lower Manhattan for political trials—first as a journalist, later as a juror, but never again as a defendant—I was still close enough to the events of the sixties that I retained a clear understanding of the true meaning of the massive structures I was entering: the towering columns of the federal court building; the barred windows rising so high at 100 Center Street, the seat of the criminal courts. And I understood that the rooms within, with their thirty-foot ceilings and the judge sitting many feet above ordinary citizens, had been carefully designed to show the insignificance of the individual human being in the face of government power.

But as a participant in this demonstration and arrest, what I could not see was the view of this event from the outside, a view which did much to increase faculty support for our cause. While we rejected the notion of the university as an ivory tower, our teachers still embraced it. The professors who walked onto campus that morning found their lovely sanctuary ringed with police. It was this shock that caused many a professor to make a final break with the university administration and support the FSM's demands. David Lance Goines writes that this was "the first time in American history that the German academic tradition, barring civil authority from the University campus, had been disregarded,"*

* Goines, *The Free Speech Movement*, 410.

and that the faculty felt the administration had treated them with contempt and so, in the end, had allied themselves not so much with the students as against the administration and the government of California.

Back on campus, the atmosphere was electric. Most classes were canceled and there was a very effective student strike to oppose the policies of the administration. Graduate students picketed many buildings and the almost eight hundred who had been arrested returned to the campus wearing black armbands with a *V* emblazoned on them. You could see their armbands all over the campus. The time felt incredibly special, as if my own action was part of something that had caused a shift in the world.

Two faculty groups, a group of two hundred that supported FSM goals and a council of department chairmen that didn't, met to plan strategy, and President Clark Kerr announced that a university-wide meeting would take place on December 7, at the large Greek Theater. The FSM met as well, and determined to have its own speaker at the gathering.

At the Greek Theater, President Kerr spoke before a huge crowd. His words about order and "lawful procedures" and the continuation of classes seemed curiously detached from the electric reality—reverberating in the amphitheater like dead language from an ancient world. But Kerr did announce an amnesty in the cases against the four students and said that the university would not initiate disciplinary action against those who participated in the sit-in, but would simply accept the action of the courts. In addition, rules for campus political activity would be liberalized. When Kerr finished his announcement, Mario Savio walked slowly up to the front to speak. To my stunned amazement—and the amazement of thousands of others in the crowd—two campus policemen grabbed Mario before he could reach the microphone and dragged him off the stage. The effect was sensational. Shocked, we all rose to our feet and roared our disapproval.

Goines believes that this one "lightning-lit instant in the history of the FSM" did more to gain support for the movement than anything else. "We all heard stories of older professors who had escaped Nazi terror," Goines writes, "and who, stunned by what the police had done before their very eyes, expressed shame and rage that they had condoned an administration which resorted to Storm Trooper tactics to prevent one student from speaking to a crowd."* Moments later, when the administration realized its mistake and released Savio, the damage was done. Ten thousand people attended the rally in Sproul Plaza later that day.

Meanwhile, a group of more liberal faculty members—the Committee of 200—drew up its own proposals, which essentially supported the FSM's demands: that there be no disciplinary measures taken by the university for events prior to December 8, and while campus activities might be subject to reasonable regulations as to time, place, and manner, their political content would not be restricted nor would restrictions be placed on the political activity of off-campus groups.

The next day, December 8, the Academic Senate met to consider the faculty's proposal. Somewhere between three and five thousand students listened for three hours as the meeting was broadcast outside over loudspeakers. When the Committee of 200's resolution in support of the FSM's demands passed by a vote of 824–115 and all amendments that would have weakened or diluted the force of that resolution were roundly voted down by large majorities, the students outside roared their approval, and many of us stood holding each other as tears flowed. Then the meeting ended and moments later the applauding students backed away on either

* Goines, *The Free Speech Movement*, 429.

side, making a path for the professors, who walked out through the auditorium doors in an almost formal procession. It was, Bettina Aptheker noted some twenty years later, "one of the courageous moments in the history of the faculty, which had not always been courageous.... Many of them and many of us were crying. Many of them and many of us came to believe that the oppression of the 1950's was finally at an end."* A week later, the California Board of Regents voted that political activity would only be regulated by the First and Fourteenth amendments to the U.S. Constitution. From now on students would be judged as citizens. The Free Speech Movement had won.

We were jubilant. As I wandered through the fogbound and rainy campus, I found my soul open and ready to receive on all levels. As I inhaled the pungent smell of eucalyptus trees and walked the charming wooden bridges over Strawberry Creek, I kept pinching myself that this place was real. The world seemed deeply good.

Later, the coldness of the law and the brutality of the Oakland police sank in. And as I read the biased reports of our struggle in the newspapers (in which we were portrayed as communist dupes or outside agitators—accounts which bore no relation to the events we had witnessed), I felt, as if for the first time, that the society around me was a place of distortion, lies, and evil. The Free Speech Movement gave me a profound understanding of the unseen institutions of this country—the courts, the jails, and the police—institutions which had never before touched my life, and which remain hidden for most white, middle-class people.

But more importantly, the FSM gave me an experience of a new kind of freedom, not to speak, to act, or to buy, but to

*Bettina Aptheker, in a speech at the twentieth-year reunion of the FSM, December 1984.

claim the power to come together with others in community to transform and to change. And the FSM was also emotionally powerful because it seemed to be a battle to wrest the control of our lives away from the clerks, the files, and the forms that seemed to be increasingly dominating our lives as students—in other words, from the seemingly invulnerable giants of technology and bureaucracy. In my own life, I had gone from a small private school filled with liberty and creativity to a high school where creativity was mixed with bureaucracy and rigidity, to a huge university where the most popular slogan referred to students as IBM computer cards ("Do not fold, spindle, or mutilate!"). The Free Speech Movement gave me and many others a sense of personal power and control over our lives.

This is true for me even though I was just a grunt, a foot soldier in this battle. I was a lowly freshman and few people knew my name. I made no speeches from the steps of Sproul Plaza, and I was never quoted in the newspapers. I sat at tables, picketed, went to meetings, listened to speeches, handed out leaflets, marched, sat-in, and went to jail.

I resisted some of the activities of day-by-day political organizing—the staffing of offices, the cooking of food. In part, this was because I knew that I was a person of ideas, not of day-to-day action. I was fascinated by theory and philosophy, but I found many political meetings deadly dull. And I also intuitively knew, without benefit of feminist analysis, that it was the female students (then called coeds) who were generally making the coffee and running the mimeograph machines. The FSM retained, as did all left movements of the day, its sexist baggage, and few were the women who made names for themselves on their own. Most of the movement's women leaders were some man's sister or some man's lover.

Bettina Aptheker was the one woman who stood entirely on her own, and many years later she would say that she was accepted into the inner circles partly because her father was a famous communist theoretician. I was certainly in awe of Mario Savio's and Jack Weinberg's oratory, but it was not to them that I looked for a model. If there was anyone whom I sought as my mentor, a leader whose style I wished to emulate, it was Bettina. Although she was described again and again in the press as an avowed communist—and was, in fact, the only actual Communist Party member in the FSM leadership—Bettina actually functioned then, as she did throughout the sixties, as a peacemaker between all factions. She was down-to-earth, optimistic, direct and unpretentious. She could cut through any argument and find the common ground. She radiated goodness, was egalitarian in style despite her party affiliation, and seemed to be without even a drop of adolescent angst. She remained for me a model of righteous politics wedded to good spirits and psychological wholeness. And she became an illustration of an important and recurring lesson in life: outward political affiliation or ideology is never the measure of a human being and it should never be the basis on which you choose your friends.

Reading Goines's book *The Free Speech Movement: Coming of Age in the 1960s* has made me understand how different my own experience was from his, and how different was the experience of women from that of men in the movement. For Goines, political activity was part of his total rebellion against his parents. He hated school and gloried in a kind of young man's liberation: he writes that he quickly saw that radical politics brought him sex and the adoration of young women.

I was a virgin when I arrived on campus in the summer of 1964, and I was still a virgin when the FSM achieved its victory in December. For me, unlike Goines, radical politics had little to do with sex; instead, it was about ideas and, secondarily, about friendships. I weighed a hundred and eighty pounds, a fact that I now understand was in part a deep feminist protest. My weight was a suit of armor I wore to maintain control of my life, so as to be taken seriously for my ideas and never seen as a sexual object. And I wasn't. Looking back, I realize that I also protected myself by not putting myself in situations that would be dangerously intimate, like the day-to-day running of a political organization. It was much safer to act from the outside, where I was always in control.

In 1984, twenty years after our victory, Bettina Aptheker addressed several thousand people at a Free Speech Movement reunion. It was the first time I had seen her in many, many years. Her words brought tears to almost every woman FSM veteran in the room. She started by saying that she was often known as the daughter of Herbert Aptheker, the communist theoretician, but she was also the daughter of Fay Aptheker, and that she would now like to introduce herself by naming herself back through her female line. She noted that most of the histories of the sixties have been written by men, and so our history of that era is partial, since the ideas and articulations and reflections of women have been excluded. Because of this, she argued, the histories have emphasized power and control, whereas the women's stories might have emphasized the dailyness of struggle, connection, and the long slow process of meaningful change. She noted that women in the sixties staffed the offices, while it was the men who held the press conferences and did the publicity. This reflected the sexual division of labor in the larger society, "but if we are a radical movement about the business of making change, we need to change how we go about our business of making change."

And then she entered deeper waters: "It was also the case that there were women who, one way or another, found

themselves in situations of performing sexual favors for important movement men. That happened. It is also a fact that
women activists were more seriously abused, physically and
sexually, both by the police, which is to be expected, and also
by men within the movement, which is something that is no
longer tolerable."

Then Bettina spoke even more personally and her words
began to illuminate my own reflections as a woman who
went through this experience. She said that as an only child,
very cherished by her parents, she was not "gendered female." Baseball was her passion, and she was totally crushed
when she could not play in Little League. She was taught that
she was intelligent and she was encouraged to speak out publicly. And when she came to Berkeley, as Aptheker's daughter,
"I was ushered into the inner circles of the revolutionary
movement in Berkeley despite my sex." She said she was
treated as "one of the boys," neutered sexually. The very few
times she was looked upon as female she was seen as "an object of sexual prey."

"I also internalized certain aspects of the oppression of
women. I believed there were men, there were women, and
there was me. I didn't want to be like other women, because
I saw the women as being subordinated and unable to speak
and unable to present their views, so I participated in the
oppression of women in the FSM"—and here her voice
dropped to a deep whisper—"for which I apologize." Many
women in the audience sat with tears streaming down their
faces. Bettina ended her speech by saying that despite the humiliating roles women were forced to play in the movement,
"we did march in the morning, and in apprehending the
sound of those streets flooded with people we heard the echo
of our own liberation. What we learned in the sixties, the
great secret as it were, is that people have the inherited wis-

dom and the collective strength to change the conditions of their lives."*

Like Bettina, I was an only child who had not been programmed as readily as others into a female role. For me, as for her, politics was a place I came to through inheritance and tradition, not through anger and rebellion.

At least a hundred former activists attended the twentieth anniversary of the Free Speech Movement. As we looked around the room at those who had come to this reunion, we realized what we were not: we were not burned-out, drugged-out sixties radicals, the lost generation described so often in studies of this period. We had emerged from the storms of the era for the most part deepened and reasonably unscathed. Most of us had experienced a kind of radiance. Most of us were leading full and interesting lives and doing more good than harm. Among us there were few regrets.

Many people have attempted to describe the energy that people felt, the intense sense of possibility, the feeling, almost universally shared, that we could change not only our own lives—in itself an amazing idea, for even that seems a fantasy to so many young people today—but the conditions of the world. And because we experienced a victory, most of us have never lost that feeling, despite the inevitable setbacks, tragedies, and changes that may have taken place in our individual lives. Most of us remain incurable optimists and most of us have been able to continue working, in some form, toward efforts of personal and political transformation.

Jack Weinberg, the activist who'd once coined the phrase "Never trust anyone over thirty," explained it this way: We had not only experienced a great battle, we had experienced what it was like to *win* a great battle, and it was the experience

* Aptheker, FSM reunion speech, December 1984.

of victory that had changed our lives. Unlike the generation that followed, who only experienced the maddening and frustrating battle to end the Vietnam War, our fight, like the civil rights activism that went before and after it, left a trail of positive change.

At the university, we had demanded our rights as citizens, argued for self-directed education, and helped to usher in a whole decade of experimentation. We'd done something to transform the world around us, and we were forever marked by the belief that change was possible. It would affect us for life, making us deep optimists about human possibility and influencing every choice from then on. As W. J. Rorabaugh writes in *Berkeley at War*, "The Free Speech Movement unleashed a restless probing of life."*

Six months later I went to Mississippi as a civil rights worker.

---

*W. J. Rorabaugh, *Berkeley at War* (New York: Oxford University Press, 1989), 47.

Mississippi Summer

W HEN I REDISCOVERED my Mississippi summer journal—a hundred and eighty yellowing, handwritten pages enclosed in a cheap, zippered case of fake brown leather—it was not the writing but the snapshots that fell out, most of them faded and overexposed, that brought a flood of recollections of a summer filled with the kind of fear that remains unnoticed when you encounter it, but racks the body when you look back from afar. And there, along with the faces of the people and their searing, intense expressions, were the weathered shacks and dirt roads of Hog Town, the black area of Belzoni, Mississippi, where I lived in the summer of 1965.

Why on earth did I go? As a nineteen-year-old I was unconscious of many of the complex tides flowing through me. I certainly believed in civil rights and had been taught from an early age to respect people of all races and nations; I had been propelled into activism at the age of fourteen, partly by family tradition, partly by friends, and also by some still-undefined feeling of moral urgency; I had walked picket lines to protest segregated hiring policies as early as 1960. But beliefs alone would not have brought me to the Mississippi Delta.

I was also fascinated with the South. I had been born in Little

Rock, Arkansas, and although I left at the age of six months, as a young girl I had always wondered if being born in the South had, somehow, marked me. I remembered every detail of my mother's fascinating stories of her years in Arkansas, Texas, and Oklahoma during World War II—even odd tidbits like the fact that lipsticks would melt in the Texas heat, so my mother had put them in the icebox—and I wanted that kind of romance and adventure for myself.

After my participation in the Free Speech Movement, I felt that the world was on the cusp of transformation. I also knew that the best leaders of the FSM had honed their leadership skills in civil rights work in the South the summer before. Training in Mississippi seemed a way to gain the serious skills needed to be an activist.

And then there was Andy Goodman. In the summer of 1964 nearly a thousand college students went south to work for the Mississippi Summer Project, where they helped to register black voters and set up Freedom Schools. The Freedom Schools taught reading skills, so that blacks could pass the arcane literacy requirements needed to register to vote. These schools also taught the history of the civil rights movement, and they helped black citizens become aware of their own rights and powers. Three civil rights workers were murdered that summer, and Andy Goodman was one of them.

He had grown up in my neighborhood. His mother, Carolyn, and my mother were friends, and Andy had gone to Walden, a progressive school five blocks from my home. Andy's murder had rocked my mother. She closely followed the story of the murders and the very slow government investigation into their deaths that followed. She fervently hoped I would not go to Mississippi and wrote me a letter urging me to choose the equally necessary civil rights and poverty work closer to home. Looking back at this letter almost thirty years later, having my own young child at home, I am amazed at how she put her own feelings forward in such a way as not to trap me, leaving me free to disagree and choose a different path, as indeed I did.

May 3rd, 1965

Dearest Margot:

I just spoke to Joe Popper. . . . He thinks white kids are needed to work with Whites more than with Negroes. Naturally I'd be happier to have you up North. . . . But that is a decision sweetheart that you'll have to make. I would not be happy if I felt you did something for my sake that you deep down didn't want to do—that only leads to martyrville. So find out all the projects that SNCC is sponsoring North and South and if there is just as exciting a one nearer to home, naturally I'd be delighted if you decided to take it. I love you very much as you know and I feel you have (as every teenager does) many hurdles to jump until you know who you really are and what it is you want from this span of years given to us humans. Naturally being a mommy I feel you've been away all year and maybe it wouldn't be such a bad idea to work closer to home—what think you? However I am giving you my blessings and love should it be the Southland you'll be in.

Her arguments were eminently rational, and not just those of a mother protecting her child. Six months later practically every black civil rights group in the country would also be urging whites to return to their own communities. They argued, with some justification, that segregation existed in the North as well as the South. But, that said, I still believe there were important reasons for whites to go south in 1964 and 1965. Blacks who tried to oppose the system of segregation were getting killed every day, and in most cases their names didn't even appear in the papers. But white segregationists who thought nothing of beating up a black person, or leaving someone dead on a lonely back road, thought again when the civil rights worker was white, educated, and might be, God forbid, the daughter or son of a senator or banker. Like it or not, white, middle-class students *were* noticed. And by going to the South, we allowed the civil rights movement to use us as hostages. As a result, segregationists could not so easily circumvent the federal laws on voting and equal access.

But at the time thoughts of political strategy were not uppermost in my mind. I simply knew that within the past two years the South had been the place where the lines were drawn most clearly—the place where NAACP leader Medgar Evers had been shot, where four children had died in a church bombing in Birmingham, and where a close neighbor of my own age and background had been murdered.

And also, truth be told, I felt a call to adventure, a need to throw myself into a new and different world and learn its lessons, to undergo a test of fire. I felt surprisingly little foreboding. Despite Andy's death, I was clothed in the typical adolescent's illusion of immortality. In the same way that I loved hurricanes and at the age of nine felt only excitement, not fear, when I was evacuated from a New England shore on the eve of a great and destructive storm, I had a desire to throw myself into the maelstrom.

I was also struggling intensely with the question of whether it was really possible to change the world. Already in 1965 there were tensions emerging between the cultural and political wings of the radical movement. Today we tend to lump many aspects of the sixties together—rock music, politics, clothing styles, sex and drugs—but a continuing

battle between the "hippies," on the one side, and the "politi-
cos" on the other, defined much of the era. At Berkeley, my
two roommates had been fairly antipolitical. They had introduced me to ideas of nihilism and human insignificance, and
I was unsure of my own attitudes. Six weeks before I went to
Mississippi I wrote home,

I am beginning to see a new class conflict that even transcends
the economic. The new rebels will reject all— including the
idea that anything can be changed. On the cover of his most
recent album Bob Dylan says, "I accept chaos ... the great
books have been written, the great sayings have been said ..."
And Dylan still sings civil rights songs and anti-war songs and
makes some commitment. But take another look at that
Beatles film again, *A Hard Day's Night*. Notice how, with the exception of a few people, they ridicule everyone. Do you have
any idea what the Beatles mean to people here? They are GOD.
I know someone who got a job in a theater to see them 69
times. One of my roommates has seen the film seven times.
Why are they idolized? Because the Beatles have freed themselves completely from the bonds of convention. Nothing is
sacred, nothing except themselves is of any consequence.

But what if my roommates are right? I wondered. Suppose
good and evil are illusions? Suppose there is no truth, no morality? How could I work for civil rights if everything is
meaningless?

As for South or North, I wrote my mother that I knew
there was important work to be done in both places. "But
going to the South is more than that. It is a selfish, but constructively selfish act. It is a chance to experience a part of
reality, a part of America, a life, a fear, a people, that can only
be understood from within. I must see what I can do before
rejecting the possibility of doing."

Looking back, I am surprised at how aware I was of my
own selfish motives, and how much I was struggling to bal-

ance these motives with ideas of justice, compassion, and changing the world. I was also probably more influenced than I would have cared to admit by my father's attitudes and his belief in putting social concerns above all. From the time I was a child, he had warned me against the tendency for an only child to be selfish. "The great task in any life," my father wrote to me five months before my Mississippi journey,

is to merge self-interest with the interest of mankind. Since all life is social life, the problem is a threefold one: first, what are your needs, desires and wishes. Second, what are the needs, desires of other people—those around you, mankind as a whole, friends, etc. And third, how to bring self-interest into agreement with common human interest. No one is perfect in doing that but whenever one accomplishes that in any area, there is a feeling of satisfaction and significance. This is also the basis of morality, ethics, the basis of positive relationships, of friendships, of love, and this also resolves the conflict of egoism against altruism, of selfishness against unselfishness.

Going to Mississippi seemed to be a way to merge self-interest with the concerns of others, as well as begin to answer many of these questions of heart, soul, and self: How much courage did I possess, how much of an activist did I really want to be, and how possible was it to really change the world around me?

By June and the end of the school term, I had decided to join a voter registration project run jointly by the Mississippi Freedom Democratic Party, an organization that was trying to gain representation for black Mississippians, and the Student Nonviolent Coordinating Committee (SNCC). Although I went alone, knowing no one else who had made a similar decision, I was part of a group of several hundred college students—mostly white, mostly from the North—

who came to Washington, D.C., the border between the North and the South, to begin our training.

We slept in the pews of a Baptist church. During a session on nonviolence, we were shown how to fall, how to "go limp" when arrested, and how to cover our faces and ears when attacked. Young women were urged to remove all jewelry, particularly earrings if their ears were pierced. Using theatrical techniques and role-playing, the civil rights organizers imitated Southern policemen and local "rednecks"; they presented a mock sit-in, followed by a demonstration of how to deal with violence. The role-playing once became so real that a young woman was pushed over and her nose began to bleed.

The instructions were familiar from the FSM occupation of Sproul Hall six months before. During that sit-in, moments before the arrests took place, the atmosphere in the room had been electric; now, in Washington, in a role-playing session far removed from real events, there was something almost surreal about the way our instructors interspersed their comments with jokes and laughter. Still, underneath the levity there was a sense of deadly seriousness. After all, we were going to a place where people had been killed. There were strict rules to follow: always travel with a partner, always have a dime for a phone call. We were entering an unforgiving world. "It only takes three seconds to disappear in Mississippi," we were told, words which would come to haunt me a mere six weeks later.

At a session on community organization, we took the parts of farmers, sharecroppers, and priests. We were told never to impose our views on local people. In one session, a woman playing a sharecropper called us communists and, to our surprise, we were advised not to argue with her, not even to disabuse her of this notion. After all, we were told, she's probably read it in the paper and it's what she thinks. "Always be in the background," the organizers emphasized, "so that the local people will make their own decisions and you, when you go, will not be needed." This lesson in noninterference was difficult to obey, like the prime directive in *Star Trek*, and we didn't always follow it precisely.

We heard lectures on Mississippi's political history and the history of voting rights. We spent hours lobbying for civil rights legislation; at one point, I and another volunteer found ourselves inside Gerald Ford's congressional office in the Capitol, speaking to his legislative assistant. She was clearly uninterested in our civil rights agenda and spent most of the time interrogating us. "Who's paying you?" she asked, and weren't we "breaking housing regulations by sleeping on a church floor?"

I remember listening to Mrs. Victoria Gray, a candidate for Congress with the Mississippi Freedom Democratic Party. "The MFDP," she said, was a means for political expression by black Mississippians. It was a chance to make democracy real, to "bring truth to the biblical saying that the words can become flesh."

It was in Washington that I first heard the singing. I had sung spirituals in City and Country and I knew a dozen civil rights songs by the time I was fifteen. But now those songs took on a full-bodied life. They swelled and roared and were so overpowering that my body and voice became one with the harmonies, the *alleluia*s and the clapping of hands. The singing seemed to be a pathway to the stars and it came from the deepest part of being.

After a week in Washington I got a ride to Mississippi with four other civil rights volunteers. The deep South of the early sixties felt more foreign than Europe. Soon after we crossed the Mason-Dixon line, in Virginia, we saw the words "Vote White, Vote Republican" scrawled on an overpass. In Alabama I felt like an enemy spy trying to "pass" as I mailed home a postcard with a picture of Alabama's Governor George Wallace standing in front of the Alabama state flag, a flag that is only minutely distinguishable from the Confederate one.

At a Georgia lunch counter the waitress practically jumped when she overheard me mention Berkeley in a casual conversation. After a week in the black ghetto of Washington, D.C., the white South hit me like a cold wind. Georgia was also where I first saw separate bathrooms for white and colored. But most segregation was, even then, more subtle. The lunch counter where we ate was segregated, but there were no signs, and most white people would not even have noticed. Signs saying "Negroes can't eat here" were unnecessary. Everyone knew the rules. This world seemed so alien, and I was so much an outsider, that it was hard to remember my mother's words: "I've lived down South and having lived there, I do not assume that every white Southerner is automatically a racist. I have met too many decent white Southerners to fall victim to that cliché of so many so-called liberal Northerners."

When we arrived in a black neighborhood in Jackson, Mississippi, for the next phase of our training, I suddenly felt I was home. I was no longer in enemy territory; I was back in a place where my values and beliefs were welcomed. There was a casual and relaxed air, and I suddenly felt safe for the first time since leaving the District of Columbia. But later, standing in front of the project office, I began to feel uncomfortable. The whole neighborhood was clearly aware that hundreds of whites were passing through, and every once in a while some strange young man would approach, take my hand or put his arm around my shoulder, and begin flirting. I was still a virgin, and just about as uptight about having sex

with anyone, black or white, as I could be. I was also someone
determined to remain in control, no matter what the cost.
"Most of the girls just don't know how to handle it," I wrote
in my journal. "It's really bad. God knows what they're feeling inside, perhaps guilt, but they just can't tell these guys
'No.' It's really pitiful." At the same time, down deep, I may
have envied them their freedom to let go.

It was also in Jackson that I experienced my first encounter with anti-Semitism. It was a very simple moment—perhaps eight seconds in all—and it was very mild, but it remains indelible, and every word in the encounter played
over and over in my mind for days. Walking down the street,
I was accosted by three young men in their twenties. "You
Italian?" they asked. "No," I replied. "You Greek?" "No," I said
again. "Oh, no," they laughed to each other, "not another
one!" Inside I raged. Was I so easy to pinpoint? How could
these black guys presume to know who I was, how could they
put me in their little box? *Me*—this so non-Jewish, Jewish
person who grew up celebrating Christmas, had sung in a
Catholic choir, continually lusted for lobster and bacon, had
entered a synagogue no more than three times in her life,
and even possessed a baptismal certificate from some Presby-
terian church in Little Rock? I was furious that my appearance was such a dead giveaway and I was so easy to categorize.

That night I stayed with Mrs. Bertha Coleman, a young
black woman in her late twenties. I never figured out how
she earned her meagre living. The house was like nothing I
had ever seen in a city. The flush toilet stood in a shed
attached to the house. The living room contained one chair,
some curtains on one window, and a shelf of bric-a-brac. The
wallpaper was faded and torn in many places. A picture of
the Last Supper hung on the wall. There was no electricity,
only a single oil lamp which served as the light for the entire
house. The small kitchen had a sink with cold running water,

but no refrigerator, and one of the windows was covered with newspaper instead of glass. A pan of cornbread rested on the stove, the only food.

I shared Mrs. Coleman's bedroom and her bed. When I awoke she had already left for a funeral, and one of her little boys, a three- or four-year-old, was sleeping naked beside me. It was too hot to use any bedcovering and I felt sweaty and overdressed in my pajamas. The cornbread on the stove did not seem sufficient to feed the swarm of children that clustered around me, three of whom seemed to belong to my host, and all of them seemed to be hungry. I divided what there was. The eldest child was friendly and talkative, but he kept on saying "Yes, ma'am," which made me feel uncomfortable. I already felt humbled to be in the presence of such generosity mixed with such poverty. A woman who had absolutely nothing had opened her home, her bed, and her kitchen to me.

In Mississippi, some of the greatest hospitality came from the poorest people. It made me realize how seldom generosity is paired with affluence and how rarely I had been willing to share my own possessions. But prosperous black families also came to our aid. Our group's training continued in Hattiesburg, where I stayed with a middle-class black family, the Dwights. Although they had five children living at home, their house was large enough to give lodging to four volunteers. The Dwights had three lively teenage daughters. I talked with them for hours, about Barry Goldwater, Lyndon Johnson, Vietnam and civil rights. "Every time I listen to these girls I am more amazed," I wrote in my journal.

I can't get over it. It is as if a whole world has been opened up to them and they are devouring it. There was no spouting of dogma, but an intelligent, even politically sophisticated discussion. I asked them where they had gained such an opportunity to think and question and they said, "the freedom schools."

The next night, I got to listen to them again, talking about school and about being jailed in Jackson. Then Mr. and Mrs. Dwight returned home. On the way home, the police stopped them, and asked to see Mr. Dwight's license which he had forgotten. They put Mr. Dwight in jail for a few minutes until he paid a nine dollar fine. It's a little thing, but it illustrates the kind of constant harassment the local people here are always up against.

On July 8, after our training was over, the MFDP interviewed us for the various civil rights projects that were taking place all over Mississippi. Then we waited for two days that seemed to last forever. While we waited, people from the local counties grew impatient and began to ask us to come with them. At one point a guy came over and asked me if I wanted to go to Mosspoint. "It's on the beach," he said, "with palm trees swaying." But the area seemed pretty middle-class, and I wanted the rural experience.

Then I heard about Belzoni, in Humphries County, but the more I heard about it, the more I was afraid. The director of the project was in jail and the phone was disconnected. We knew that it was a "tough area," but not much else. As we waited around I put myself on one list and then on another, and finally decided on Belzoni. That evening we heard that a car that had left for Greenwood had been firebombed. Although no one had been hurt, we decided to delay our journey until daylight.

There were six white volunteers who went to Belzoni. I was the only woman. The men lived in the Freedom House, an office with beds, books, and typewriters. Nearby was Mary Thomas's store, a place to eat breakfast and wash up. Two houses away from the Freedom House was my home, with the Lee family. This description is from my journal:

July 10, 1965. I live on a dirt street. Geese and chickens and, of course, people are its travelers. This morning I woke up at 6:30, to the sounds of roosters crowing and a voice on the radio giving the agricultural news and the weather for the Delta. Time to begin the process of washing. The water is outside. There's a large television, a radio, but no toilet, only an outhouse in the back, where the hogs and chickens live. All water (cold) comes from an outdoor faucet. To wash dishes or clothes, you fill a pan and get on with it. As for bathing, there's a tub over at Mary Thomas's store. There is real poverty here, and fear, and apathy, and beauty too. There are sunflowers everywhere, and kind people and sad people, and people who make two dollars a day picking cotton on plantations.

The Lees' house was that strange combination of poverty and abundance so common in the black American South of the 1960s. It was comparatively ample—six rooms—and it had electricity and a television, but it lacked indoor plumbing or running water. There was a pump in the backyard and you brushed your teeth by taking a glass of water, swishing the water around in your mouth, and spitting it out over the back porch onto the ground, watching the mixture of water, saliva, and toothpaste form patterns on the grass and dirt below.

But in some ways the house was pretty luxurious for Hog Town; it even had a telephone. Most of the houses were shacks of wood and tin, with torn tar paper for covering. Hens and roosters would peck for food in the dirt streets, and since there was no drainage system, during a rainstorm the roads became rivers that were often more than ankle deep. It was all in sharp contrast to the white part of town, with its elegant courthouse with stately Doric columns.

The Lees had twelve children, six of them living at home. A beat-up red Ford pickup truck sat in front of the house, near a patch of weeds and a couple of old tires. At least four dogs wandered around nearby. The backyard contained the outhouse, pigpen, and chicken coop: it was crisscrossed by clotheslines and surrounded by sunflowers.

I will never forget the two dusk-colored pigs that rooted around in the mud and slops, because one night, around 4:00 A.M., I padded barefoot out the back door, struck out across the yard and over to the outhouse, and sat down for what I hoped would be a very quick pee. But suddenly the wind rattled the door, the outside wooden latch slipped into its holder, and I was locked inside, listening to the pigs snuffling and snorting in the black night. It took about fifteen minutes of frenzied shouting until one of the Lee kids came to the rescue, creating a good enough story to give the neighborhood a few laughs for at least a week. The Lees, I am sure, thought I was a peculiar addition to their family.

Mrs. Lee was a slender woman with high cheekbones, ebony skin, and fine features. Her hair was severely pulled back and she stood straight and proud. She read her Bible regularly, quoted from it often, and applied every passage toward a practical purpose. For many of the blacks in Belzoni, ground down from years of poverty and fear, heaven had become the only reward and funerals the only happy social occasion. Not so for Mrs. Lee, whose civil rights activism was out there for anyone to see, since she fed me and gave me a bed. "God only helps those who help themselves," was one line I heard often in her house. Under her inspiration I read the New Testament that summer, word for word.

In 1965, Belzoni was a small town in the middle of the Delta. Most of its residents were black, yet not a single black person was registered to vote. In 1961, a farmer named Herbert Lee led a voter registration drive in the area. Four hundred people turned out to register. The next day, while he was sitting in the back of his pickup truck, Lee was shot to death by a white member of the Mississippi state legislature. His death inspired one of the most beautiful songs of the civil rights movement:

We've been 'buked and we've been scorned,
We've been talked about sure's you're born.
But we'll never turn back,
No, we'll never turn back.
Until we've all been freed and we have equality.

We have hung our head and cried
For those like Lee who died,
Died for you and died for me,
*Died for the cause of equality.**

The Belzoni project had a staff of four. One of them, Robert, was in jail. The others were Ellis, Matt, and Johnnie. Johnnie was tall, even a bit gangly. He had prominent cheekbones, long arms with slender fingers. He smoked constantly and drank heavily, but he was smart. By the third week he had psyched me out. "You're an explorer," he told me, before I was really ready to admit how large a motive exploration was in my journey to Mississippi. Then there was Matt, a large guy who said little. He wore a banded straw hat and sunglasses, and was a constant, imposing but silent presence. Lastly, there was Ellis, certainly the most suave of the three organizers. He looked cool and smoked a pipe. The six volunteers included Bernie and me from New York, Ben from California, and Bill, Dan, and John from Wesleyan. Wesleyan University was helping to fund the project.

Belzoni had several prominent black families. The wealthiest citizen was the local funeral director, and he was sympa-

* "We'll Never Turn Back," *Sing for Freedom: The Story of the Civil Rights Movement Through Its Songs*, ed. Guy and Candie Carawan (*Bethlehem, Penn.*: Sing Out Publications, 1990), 93–95.

thetic to our goals. But the family most active in civil rights in the area was the Hazelwoods, independent farmers who were working on a government project with over a hundred acres of their own. Daddy Hazelwood, the eldest, had the kind of face that leaps out at you from old photographs. He was tall and thin, with a sensitive, beautiful, bony face. But it was his long hands and expressive fingers that told the most. This was a man who could neither read nor write, but at every meeting he would utter the most moving phrases. Intelligent and articulate, his low, sweet, trembling voice could make you cry.

In the past few years, Belzoni high school students had succeeded in desegregating the public library and had made various unsuccessful attempts to end segregation at the movie theater. They had also attempted to desegregate the ice cream parlor, which had seats and shade trees for whites only. Much of our daily work was door-to-door canvassing, trying to convince people to register to vote, and to sign a petition to get the streets paved and put in a drainage system and a few lights. To an outsider it must have seemed very simple, even easy, but it was a losing proposition. Most people were too scared to sign the petition, and even more scared to confront the registrars.

July 11th. It's Sunday and we all went to church. Bernie, John, Matt and I went to New Hope Baptist church to hear Reverend Johnson preach. He was bold for Mississippi. He based his sermon on a passage from Kings—about not running, but standing up. By the end of the sermon he sounded like a rock and roll singer, and two young women were filled with the spirit and had fits. Reverend Johnson really paved the way for us. He talked about how Negroes were still in bondage and then he introduced us, by talking about white college students coming to the South. Afterwards John talked and mentioned the petition. Then Reverend Johnson urged his congregation to sign the petition and to register to vote. Afterwards, there was an incredible feast: chicken, cornbread, stuffing, okra, sweet potato pie, and the church ladies were so insistent that we eat that I must have had six pieces of pie and cake.

July 13th. Yesterday, we went over to the Hazelwoods to help them chop cotton. I had thought that chopping cotton was some special process where cotton was somehow chopped. But it is simply weeding with a hoe. It was very hot, but good to be doing something physical for a change. After a while we went back to the house, had a good meal, had a nap and went back into the field again. I drove the tractor. Since I had never driven anything before, I was so excited and scared that I held on to the wheel so tightly that when I reached the field my hands were hard to unclench. The spirit of the group was great and the work was really fun.

What I did not mention in journals or letters was one of my most vivid memories of that day: watching a helicopter spray insecticide over the crops, drenching us in a rain of DDT or some equivalent. How easily we were poisoned. No one else mentioned it. Bernie, the other volunteer from New York, told me years later about returning to Mississippi and sitting down with the Hazelwoods as they watched a baseball game on television. Someone picked up a can of insect spray and casually sprayed the house every few hours.

July 15th. Tonight we learned a bit about canvassing, fought off the bugs and sang freedom songs. One must get used to a completely different pace of life. We go slow. It all seems as yet quite different than I expected. I expected fear. There is relatively little as yet. I expected little sleep, there is a good amount.

Dear Mom:

I would like to try and piece together many of the feelings one gets here, but I really don't know if they can be expressed in a letter. We are a strange group. So far there hasn't been anything that in one's wildest imagination one could call an incident. No police, no local "red-necks," nothing.

The other day I was canvassing on that petition I told you about. I went with Ellis, a staff member. Here we were, a white girl and Negro boy going house to house talking with people. A couple of cars passed, but except for the rather startled glance of one white woman, nothing. But my attitude is far from carefree. It greatly disturbs me that the typical attitude of southern whites is that obviously I am sleeping with Negro guys, when, knowing me, I'm not sleeping with anyone. The day after, I went canvassing with a girl, Mae. We went quite close to the white community. Many people saw us without comment.

I do feel that deep down inside me is some indefinable barrier. I don't know where this barrier came from, you certainly don't seem to have it. Here in the Negro community I don't notice it most of the time, in fact, I feel very much at home, but I wonder if I will ever be able to have a real heart and soul talk with anyone. When I am in the Negro community, the distance I often feel between me and Negro people all but disappears. There is a barrier with guys and sex, but I think that's a problem I have with all guys. But generally it is only when I am in the white community or see a white person driving a car or entering a store that the barrier suddenly comes back. It is as if a little inner voice is saying, "You live here. You're white." And then I wonder about this little part of me, deep down, that scares me. Maybe I am not as much of a revolutionary as I would have myself believe. I am often ambivalent, at times terribly extremist, at other times all for compromise. And of course, I can go home whenever I want. I can be here for two months and then I can slip back into security. And there is a part of me that will love a bit of this slipping back. But these people are heroes. They have no security to begin with, and once they step out into the struggle, what little security they have is gone. I really don't know where I would stand if I was a Negro sharecropper and stood to lose my life, or my job if I just signed a piece of paper asking for better drainage, a bit of pavement and some street lights. When one sits at home it is easy to say that one would like to be working continually in this way and live one's life this way, but do I really? God I hope I will never be a sell out! But I find that I am yearning for normal things. At the moment, all I want to do is go dancing for hours.

There is singing outside the freedom house. Those freedom songs have something almost mystical about them. They make you light up with happiness no matter how you are feeling. Then there are other moments too. Sometimes people can show their appreciation in secret, silent ways. Today as we canvassed a truck passed us filled with peaches. Two whites were in front, the Negroes in the back, and they rolled us a couple of peaches when they saw us passing.

Canvassing was often a depressing experience. Day after day we would knock on doors and ask people to sign a petition to the mayor for paved streets, streetlights, sewers and fire hydrants. On a typical day, after knocking on doors for two hours, we had three signatures. We met teachers who were afraid to "step out of line," and pensioners who were afraid they would not get their checks. The fear was palpable.

Sometimes all the people who lived on a block would suddenly back out on the day they had agreed to go down to the courthouse and register to vote. People would be so very polite and obliging; they would tell you they were going to go, but when you came to pick them up they had disappeared; they were in the fields, at work, or, most commonly, "sick."

And many people *were* ill. Belzoni had no black doctors. We entered many shacks where elderly people, mainly women living alone, were too sick to move about. Many who hobbled to the door to let us in had large black circles under their eyes, or even large patches of darkness. Often their limbs were thin and their bodies frail, their movements weak. "We sure could use a doctor here," I wrote home.

Dear Mom:

Have you ever seen a child whose navel has not been properly knotted when they were born, and the thing grows and protrudes as the child gets larger? There are many children like this here.

But do you know what is the most amazing thing being here? I am living among people who have been physically and spiritually maimed for 300 years. Their houses are falling down, and they get exploited every way they turn and yet the most fantastic number of them have not lost their spirit and their love of life. God! Think of the dead people we know, and then meet these people! They still have an amazing amount of joy inside them. Spiritually, I wonder if we have anything to offer them at all.

After only ten days in Mississippi, I had to fly to California to be sentenced for my part in the Berkeley protests. A couple of the project leaders drove me to the airport. We were very late. Driving was a whole new experience for us in the South. The volunteers would always drive ten miles below the speed limit and obey every signal. The locals, the old hands, and the staff would drive as fast as possible, although often with great skill, as if to say "It's better to get out of danger fast." On the way to the airport I cowered in the back while noticing that the speedometer was often reaching ninety miles an hour. But I made the plane. Just barely.

I remember relaxing in the cool, air-conditioned San Francisco airport. Compared to Mississippi, the city itself was positively wintry. Berkeley seemed almost psychedelic: the beautiful green lawns of the campus, the clusters of flowers planted everywhere; the cool air, low humidity, and cloudless blue sky. For thirty-four hours I reveled in a heavenly feeling of cleanliness.

Tensions at the courthouse were high, and sentences were harsher than expected. Our lawyers argued that we should accept probation, at least until the appeal process came to its end. Some of the militants attacked the lawyers, and before sentencing one defendant made an eloquent statement about his commitment to civil rights and how this commitment might necessitate such actions again. He then said he could not accept a probation that would prohibit him from fighting against injustice. His words unlocked the pent-up feelings of many in the courtroom and resulted in a spontaneous outburst of whistles, shouts, and applause. Shocked, the judge furiously pounded his gavel and cleared the courtroom. Later, at a meeting, some of the lawyers pleaded for decorum; one must play by the rules of the game, they said. "We lost the game!" someone bitterly called out. In the end they were missing some piece of paper pertinent to my case and postponed my sentencing until I returned to school in the fall. It was a total waste of three days and a $258 plane fare.

I was nervous on the flight back, and as I flew into Hattiesburg I began getting really scared. It was as if the quick
change of scenery unlocked hidden feelings. Outwardly Belzoni had been calm and I had not noticed the undercurrent
of white menace. Once I was back in Belzoni my fear quickly
subsided and became, once again, a natural and almost unnoticed rhythm in life.

Dear Mom:

It was strange going to California—the relief from
constant sweat, the luxury of cool air, cleanliness, toilets, hot water and washing machines. The concept of
"roughing it" is not original. But when you live here for
a while, you begin to realize that there is no respite from
these things for the people who live here, ever.

On July 21, seven men and women became the first blacks
to successfully register to vote in Belzoni. But as the days
went by our progress was frustratingly slow and tensions
grew between the volunteers and the project staff. Johnnie,
our project leader, was often drunk, and occasionally talked
like he was drunk even when he was sober. A number of black
leaders in the local community felt he was sabotaging the
project. A major supporter told us he was reluctant to give
the project more money because he feared it would go for
drink. Despite the fact that we were finally beginning to register a few people, a number of the volunteers felt that there
was no hope for the project unless there was a change in leadership. Then, one night, two volunteers and one of the local
workers, a young man called Ora, were followed by two
white men when they got out of a car to attend a meeting of
the Mississippi Student Union. They were called "bastards,"
"scum," "nigger lovers," "motherfuckers." Ora and another

black guy pretended to throw some stones. A few other cars cruised by the meeting place during the evening.

The next day I went to Mary Thomas's store to wash up, and Johnnie walked in. We started talking and drinking coffee. I began to tell him my misgivings: that what I was doing in Belzoni was superfluous, even harmful; that I was living with the Lees, enjoying their generous hospitality, but not paying them back by working as hard as possible. I was worried, I said, that when the volunteers left, and then the staff left, there would be no real local movement and the few active people—like the Hazelwoods, Mary Thomas, and the Lees—would be targets. The few registered voters, the few who had spoken out, would be left to the mercy of the local whites. "Perhaps," I told Johnnie, "we should leave now, before we're too committed, or maybe we should get new people."

Johnnie replied that I didn't really understand. "The staff has been canvassing for ten months and they're tired." And that was certainly true. I thought of what it must feel like to knock on doors day after day, month after month, and get nowhere. It was hard to grasp. "I know that," I said, although perhaps I didn't. "When I was going out canvassing with Matt the other day, he refused to even knock on the door at ten houses. He 'knew' they would never go down and register, so we never even tried. But the volunteers, who haven't had time to be discouraged, would have gone to every house. Perhaps," I ventured gently, "you have to evaluate if by being so tired you aren't contributing much to the movement."

"Do you mean I'm hurting the movement?" he asked me point-blank, and I, unwilling to court conflict, afraid of anger and wanting to be liked, backed off. "No, I don't mean that," I said, though it was exactly what I meant.

Just as I uttered the last syllable, another volunteer, Bill, walked in and sat down at the table with Johnnie. "Yes, you *are* hurting the movement," Bill said, and he went on to say the things many had been saying over and over again in private: that Johnnie's drinking was hurting the project, that local blacks with funds would not give money for fear that it would be drunk up, that the Hazelwoods and many of the good local workers were unhappy. If the staff was too tired, said Bill, then there should be fresh staff. It was what most of the volunteers had felt for a while.

The staff meeting that took place later that day was exactly what everyone feared: staff against volunteers, black against white. Some of the volunteers argued that many civil rights organizations believed in rotating people so that activists wouldn't get totally burnt out, and that we should let the local people decide the fate of the project. But much of the discussion centered around complaints about personal behavior. When several volunteers suggested that the present staff was burnt out, Johnnie and Ellis responded with fury. They didn't care what people thought, they said, they were staying. Matt sat on the floor, his back to the wall, as usual saying nothing, and I still believed that somewhere inside his silence was a great wisdom if only one could coax it out. I remember that I said very little.

"The volunteers feel like we're doing nothing," I said. "We may only be here for two months, but we do have one thing —new energy. Unlike you, we haven't been banging our heads against a brick wall month after month. The staff hasn't helped or directed us. I feel I've done very little." Johnnie replied that the project should get rid of some of the volunteers.

At the end of the meeting the staff said they would decide whether to take the issue to the local people, or try to get some new staff, or tell the volunteers to leave.

July 26th. Johnnie is leaving for a few days, taking a vacation. I
spoke to Mrs. Lee and she totally supported our point of view
and said that the staff had been trying to oust the most productive volunteers. Who knows what will happen?

The other day, while swimming in the Yazoo river with the
Hazelwoods, I began talking to Dan, one of the volunteers. He
says little but seems to be a lovely and sensitive person. We
were both depressed at the slow pace of change here and
agreed that there didn't seem to be much hope for improve-
ment. Dan says he hasn't discovered his role in the movement
yet. I don't know if I even have a role.

Yesterday I attended a funeral. Funerals are the greatest social occasion here. Families are large and relatives come from
all over. But there are numerous people who have never met
the deceased and know the relatives only slightly, who attend
the service anyway. I had the strangest mixed feeling about
the whole thing. The service was simple and beautiful and the
minister did not dwell on sorrow, but on Jesus and heaven.
The buffet was delicious and it was easy to feel at home. But I
kept thinking how sad and grotesque that funerals are the
main social event here, it's as if the only joy and celebration
comes when someone leaves this earth and going to heaven is
the only way to end pain and suffering.

If my diary entries and letters home were reflective, my
mother's letters to me were practical and somewhat frantic.
She had joined an organization of parents whose children
had gone down to Mississippi, and she was heavily involved
in fundraising for urgent items.

July 28th

Dearest Margot:

I am groggy from sitting at this typewriter for the last
four hours. And all of it is related to the Mississippi Parents Project. There is an urgent need for funds for communication. Car-to-car radios, repair of radios, tele-
phones.... If you read the national press, except for an

occasional demonstration all is quiet. Yet there are daily
stories of beatings, terror and arrests about which you
hear nothing.

There are places that don't have a phone, and as for
putting radios in cars, many projects don't have a car. Who
knows if there had been a radio in the car last summer, the
three might still be alive. So I just made up a list of 106
names of people I know to whom I'm sending letters asking for money for just that—radios and communication
set-ups for the safety of the civil rights workers, specifically
in Mississippi, and also for the rest of the South.

What I want from you immediately is a short resume of
the communications set up in Belzoni. Any printed means
of communication, radio, telephone, car, etc.

You write that it is quiet in Mississippi. Naturally it is
quiet. Did you know that all residents have received letters
from their Congressman to keep low and not make trouble. They know the challenge to unseat the congressmen is
up and how it would look if there were violence because of
attempts at voter registration. Just wait. What I'm afraid of
is what will happen if there is a good chance of a big vote
to unseat the Mississippi delegation.... love, embraces and
kisses, Mom.

Dear Mom:

We have a telephone as of a week ago, and we have
one car. We had a radio which seems to be broken. We
would have to go to Jackson to get it fixed and no one
seems to be going to Jackson soon. Besides the radio, our
only real problem is being at the mercy of local operators when we place our calls. Often the operators mess
up our calls, connect us to dial-a-prayer, or to a number
that rings constantly with no answer.

———

On August 3, five of us decided to go out into the country and canvass: Bernie, Ben, John, Ora (the only local, the only black), and myself. As our car passed through the small town of Isola, we noticed a blue-and-white pickup truck following us. As we drove by a gas station, the truck stopped and picked up another man and continued to follow our car, even when we stopped twice for directions. We finally found the people we were seeking, the Curtis family, known to be sympathetic to our goals. We stopped the car and talked to Mr. Curtis, a farmer, as he stood in his yard. The truck stayed close behind.

Mr. Curtis told us that we were crazy to come out there in broad daylight. He said he recognized one of the men in the truck, a local gas station owner and an active member of the White Citizens Council. It was becoming clear that we should not be there, that he should not be talking to us, and that we should leave as soon as possible. But we argued about it a bit, since we had wanted to canvass outside of Belzoni and finally we were doing it. But everyone agreed that we should go back by a different route, one that did not go through Isola. Going through Isola in a car with blacks and whites had been like waving a red flag in front of a bull. It was a big mistake.

The pickup turned around and passed the house again. We started driving. At an intersection, we saw another pickup truck waiting for us. We turned and they followed.

And then we took the wrong turn, and suddenly we were speeding down lonely and unknown dirt roads, lost among deserted cotton fields, kicking up clouds of dust as Ora floored the gas pedal, rushing at ninety miles an hour, the two pickups staying close on our tails. We noticed that both of them had radios, and that neither had visible license plates.

Suddenly the second truck rammed into us as we turned onto another unknown road. We sped on until we came to a dead end on a deserted plantation. We turned the car around to find the two pickup trucks blocking our way. There were ditches on either side of the road. We were trapped.

Several white men got out of one of the pickups and came up to our car. "This is private property," one of them said. "What are you doing here?" We said we had lost our way. One of the men told Ora to get out of the car and start walking, which he did. Then they told the other male volunteers to get out of the car one by one. Ben was the first to emerge. One of the men punched him and he went limp in the nonviolent resistance pose we had all been taught; his glasses went careening onto the ground. Next, Bernie was told to get out of the car, and he too received a punch; he went limp so fast the punch may not have really connected, but he was kicked several times in the back. Then one of the men came over to John, who looked like the perfect all-American guy. "Won't you say anything?" one of the men said to John. John remained silent. Then he was asked if he had a black or white father. John replied, "White." The man called John a coward for not fighting back, and other names. Then John was punched a few times, too.

I sat in the car alone and untouched, mumbling over and over to myself "Oh my God, oh my God" as I watched each person get beaten and go limp. Time stretched. I found myself completely unheroic. I was neither calm nor collected. Chaotic images of being raped or killed pulsed through my head.

At last, surely only moments later, the white men ordered the volunteers to get back into the car. We started off, one pickup in front and the other behind. We passed Ora and stopped to talk to him, but the pickup truck in front of us stopped, too. The men got out and came up to us and said, "We told you not to pick him up. He walks." I didn't notice that several of the men were carrying pistols, but others did. We started our car once more and drove, one pickup in front, the other behind, until we reached the paved road leading to the highway. At that point they let us go on our way.

As we drove back to Belzoni a highway patrol car passed us. In any Northern state we would have stopped it and asked for help, but here the police were not necessarily our friends.

When I got back I was trembling, much more fearful than at the time of the actual incident. I was frantic with worry for Ora's safety. Johnnie and Matt left instantly to look for him. They took their guns. We had broken an absolute rule: never leave anyone alone. Shortly after Matt and Johnnie left, Ora came back. He had hidden in the cotton and corn fields until he found a ride home with a farmer. But the brute fact was that four white volunteers had left a black local activist in a deeply dangerous situation. The incident provided painful lessons: never travel without a radio; never travel without someone who knows the roads well. Against all common sense, we had gone through a small town known to be unfriendly. We were in a white station wagon and many of the cars donated to the civil rights movement were white; it may have been that our car was easily recognized.

When we returned to the Freedom House we wrote out affidavits and placed calls to the county attorney, the sheriff, and the FBI. The FBI arrived in the morning and took pictures of John and Bernie and Ben, but there was little evidence in the way of external bruises. Unlike the agents in the film *Mississippi Burning*, these FBI officers were exceptionally unpleasant.

We later learned of a possible explanation for their hostility. Apparently, a few days before, a Mississippi Freedom Democratic Party newsletter had urged blacks to refuse to serve in Vietnam. It is not our war, the newsletter said, noting that blacks were getting killed in far greater proportions to whites. Unknown to us, this had become a leading story in the *Clarion Ledger*, an important Mississippi newspaper, and had precipitated strongly worded rebuttals from the NAACP and the AFL-CIO. The Mississippi authorities were incensed. In our case, instead of investigating the beatings, the FBI started questioning my fellow volunteers. When they found out that Ben had just turned eighteen and hadn't yet registered for the draft, they had what they needed. They came back the next day, took Ben down to the nearest draft board, and threatened to prosecute him for draft dodging. As for our case, they said they could only file a report since they had no jurisdiction to make arrests. "Even if we saw the violence ourselves," they said, "we could do nothing unless it was a federal crime."

The next staff meeting was explosive. Johnnie was furious and blamed us for going through Isola. We didn't understand Mississippi, he said, and we didn't know how to protect ourselves. The argument continued for hours. John repeated that the white volunteers didn't want to lead the project, but that the staff was doing nothing. Johnnie said the staff had no plans to leave. I decided it was my own time to go.

August 6th. This day, my last in Mississippi, has been one of the strangest days of my life. I have such mixed feelings at leaving all these people. I feel glad to leave the horror, and guilty to let them stand it alone.

I decided I would go home by way of Little Rock, the place where I was born. I got to the Lafayette Hotel at about 3:00 A.M. It was hard to sleep well; the air-conditioned room seemed like an iceberg. I had vague and slightly scary dreams about leaving Mississippi, but Little Rock seemed even more frightening, and the feeling of fear and strangeness grew with the day. Such dissonance! First the hotel, which was such luxury after the Lees' shack. Then looking at the state capital building in the morning and realizing that I was no longer a civil rights worker but simply a tourist, someone to be smiled at, to be welcomed, to roll out the mat of Southern hospitality for. In one moment I had stepped from fear and poverty to whiteness, wealth, and Southern tradition. I felt like I was "passing," faking it, discarding the role of "nigger lover" for the one of "Little Rockian returning to her place of birth." I was entering the kind of homes I had been afraid to walk by. I could laugh loudly on streets like those I had silently and swiftly passed, and talk with people I had hitherto avoided.

Little Rock seemed like an active, bustling town, clean and attractive. But everything glowed with whiteness. And suddenly, I felt an inner terror growing within me, becoming unbearable as the day passed. It was the sudden turning off of six weeks of reflexes that I had slowly built up—a sudden switch.

Dr. Christopher Bromley had been my pediatrician for my first six months of life. The Bromley family welcomed me, would not let me pay for my nights in the hotel, and took me to a local art center for lunch. The atmosphere was quiet and tasteful. But I was already in shock. The white Southern drawl that two months ago I had found enchanting now caused prickles on the back of my neck. On the issue of civil rights, the Bromleys asked me didn't I think the Negroes were happy the way they were? They believed that outsiders were making the situation worse, and that new civil rights laws were changing the Constitution in drastic ways. This would only become apparent in a number of years, they assured me, and then it would be too late. I realized that these incredibly generous and hospitable people were far from the liberals I had expected, and were in no way aware that I was the very kind of outsider they condemned.

The Bromley family's neighborhood was filled with the large homes of wealthy business executives, doctors, and politicians. The Bromleys' house had twelve rooms, and was graced with large and lovely gardens. There were two maids. I was introduced to them, but it was clear that it was inappropriate to shake their hands. I began to feel jittery inside and I started to tremble.

Later, as one of the Bromley daughters drove me around Little Rock, I began to feel more at home. She was warm and open, a college student at a university in the Midwest. I began to feel more at ease. She disagreed with Governor Wallace, she said, but then she talked about the guy she was seeing, whose family owned half of Arkansas's plantations and who "really hated Negroes." I kept thinking of Isola and the men in the pickup trucks. When we returned she went upstairs to put her hair in curlers, and I was alone in the living room, playing records—John Reed, Stan Getz, and *Goldfinger*. I tried to read, but the pounding, spine-tingling music from *Goldfinger* increased my sense of dissonance and discomfort. Finally one of the maids came in. I shook her hand and we began to talk.

The Bromley's other daughter was more troubled about race than her sister. She said that she loved one of the maids almost as much as her mother. She added that a wonderful Negro boy used to be a great friend, but now it felt uncomfortable to be together, and that hurt. This was a recent change, she said; it happened when the Little Rock schools were desegregated. "I think you're wrong in thinking that the change in your relations has to do with the civil rights crisis," I said. I told her that the situation she was experiencing was a fundamental hurt that occurred over and over in

Southern tradition: that as whites grew up they had to distance themselves from the black friends they had played with
in childhood.

That night we sat in the garden and watched the night-
blooming cereus, a cactus with an exotic white flower that
blooms for one night only and wilts by morning. When it
opened, it had the most exquisite smell, a dark and subtle
perfume. I sat and watched it and sniffed its fragrance for
a long time—it was just like this world I was suddenly in,
so rarefied.

The next day we passed Cammack Village, where my parents had lived during the war. We stopped by the old St. Vincent's Hospital, where I was born, which now was a black hospital, and I went up to the third floor to see the newborns.
Later that day, Dr. Bromley took me with him to the new St.
Vincent's and we found my mother's admission card, and the
chart of baby Adler's weight gain. I was a preemie and had
spent thirty days in that hospital. "The hospitals are integrated now," Mrs. Bromley told me. "It's a shame, because it's
made many people feel uncomfortable."

Suddenly my body began shaking. "I have to go home," I
wrote in my journal. The dissonance between my Belzoni experiences and the Bromleys' lily-white gentility was too
great. I felt that I might explode if I didn't get out quick. I
packed and left on an evening bus. As the South receded, I
felt myself relaxing, for the first time in months. But, watching the scenery pass by, I was unsure what lessons I was carrying home.

I was no clearer about my role as an activist and I continued to doubt my courage in the face of danger. I believed
even less in authority, and less in the institutions of the state.
But at the same time I was more humble. I realized the black
families of Mississippi had given me food, housing, and edu-

cation—guidance in living in a different world. It seemed to be much more than I had given them.

I never had the courage to sit down with Mrs. Lee and ask her about the reality of her God, nor did I sit with Johnnie and ask about the truth of his life. I was too young and too uncertain to open every pore to the experience around me. I also realized that while many of the people I had worked with were not saints, they *were* heroes. People can be heroes and still be deeply flawed as human beings. Oppressed people are often crippled by their oppression. The miracle was that so many of the people I had met in Mississippi were open, generous, and whole.

Only days after my leaving Mississippi, President Lyndon Johnson signed the Voting Rights Act. Suddenly, with the force of the presidency clearly behind it, voter registration picked up all over the South. Registrars began to accept anyone who was reasonably literate, although scores of complaints were still being filed with the Justice Department. Within two years, more than a third of the eligible blacks in Mississippi had registered. The Voting Rights Act changed the face of Mississippi politics forever. Today the roads in Belzoni's black neighborhoods are paved, and blacks hold elective office. Our own role—the role of the white civil rights workers who ventured South—remains much less clear.

About seven or eight months after I returned to Berkeley, I walked across the campus on a beautiful spring night. As I came up a hill toward the northside exit of the campus, I approached a deserted section, a path overhung with eucalyptus and pine. Suddenly a slender black man jumped out of the bushes and grabbed me. "Kiss me a thousand times or I'll rape you," he said. The first thought inside my head—as everything became deadly still and time seemed to stop—was "Hey, this can't be happening to *me*—I was in Mississippi!"

Then, for some blessed reason, I became totally calm. "But you don't even know me," I said quietly. "How boring to have sex with someone you don't even know." He was so taken aback that he let go his grasp and I ran, and ran and ran, until I walked up the steps of Hoyt Hall, the student co-op building where I lived, and began to tremble uncontrollably.

"Call the police," everyone said. But I hesitated, for the police, whether arresting me in Berkeley or investigating a dangerous incident on a lonely plantation, were my enemy, not my protector. "Call the police!" everyone said over and over. After all, I wasn't a black person living in Mississippi or Harlem. I was a white middle-class woman. And in white America, for such a woman walking alone at night, the police are usually a blessing.

With different messages at war within in my brain, I finally dialed and spoke. My voice was wobbly. I told the police what I knew and where the man was. "Will you press charges?" they asked. My voice was frozen. I simply couldn't say yes. Given what I had experienced in the South, how could I put any young black person into the hands of the police? "Just get him out of there," I said. "We can't do anything if you won't press charges," the officer said. I hung up.

It took me many years, decades even, to be able to hold in my brain simultaneously the different truths of my experiences.

A Question of Enlistment

WHEN I RETURNED to Berkeley after my summer in Mississippi, I was soberer and a bit disillusioned. I had left the battles in Berkeley feeling a sense of limitless possibility. Tumultuous changes seemed to be happening everywhere and it was not hard to feel a sense of purpose as one helped to implement them. There was a sense of inevitability, like riding a wave as it surged to the shore. But in Mississippi I saw another, perhaps truer, picture of the daily life of struggle. The work of a civil rights activist seemed frustrating and difficult, the rewards unclear and victory less certain. I continued to believe that the only work worth doing in the world was helping to change it, a belief that came from the heart as well as from family tradition. But I no longer believed it was always an easy or joyous task. I believed I should throw myself into "the revolution" at the same time that I continued to wonder about the level of my own commitment.

In a journalism class at Berkeley taught by Peter Steffens, son of the great muckraking journalist Lincoln Steffens, I was captivated by a story in Vincent Sheean's *Personal History*.

Sheean, a well-known war correspondent of my parents' generation, fell madly in love with an American communist named Rayna Prome when he met her in China during the 1940s. Prome had dedicated her life to the cause of world revolution, and she determined to travel to Moscow where she would be trained to become a "revolutionary instrument." (It wasn't exactly clear to me what a revolutionary instrument was, but the emotional sense was clear. It meant a certain kind of purity; it meant someone who was totally committed to working for change, someone who would put this above all else, including love, career, and all personal, selfish desires.) Sheean was passionately in love and desperate to talk Prome out of this decision. He followed her all the way to Moscow, and for three days and two nights they argued. Sheean wanted a relationship with a real woman, a human being, and he insisted that if Prome dedicated her whole life to revolutionary struggle she would lose her soul and sense of self. He offered her love and companionship, but it was not enough. She was on fire with politics and she turned him down. After he lost the argument, he asked Rayna to spend one last evening with him, and they went to a party at a state function in Moscow.

They danced—Prome frail and splendid in a golden dress—and, in a symbolic ending worthy of fiction, she suddenly suffered a blinding headache. Sheean took her home and bid her good night. In the morning she was found dead of a brain aneurysm.

I'm not sure why this story obsessed me for many years. I once thought that it symbolized a tension in my soul between journalism and revolution, but at the time I had no thoughts about being a journalist. More likely, I deeply desired to commit myself totally to something, but to what? Sheean and Prome were two sides of myself. I was struggling between commitment to the world or commitment to the life of the mind and spirit. The world I knew was one of either/or: of body or soul, reason or emotion, mysticism or science, this world or some world after, commitment to the group or commitment to the individual, socialist revolution or capitalism. Today one could say that all those dichotomies of my youth were unnecessary, that many things are not either/or, but rather both/and. But at the time I thought I had to make an irrevocable choice.

At Berkeley, the heady euphoria that followed the victory of the FSM had deteriorated into the bickering of a hundred small and increasingly dogmatic left-wing groups, a mix of Maoists, Trotskyists, democratic socialists, and anarchists. The Communist Party seemed to be one of the only groups that was fighting that trend, working toward unity among the groups. Meeting party members at Berkeley forced me to reevaluate my long-held ideas about them. And I was intrigued.

Of course, the Communist Party was part of my family history. My grandmother, Raissa, had been active in the Communist Party of Austria, but was thrown out for her friendship with Trotsky. My mother, Freyda, told me with great gales of laughter about how she was refused admittance to the Communist Party in the 1940s; the head of the local chapter just laughed in her face, or so the story went. "You?" he sputtered. "But you're entirely undisciplinable!" Even my father, who I'd always assumed had been a party member, since he refused to answer the question during my youth, confided to me in his nineties that he had never trusted the party functionaries, and preferred to be a "fellow traveler," a sympathizer on the edges.

When I was growing up in New York City, the Communist Party seemed a joke—populated solely by FBI informants and elderly leftists desperate for young blood. A meeting I attended when I was thirteen tells it all. I had seen an advertisement for the thirtieth anniversary celebration of the party's paper, *The Worker*, and, on a lark, I went with two friends. The experience was bizarre. At one point a middle-aged woman who spoke stridently and brandished a cane made an incredible gaffe: "... and the so-called people of the captive countries—" she said, "I mean, the people of the so-called captive countries." That woman became for me a metaphor for the CP of the 1950s— people who were old and dogmatic. Alas, I was too young to appreciate that the elderly black man (in his nineties) who followed this woman to the podium was none other than the renowned scholar and activist W. E. B. Du Bois. It was one of his last appearances.

On the surface, the Communist Party seemed as irrelevant in Berkeley as it had seemed in New York. Although the press accused the Free Speech Movement of being controlled by communists, with the exception of Bettina Aptheker, the party seemed invisible. And in fact it was small; the Berkeley chapter had about seventeen members.

One afternoon I sat with Bettina on the terrace overlooking the Berkeley campus. "I see myself as a sort of a fire brigade," she said, laughing. "All these left groups fight and create all these fires, and I attempt to put them out." Unlike the rigid elders I had encountered in New York, the Communist Party at Berkeley seemed to be a small group of young people who were desperately attempting to create unity and a common agenda for Berkeley radicals, perhaps an impossible task.

Bettina had a calm sense of herself. She always seemed so optimistic and able to act with ease. In contrast, I was plagued with doubts. I noticed that it was her communism and belief in "history" that allowed her to act: no matter how hard the battle, how frustrating the daily events, she believed that the future was assured, the revolution a matter of course. As I sat listening to her, yearning to be so strong, thinking how happy I would be to go into battle with a firm yet calm and gentle demeanor, always looking on the positive side, I had an epiphany. I realized that it didn't matter if history was truly on her side. Even if her beliefs were unfounded, they gave her the courage to act. And by action she might bring about the very change she was seeking. It took me many more years to understand the much more subtle notion that an action may bring about a very different set of effects than those desired. But in 1966 I began to study Marxism seriously, hoping somehow to will such a belief in myself, to create a bulwark against the barrage of doubts that constantly assailed me.

In a way that may be impossible to understand today, Marxism seemed a powerfully beautiful philosophy. It ordered the world, provided an explanation for injustice and inequality, and provided a vision (albeit ethereal) of a golden world where the only problems were human problems: sadness at death and loss, occasional envy and greed. The large structural problems of oppression and inequality would be vanquished. Vivian Gornick's *The Romance of American Communism* gives a sense of this vision when she quotes a woman who says that reading Marx was like having "fireworks exploding in your head ... like I was discovering the world for the first time ... as though the world had been a blurred photograph and now suddenly I was seeing a clear print."*

Marxism gave us something else—something I still believe today, even though I am now suspicious of most grand theories. Marxism says that nothing is exactly as you think it is. There is no such thing as a pure idea; nothing stands completely alone, but instead is tied to a thousand other things. Everything you believe to be an eternal truth is colored by your class, your race, your gender, and by a thousand other influences that have made you who you are and built up your thoughts and values. And this is true not only of everything you believe, but also of everything you read in a newspaper or see on television or hear in a speech.

* Vivian Gornick, *The Romance of American Communism* (New York: Basic Books, 1977), 65.

As my appreciation for Marxism grew, I wondered if the Communist Party could be the vehicle for my revolutionary struggles. And just as I began to consider this, I received two invitations to dinner in the same week. Since I had never been invited to dinner even once in my two years at Berkeley, this was, to say the least, odd.

The first dinner was with an old friend from elementary school. She was two years older than I, not a close friend, but a connection to home and New York. I had not known that she was a member of the Communist Party, but it became the central theme of our talk. Like Bettina, she was warm and funny, and unlike many of the radicals in Berkeley, she did not speak in jargon.

"I wasn't supposed to go to Berkeley, you know," she laughed.

"Why not?" I asked.

"Oh, you know," she said, "I was told it was like bringing coals to Newcastle. But I didn't care. I went anyway."

"You mean the party told you what school they wanted you to go to?"

"Oh, nothing quite as formal as that. I was just given to understand it would be better for the party if I went elsewhere—you know, a small university in the Midwest. But I didn't care. I wanted to go here."

"Are there lots of things you have to do in the party that you don't want to do?"

"Not much, really. We're all supposed to sell *The People's World*, you know, the party newspaper, and no one ever wants to do it. It's a terrible newspaper."

I left the dinner as unsure as ever. I pondered whether I would ever be willing to go somewhere I didn't want to go, or do something I didn't want to do, just because an organization thought it was the best decision. I thought about Rayna Prome deciding to give up her personal life for the cause of revolution. It seemed righteous and noble, but I doubted I could do it. The nub of the problem was the party's belief in "democratic centralism." This was the idea that you might disagree and argue about an issue, but once the organization made a decision, you accepted it, and you never made your disagreements public outside the group. While most American corporations have a similar policy, it was not something I could agree with intellectually, and emotionally I couldn't imagine being willing to adhere to it.

By the time of the second dinner, with Bettina Aptheker, I felt an enormous weight upon me. By then I understood that these dinner invitations meant that my friends in the party wanted to recruit me. It made sense on some level; it was the opportunity to do what beliefs, family heritage, and morals required. Bettina and I sat and talked about life and Berkeley, and Bettina never brought the subject up, until finally the pressure inside me was so intense that I let it bubble to the surface myself.

We talked about my misgivings about the party. We talked about democratic centralism, and about the contrast between the totalitarian party structure and the warm, generous, loving people inside it. This human presence seemed so much more real than distant party directives, real or imagined. At the end of the evening I was invited to a meeting as a guest, and I decided to go.

As I waited for this event to take place, I continued to read Marx and argue about politics with my best friends. I was living in Hoyt Hall, a student co-op for women. The kitchen was always open, coffee was always available, and there was a deep comfort in living in a community of women. That sense of community was strengthened by the work shifts we did each week, cleaning toilets, vacuuming rugs, and preparing meals. But the sense of community I experienced there was still not enough.

Neither of my best friends at the co-op were committed activists. I had already learned a central truth—that my comrades in politics would not necessarily be my closest friends.

But though my friends never joined my political or spiritual excursions, they sat up with me and argued for long hours. And their arguments were not so different from those made by Vincent Sheean to Rayna Prome: that the party was rigid and dogmatic, that it would stifle my freedom, and that ultimately it would not nourish my yearning for community. When the time for a decision was at hand, I, unlike Rayna Prome, was still uncertain about what to do.

The meeting of the Berkeley chapter of the Communist Party took place in the cosy living room of a private home. Most of the seventeen people in the chapter were there. A couple of them were activists I knew, but most were strangers. One member was sick. I listened to a discussion of how she was doing, and whether people were going over to see her, to bring her soup and groceries. I was riveted by the sense of caring in the room; it was as if this small group of party members, most of them unknown to the activists of Berkeley, was fragile. Despite the sense of revolution in the Berkeley air, these communists still found that secrecy was necessary because of the cold war. I wondered what it would be like to live in a community of such warmth, to find a bowl of chicken soup on my doorstep the next time I had the flu. I yearned for such community, and yet I feared it would strangle me.

Just as my old friend had told me, there was a discussion of selling the party newspaper. There was a lot of laughter, no one wanted to do it, and there were some friendly admonishments to do better in the future. At the end of the meeting, there was a section called "Good and Welfare." Imagine a self-criticism session, but warm and fuzzy and gentle. Everyone spoke in turn. People talked of mistakes they had made and sought advice from the group. There were two other invited guests, and when their turn came they both said they had decided to join the party. And then it was my turn. "Oh God," I thought. "I'm last, and the two others joined."

I suddenly knew that I couldn't join them. The sad, fierce

only child inside looked out at the party and the guests and felt a stranger in their midst. I longed deeply to be part of such a caring community, where everyone worked for shared values. But at rock bottom I knew I was never going to feel comfortable being told what to do, whether by the party faithful or anyone else. I would always be an outsider—fighting for community, yearning for it, yet afraid of its imprisoning ties.

I don't remember my exact response that night. I think I said that I had too artistic and anarchic a temperament; that I believed in socialism, but as much as I envied their community I could never be a part of it. They were respectful and decent. Unlike the Mormon missionaries who had been ringing my doorbell ever since I signed the guestbook at their temple in Salt Lake City, they did not even urge me to reconsider. Later, one of them told me that he felt it was a weakness of the party that it couldn't accommodate people like me.

They asked me to work with them on common issues, but once I walked out the door of that living room I felt a terror— a residue, perhaps, of the 1950s McCarthy period. I remembered that hundreds of people had been interrogated and brought before investigative committees, that many had taken the Fifth Amendment rather than inform on their friends, and that some had gone to jail because of it. I remembered my father's instruction never to ask or answer the question "Are you a Communist?" And so I felt a fear that having rejected the party, and these members who had taken me into their confidence, I had no right to know them, or even remember their names. Although the danger seemed remote, there was always the possibility that I might be called before some investigative committee. I retreated into my studies and I willed myself to forget them. And most of their names are lost to me now.

It is strange to think of this today, when communism appears to lie on the "ash heap of history." Marx's economic theory may be discredited, or, at the very least, unproven and untried. But the core legacy shared by those of us who went through a serious encounter with Marxism has little to do with economic theory or even communism. It is this: when we look at the world, even today, we take nothing at face value. We are always looking for the unseen relationships.

How different would this book be, I must constantly wonder, and how different my life, if I were not from an atheist, Jewish, semi-Marxist, upper-middle-class home? If I were not a woman and standing at a certain very particular point in history? How different would these stories be if everything I believed in hadn't been influenced by the progressive education of City and Country, and by certain teachers at Berkeley? And to take it even further, and, most oddly, in a direction that Marx himself would never have taken it, how different would the lessons from these experiences be if my ideas over the last twenty years hadn't been influenced by thousands of books: writings on nature, philosophy, religion, ecology, utopias, dystopias, feminism, ecofeminism, and (if truth be told) the ideas, the different landscapes, and the realms of possibility presented in science fiction.

Looking back, it seems oddly fitting that just as my mother was rejected by the party for being too anarchistic and "undisciplinable," I declined membership for similar reasons. The struggle to change the world is certainly more difficult without a grand and glorious theory that gives people the confidence of victory. But when barbarism is at the gates,* it is still important to struggle against it, despite our doubts.

---

*"Socialism or barbarism" is a phrase attributed to Rosa Luxemburg; in writing this last paragraph I was powerfully influenced by a speech by Mario Savio at the thirtieth anniversary of the Free Speech Movement, in Berkeley, California.

A Left-Wing Nun in the Summer of Love; *Or, If This Is the Sixties, Where's the Sex, Drugs, and Rock and Roll?*

CHAPTER 7

MARIJUANA—"grass"—was the recreational drug of choice for much of Berkeley in the mid-sixties, but although I smoked grass many a time, there was only one real drug for me. One that would remain the sweetest and the most soothing, the most reliable, and certainly the cheapest drug on the market—the drug I could consume until my senses were sated, until I felt large and therefore strong enough to encounter the world, until I fell into unconsciousness and sleep, until all pain was numbed—my drug of choice: food.

Despite an upbringing of freedom and progressive values, by the time I was a teenager I was completely alienated from my body. I could remember an earlier time, when my body had been a friend and ally, simply by opening up an album of candid photographs from my childhood. Whether picking out notes on the piano or playing with suds in a bubble bath, the utter self-assurance that radiated from the being in those pictures was awesome. Later, as an adolescent, I would look at these photographs and weep. I would think back with amazement to those summers when my whole family swam nude on the beaches of Chilmark and Gayhead with a lack of self-consciousness and an easy sense of freedom that it no longer seemed possible to attain.

Puberty, my parents' divorce, my father's exit from our home, and my mother's illness created a new world of uncertainty filled with feelings of distrust, abandonment, and lovelessness. And it was just at this moment that the boys in my school—who'd been my friends from the first grade on—began their clumsy attempts at affection, which changed them from companions to alien beings with strange desires.

Some of the girls in my class seemed to find their new roles easily; others of us, once so sure-footed, stumbled. The dance parties that suddenly materialized were gloriously painful, and I was doomed from the start: I just couldn't flirt. I watched my friend Lucy, whose face was filled with freckles and whose hair flamed red, begin to flex her flirting muscles, and I found myself unable to mimic her. I was disgusted at such a profoundly dishonest form of communication, yet I also yearned for the skill, and began to feel I was flawed in some basic way. It took me years to realize that I couldn't flirt because I lacked good role models; my parents' relationship was hardly playful, and it was not until my college years, when I saw my mother interacting with her friend and lover, Ed, that I got my first good lessons.

Not that I didn't have infatuations. As I sat in my room, listening for hours to the radio's parade of hit songs in 1958 and 1959, I began the first of countless fixations on tall, blond, good-looking boys, most of whom passed me by without a glance. I gave them words, dreams, fantasy conversations. I filled them up with my illusory perceptions of their goals, dreams, and desires, all of which sustained me but most certainly had almost nothing to do with them. And in each case I believed that somehow I would get beyond their oblique sentences and emotional silences to some great depth of feeling that lay within, to be revealed with time and patience.

And, like millions of adolescent girls before—and after!—me, I found that food was an always reliable bulwark against loneliness. Oh, what solace it provided! What comfort and pleasure without threat! By the age of fourteen, I could eat an entire box of doughnuts on a subway ride home, devour an entire chocolate cake at one sitting, or shovel a half-gallon of ice cream down my throat. I was a typical secret eater who ate three cookies publicly and slid another five under the table. I would enter bakeries, order enough cake or cookies for a dozen people, and leave with my purchase in a box tied with string, to avoid the embarrassment of being seen with such a large order. But as soon as I walked out onto the street, the string was off, the box was ripped apart, and I was tearing off pieces with my fingers. During high school I would occasionally sneak into the Russian Tea Room, where I would order as "take-out" their richest dessert, a marzipan potato with a creamy filling and chocolate pieces in the center. In the early sixties it cost fifty cents. By the 1970s, it cost three dollars, and I returned to donuts. By the time I was fourteen I weighed a hundred and fifty pounds; by the time of my sophomore year in college, I hit two hundred.

My mother, so wise in other ways, was devoted to the medical and psychological models of the time. She sent me to a therapist, and to a diet doctor who gave me little green pills that must have been placebos since they didn't seem to do much of anything. Whatever was in them, they were probably less dangerous than the occasional amphetamine I was given by friends in college, and which produced such a state of euphoria that despite my two hundred pounds I could run up four flights of stairs without stopping. The diet doctor also prescribed thyroid pills, although as far as I know, I have never had a thyroid deficiency.

I tried the various fad diets of the period, and even went to a "fat farm" where I went on a nine-day fast of nothing but water. It was far from a spiritual experience. The residents sat around, reading or watching television. Besides several young women who were dieting so that they could gain parts in movies or plays, the population was mostly middle-aged women who drank cups of warm water and talked obsessively about the food they would consume when they returned to the world. Many of them came back to this retreat year after year.

I also wandered into Weight Watchers, but the organization had just begun, and its rah-rah cheerleading kept this alienated high school student from appreciating the program's finer points: that one must cast aside notions of perfection and that life can always include at least a little bit of chocolate.

My weight was not my only concern about my body. By the time I was a freshman in college, I was convinced that I carried a deep and secret flaw; I knew I was *deformed*. And the moment when I received incontrovertible proof of this fact was the day I was arrested in Berkeley, in 1964.

I was sitting on the floor of the jail, in a holding room with dozens of other women, when the universe decided to choose that very moment to give me my period. I could feel that warm and greasy feeling as my underpants received the first spots of blood, but there were no sanitary napkins to be found. One young woman lent me a tampon, but I had never used one. I tried to remember how my mother looked, standing in the bathroom, one leg slightly bent, the other raised, with her bare foot casually resting on the toilet seat, easily inserting the tampon while carrying on a running conversation. I knew that you were supposed to be relaxed when you did it, which, at the moment, in this place, seemed inconceivable, and I knew that people who had had sex often used tampons easily, and that virgins sometimes found it difficult. I was still "intact," as the old expression went, and wondered if the tampon would work. But, being desperate, I went to the toilet, unwrapped the tampon, and tried to find the *hole* and pushed. It just didn't seem

to be going anywhere, and the more I pushed the more it hurt.
It hurt like hell, in fact. I rested and tried pushing again,
crunching up in pain. The more I willed myself to relax, the
more tense I became. Being eighteen, I didn't think about the
fact that I could not have found a worse environment to try
something new. I'd had no sleep, guards were all around, I was
in a public toilet, and at least fifty women were sitting on
the floor nearby. Instead, I began to believe—a belief that did
not truly leave me until I spent several years in a feminist
consciousness-raising group, a decade later—that I had a secret
defect. I may have looked like a normal woman on the *outside*
(although I also secretly believed that my excess weight was
some kind of signal to the world about my inner defects), but
on the *inside* I was flawed: *I didn't have the hole!*

I have brought several audiences of college students to hysterical laughter by telling them this story. Other women
laugh—and I can laugh about it too—because our fears were
so similar. Like millions of young girls, I found my body turning into something strange and alien during puberty.

In the Berkeley of the mid-sixties there was an extraordinary amount of experimentation with sex and drugs, but that
doesn't mean that love filled the streets. There was as much
sadness, tension, and anger as there was love. Many of us were
simply too young to love well. As for me, although I may have
looked a little bit like a hippie, I remained a left-wing nun.
Mine was the ecstasy of politics, not of the body. Although I
met young women who counted their conquests like many a
man, my sexual encounters were few and almost all of them
were unsuccessful.

I went through my freshman year with my virginity intact.
The next fall, after Mississippi, I fell in love with a student I'll
call Al. He was tall, blond, smart, and funny, the type I was always attracted to from afar, and we had intense talks together.

But I was at a great disadvantage; there was no way I could compete with another student who had not only jumped into bed with him immediately, but managed to shop and cook for him—quite a feat since he lived in a student dorm and supposedly ate his meals in a common dining room. To provide the food for these home-cooked delicacies, she would run to the local grocery store every few days, buy about five dollars' worth of food, and secretly slip more than three times that amount into her knapsack. For years I was completely at a loss to understand why this young woman would do this, and why he wanted it. Finally I asked him. His answer: "Why, my mother always cooked for me," he said pleasantly, oblivious to his sense of entitlement.

Still, I was infatuated, perhaps not enough to cook or steal, but enough to decide to go to bed with him. But I was tense and jittery on the night of our attempt, and the experience was as painful as my attempt to insert that tampon in the Alameda County jail. I stopped him in the middle of the act and tearfully admitted defeat. He was gentle and forgiving, but I turned away, ashamed. I was convinced more than ever that something was dreadfully amiss.

Al eventually married a lovely woman who cooks for him just as his mother once did. When I saw him at a Free Speech Movement reunion he said he missed the intense conversations we'd had in the old days. As my mother would have said, "You make your bed and you lie in it."

I finally ended my virginity in the spring of 1966, with a young radical engineer. He was smart, a bit nerdish, sandy-haired, and a loner—not so different from me. He was deeply uneasy with his emotions, and he washed his hands too often. Our relationship was strange but tender. We were friends and partners in radical politics, but also souls who twined together because of our mutual loneliness.

Once, when we were walking down Telegraph Avenue in twilight, arm in arm, he noticed a couple walking by, embracing. "See," he whispered poignantly, "we're just like them!" To all the strangers who passed we looked like two ordinary people in love, not the lonely, odd creatures we seemed to ourselves, who clung together for support, to ward off an inner darkness.

Our sex was disastrous. We were both virgins, so we fumbled terribly, and although neither of us was able to say it out loud, I think we were both mortified at the clinical experiment that resulted from our poor efforts. When he entered me, finally, I certainly felt no pleasure, and the sense I had of being some kind of freak persisted, a feeling that would stay with me into my late twenties, to be washed away only slowly and gently by a combination of consciousness-raising meetings with other women, ceremonies in the nude, a bit of therapy, a tincture of time, and, eventually, better sex.

Many years later, at an FSM reunion in 1984, we found each other again, and although we didn't put all these feelings into words, we determined to do well what had been so botched nineteen years before. We found ourselves in bed, as adults, in a romantic setting with candles burning, both of us more able to give and receive the gift of pleasure. I had been monogamous for a number of years (with the man who would become my husband), but I instinctively knew that we had to come together for this one night to prove to ourselves and each other that we weren't still those inept adolescents who had brought only misery to each other.

I am only now beginning to understand what mixed messages about sex and sensuality existed in the culture then—and exist now—and how these attitudes affected my life. In the world of my childhood, the 1950s, the word used for a sexually unresponsive women was "frigid." Even after my unsuccessful attempts at sex, I couldn't believe that the word applied to me, since from the age of seven I had achieved pleasure with ease as I lay on my stomach in my bed, in my own private realm of fantasy. Given the values of my home, no one told me masturbation was anything other than normal, only that it was something you did in private. But by the time I was a teenager I had drunk in an assortment of cultural messages, and "knew" that it was a "lesser" form of love, "immature," as the Freudians believed, and at least a tiny bit shameful, something you did not talk about to others.

Other forms of sensuality were easily available—my mother's hugs, the comfort of back rubs, having my hair brushed and braided, the aroma of certain foods, the glorious mess of eating lobster, the sleek, smooth feel of water, and the ecstasy of letting a wave carry me to the shore. But I saw little physical affection around me that seemed genuine. And this business of "having sex" with other people didn't connect with any sense of warmth and pleasure and freedom. So, in the allegedly free and honest sixties, when I finally did have intercourse— and I did not have much of it—I, like so many other women, gave pleasure to myself and faked orgasms with others. Many years later I came across *The Hite Report*, a book created from the voices of several thousand women talking about their sexual experiences. The book contained this startling and illuminating statistic: seventy-five percent of the women in Hite's survey said they did not achieve orgasm easily through penetration. As I remembered my sexual experiences in the sixties, particularly the deep shame I felt, utterly convinced that I was defective and that *everyone else* was assuredly having the most fulfilling experiences, I reread the sentence over and over, feeling my whole body begin to glow. For two days I was ecstatic, high as if on drugs, euphoric with relief and the comfort of my own normalcy.

But it wasn't until I was in the company of women, in one of the many hundreds, perhaps thousands, of consciousness-raising groups that formed in the early seventies as part of the second wave of feminism, and was listening to the stories of women and telling my own, that I began to understand how similar were many of the threads in our tales, and how ridiculously and wonderfully ordinary we all were.

My group began in 1972, with about eight other women from my neighborhood. The feminist group Red Stockings sent out volunteer facilitators to CR groups that were starting up, and one of them came to our first meeting to give us some ground rules and a list of suggested discussion topics. The rules were simple. Each week we agreed to a topic for the next week. Everyone sat in a circle and spoke in turn, perhaps for ten minutes. There were to be no interruptions. This simple idea was revolutionary because in the seventies, whether sitting in a restaurant or reading a newspaper on a park bench, women were seldom left alone. They were almost always interrupted, even accosted, by strangers. After everyone spoke, there was a time for general discussion, with some attempt to look at the common themes in the stories we shared.

At one of the earliest meetings, a woman who looked like she had gotten all the breaks—tall, thin, elegant, and self-possessed—confessed that in fifteen years of marriage she had never had an orgasm, and that she had never disclosed this fact to her husband. After the meeting she went home, told her husband the truth, and that week had the first satisfying sexual experience of her life. The changes in the rest of our lives were different in nature and perhaps not as abrupt, but over the long term they were just as dramatic. For some of the women it was the first time they had been in a place where their innermost thoughts were valued. For myself, I realized that almost every "weird" thought or feeling I had carried around inside, convinced that it was the product of some personal defect, was shared by millions of other women, or at least by eight of them.

The topics we discussed—childhood, high school, mothers, fathers, our first dates, menstruation, sex, work—brought out into the open the patterns of our lives. For many of us the experience was more radical than any therapy.

We shared truths that my mother had not been able to teach me, despite the progressive nature of her beliefs. She did not really know what to do with her desperately overweight daughter who was not eager to go out on dates, who preferred to attend political meetings or stay home reading books. When it came to women and men, my mother often resorted to the clichés of the time. "Don't finish your food before the man you date," she told me, "or you'll threaten him." Despite the radical way she had departed from her own traditions, she was not a feminist in today's sense. She had stopped work in the 1950s, had spent twenty years in a traditional marriage, and she died just as the second wave of feminism began.

I did have *some* moments of peace with my body as a teenager. I was visiting my friend Kathleen Cameron when, at the age of twelve, my first period suddenly arrived. Kathleen's parents brought out a bottle of wine and toasted my entry into womanhood. I have rarely had a menstrual cramp, and I've long wondered how much this was genetic luck and how much it was the result of knowing from the first moment that menstruation was an event to be celebrated. "They never did that for me," Kathleen confided in me many years later. In our society it is often easier for friends to provide what family cannot.

But it would take more than this moment of celebration, and more than a CR group, to change my feelings toward my own body.

During the same year that I began meeting with the group of women, I joined a group of men and women that worshipped

nature in the nude. This marked the beginning of my explora-
tion of Pagan spirituality, which eventually resulted in my book
Drawing Down the Moon. I found the group's attitude toward the
body liberating. For the first time since childhood, I was back
in the easy nudity of my parents' generation, where nakedness
had more to do with freedom than sexuality. People's bodies
just *were.* The fat, the thin, the old, the young—sagging bellies,
wrinkles, protruding veins—all were accepted and none of
this was the measure of one's worth. No one had a perfect body,
everyone had numerous blemishes and imperfections, and sitting around among all these variations, it was possible to exult
in the amazing discovery that no one cared. There was something extraordinary about discussing life, spirituality, and politics, with ten or twelve people while completely in the nude.
Many of the prejudices I had held for years against my own
form melted away.

But accepting my body was one thing; dealing with sex
and sexuality was another. I didn't understand that most
people are not naturally good at sex, and that for many
people, ease and joy in sexuality doesn't come until *after* they
are thirty. Most people get better at sex with time; some
people live perfectly fascinating lives and never get very
good at it; and—dare I say it?—some people find a great idea,
a fascinating conversation, a deep comradeship, or even an
extraordinary meal just as satisfying. Music can raise the soul
and body to heights of energy and delight. Community action and protest can make the skin tingle and the juices rise.
And what of religious ecstasy and the altered states produced
by ritual? There is very little place in our culture to talk
about forms of transcendence other than two bodies rub-
bing against each other.

I didn't feel ready to experiment with sex until 1974. During the next three years I learned many truths, including the

fact that I was never fated to be a sexual athlete. My experimentation began at the Minneapolis wedding of Tim (now Oberon) and MorningGlory Zell, which was held during a convention of Witches and Pagans. The Zells planned an elaborate ceremony that would join them for all their lifetimes, not just their current lives. While this idea may have seemed grandiose, given America's track record for marriages during even one lifetime, my friends were known to take risks on a grand scale.

On the day of the wedding, I wandered back to the hotel room I was sharing with several people, only to stumble upon a small orgy. There were two couples making love on the beds and only one person in the room was known to me. I had never participated in group sex. I panicked but I was also fascinated. I wondered what it would be like to just throw myself into such a situation and experience a rare uncontrolled moment.

Instead, I went out of the room and called a friend in New York, a man with a wealth of sexual experience. "What shall I do?" I practically wailed into the phone. "There's an orgy taking place in my hotel room, and I don't know what to do." "What do you want to do?" he asked, playing therapist for the moment. "I don't know. Part of me wants to experience it, another part wants to run and hide." "Why not go for it?" my friend suggested. I went back into the room, sat on an empty bed, and thought about taking my clothes off. A very long minute passed. Just as I started to pull my top off, the door of the room opened and an elderly man who had been pursuing me during the weekend walked in. He took one look at the scene and began unbuttoning his shirt. I pulled my top back on hastily, said "Oops, I forgot to make an important phone call" (a strategy that has always worked wonders for me), and ran out of the room. So ended my first orgy.

The wedding took place later that afternoon. The ritual was moving and poetic. As the reception ended, the newly wed couple asked me if I would come back to their room and "share their nuptial bliss." I was momentarily stunned, but two hours later I was sitting in their bedroom with five or six other people, talking and eating, and just about everyone was nude. Again I found myself both panicked and amazed, torn between desire and dread. I did notice that Tim was the only man, something I began to ponder at length only much later. I was intrigued with how totally comfortable Tim and MorningGlory were in their bodies, and I found myself in awe and a bit envious of their relaxed self-assurance. I allowed myself to undress, and lay down in their bed. Then, through some amazingly self-protective instinct, I became like a 1950s housewife, overwhelmed with fatigue. I curled up in the large bed and fell asleep. When I awoke several hours later, the Zells were sleeping peacefully beside me. So ended my second orgy.

A few months later I had a third experience with group sex that changed all my ideas about both sex and love. I visited a woman who became a symbol to me of what real sexual liberation is about, and of how fragile it is in our culture. At the time this woman was involved with a complex and inordinately handsome companion. The woman, then thirty-nine to my more youthful twenty-eight, was at that point, like myself, rather heavy, and few would have considered either of us conventionally attractive.

After I spent a lovely night at her house, she asked me if I wished to join her and her partner for lovemaking. Although I was startled to be given such an invitation, I decided to throw caution to the wind, perhaps because her partner was so stunningly attractive, or because they were both my friends.

He *was* a tender and considerate lover, and I found myself almost in tears at how beautiful an experience I was having. But all the while I wondered, "How did she have the strength to do this? How could she not be jealous? Especially since, like me, she is fat and she is almost middle-aged, and certainly not particularly attractive?" After our lovemaking we lay back and drank freshly brewed coffee as the sun lit up the morning and I tried to think of a way to say some small part of all those old thoughts about beauty and possessiveness— the legacy of our culture—that were running through my brain. I chose my words carefully. "How can you do this, so willingly, and not be jealous?" I asked. She looked at me, straight to the heart, as if she had heard both my inner and outer voices. "You know," she said to me, "when you become truly mature, you will learn that physical beauty is the least of what's going on in any truly important relationship." My friend taught me a great lesson about the superficiality of image, and about the depth of sensuality and love that can exist based on deep friendships and soulful connections.

A year after this sunny morning I began the research for the book on modern Paganism that became *Drawing Down the Moon*. In all my travels around the country, from Los Angeles to Chicago to Philadelphia to a pig farm in Missouri, I actually came across very little sex. Oh, people talked about sex, people theorized about sex, people wrote articles about sex—but I didn't *see* any sex. Perhaps, because I was primarily on a quest for ideas, I may not have even seen some of the sex that *was* there. The only exception to this was when I made my pilgrimage to St. Louis, to interview the Zells.

Tim and MorningGlory were living in a predominantly black suburb of St. Louis. When I entered their home I found eight or ten people collating their magazine, *Green Egg*, which, in 1975, was the most important Neo-Pagan magazine in the country. It was just around Halloween time, Samhain, as Pagans call it—the Celtic new year, one of the most sacred festivals in the Wiccan and Pagan calendar. The room was overheated and most of the volunteers were nude. They were eating popcorn, and feverishly busy putting together the journal.

The Zells, and others who have joined their family, are among the few people I know who have practiced group sex continuously, lovingly, and pretty much successfully for more than twenty years. Oh, I've come across countless others who have told me of their successful polyamorous relationships, but usually when I see the partners there's at least one member of the group who looks a little sad and tense around the eyes, or has suddenly gained forty pounds, although the new threesome or foursome is "working out just fine." But the Zells are an exception.

During my week-long visit, the Zells simply assumed that I would share their life and their bed. I decided, once again, that I would allow myself to be swept along. Reuniting with the Zells, without the frenzy of a wedding, was gentle and loving. Every once in a while I would look up at the ceiling and see our bodies intertwined in the mirror above; in the dimly lit room we seemed like forms in an impressionist painting, perhaps by Renoir, with soft hues fading one into another. But for them, sex was an easy act of joy and friendship, while for me it was still filled with unease, something occasional, something I did best alone. I was awed by their naturalness, how it was something they did happily, morning and night, whereas for me, even when I was in a relationship, twice a week was a lot of sex.

By the end of the week, I was secretly a wreck, although each of the experiences with these adept and experienced lovers had been gentle, passionate, even romantic. The old voice inside returned with its eternal questions: Why am I having problems with this? Is there something wrong with me?

When I arrived home in New York, I was frayed at the edges, so confused about my own thoughts and feelings that I went to a therapist. Fortunately, she was one with some wisdom and wit. After I described my experiences and feelings of inadequacy, she turned to me and said, "You know, there are champion skiers, and champion tennis players, and champion golfers. These people are just very good at sex. They are experts. But not everyone is a sexual athlete, or is supposed to be." I found myself laughing with relief. I was more relaxed about sex after this advice, and eventually did manage to have one or two joyful encounters with these various friends. But in the end I decided that for me, a greater sense of personal comfort came with a more monogamous life.

But if sex was less mysterious, beginning and sustaining a meaningful relationship was still baffling. Achieving meaningful friendships seemed hard enough. My mother had advised me from an early age that "the only way to meet an interesting man is to live an interesting life," what we might now call the "build it, and he (or she) will come" theory of relationships. I also understood, by the time I was a teenager, that even a hint of inner desperation could turn a potential partner away. Despite this knowledge, except for those few experimental encounters, I spent most of the early seventies celibate and alone.

And so I came to wonder if my problem was *men*. Perhaps I was really gay, and should try a relationship with a woman. But all my teenage fantasies and infatuations were about boys, and I had always assumed that most lesbians had rich fantasy lives filled with women. When two close women friends had, at different times, suggested a sexual relationship, I had cringed and begged off, never sure why. The idea that women could choose women, not necessarily because of strong feelings for women from an early age, but because women were more interesting than men (something that was frequently true as they went through the extraordinary changes that came with the flowering of feminism in the 1970s) had not occurred to me; I was simply noticing that men were not coming into my life, and trying to make my peace with that fact. So I walked up to the most beautiful lesbian woman I knew and, taking a deep breath, in halting phrases, suggested, in the words of the day, that she "bring me out." She agreed.

She came to my bedroom and we undressed and lay in the queen-sized bed that had once belonged to my mother, who for all her liberation, would have never taken this path. Side by side, body to body, I marveled at this beautiful woman with long, dark hair, thin as I could only dream myself thin. In fact, as I lay in her arms and felt her soft hands caressing my shoulders and back, I realized that, in part, I was not really making love with this other woman, for she and I, although we had known each other for a number of years and had shared many beliefs and values, had not really shared an intimate friendship; instead, I was making love to the me I wanted to be. I found it as difficult with her to let go and be deeply receptive as it had been with men.

And all at once I was shocked into a basic truth—that for most humans, despite the theories of assorted schools of therapy, there was rarely such a thing as a sexual problem, but only human problems which manifested themselves in every aspect of life, including sex. I understood that once I accepted my own body and mind with ease and joy, I would encounter others as themselves, not as I desired them to be. Until I did that, I would be unable to really know any person

I encountered; instead, I would merely create a fantasy being through obsession and infatuation, a creation in no way connected to the real person of flesh and bones before me. It was the last and best lesson from this series of explorations. I had learned that my political comrades were not necessarily my best friends, that friendship was more important than sex, and that I took to things slowly, at best. Now I was learning how to free myself from the poisonous cycle of infatuation.

But back in the spring of 1967, I wasn't so wise; I was seeking an infatuation that would consume me totally. I was looking everywhere for my beloved, and I was ready to find him anywhere, in a letter to a newspaper, in a solitary figure sitting in a cafe. I was no longer a virgin, but just barely, after the sorry experiment with the radical engineer.

On my twenty-first birthday, in April of 1967, on the inside front cover of a journal, I wrote two very odd birthday resolutions: "to look at people" and "to do whatever you need to do to make this year the year of love."

I had broken up with the engineer. I had ended a relationship with another young man who was only passionate about rock music and who managed to fall asleep during the lectures of the one professor I most admired.

Looking through that little black journal, alongside four pages of what can only be described as a Marxist analysis of the film *Morgan* (which I attended seven times) I found three pages of pathetically earnest notes on Erich Fromm's *The Art of Loving*: "Giving is not 'giving up' ... giving is the highest expression of potency. I experience myself as overflowing, spending, alive, hence as joyous." "Not he who has much is rich, he who gives much." And, written underneath, "I want to give so much and I feel I can give nothing and cling to people afraid that I will lose them, want to hold them because I am lonely."

But as in the historical and science fiction fantasies of my teenage years, where the hero was always "the other"—the persecuted Quaker in colonial times, the Athenian boy making his way in a harsh Spartan society, the telepathic agent in a world where telepathy is a crime—so my loves at Berkeley were also "the other." The first "other" that I found was a dark, poetic communist, just like the people in my high school fantasies. I will call him Andrei. He was an exchange student from Romania, a graduate student, and for most of the two and a half months I was obsessed with him I didn't even know his last name. I probably talked with him for a total of ten minutes, but I spent days wandering the campus looking for him, spent hours searching the 27,000 names in the student directory to find his name. I dreamed about him. I created in my mind an entire galaxy around his being.

One day I saw him on the terrace of the student cafe during one of my searching prowls. We were suddenly face to face and talking. My actions during this encounter were bizarre; I even said, "Thank you for your existence." I hadn't been this dopey since I was thirteen. Five weeks later, in mid-April, I was still obsessed, writing insipid drivel in my journal. Looking back on these words years later, I can only think I must have been stoned. But chances are I wasn't.

To Andrei:
It matters not that it is only dream and not truth, but for a brief time I knew that I was a part of humanity, that I could truly give myself to something and that feeling was magical; that I could be happy for others and content in myself.

Oh it hurts me that you do not call, and I still wonder if you think my face is flawed, or if you think me too young, or unintelligent, or is it that I do not know a Slavic tongue.

Yet I thank you for your self and for your flexibility. For if you are the one I blindly ran to on impulse, then the human species must contain others with such richness ...

And so on and so forth. As my husband said to me after I unearthed this journal, "It's so sweet, you could have fallen in love with a dog, with anything that came your way at that moment." And it may well have been true—the object of love was irrelevant; I was on an emotional and philosophical journey.

Only one week after I wrote the diary entry addressed to Andrei, I began a far greater obsession, one that would block him from my memory for many years. Marc Anderson, an infantryman stationed in Cu Chi, Vietnam, wrote a letter to the *Daily Californian*, the student newspaper at the University of California at Berkeley.

Soldiers on Two Fronts

CHAPTER 8

A VIETNAM SOLDIER SAYS "MARCH FASTER"

April 23, 1967

I've heard rumors that there are people back in the world who don't believe this war should be. I'm not positive of this though, 'cause it seems to me that if enough of them told the right people in the right way, then something might be done about it, or someone might consider doing something about it, or someone might consider thinking about doing something about it.

At least they wouldn't continue living perfectly assured that everyone agrees with their little ways of ethnocentric thinking. Right? I've been waiting for you to organize. I guess that'll be a long wait. But in the meantime, would you please march faster?

You see, while you're discussing it amongst each other, being beat, getting in bed with dark-haired artists, substituting Mao for LSD (which proves he's a dope), deciding who should really run the school, and all the myriads of other equally important stuff, some people here are dying for lighting a cigarette at night, or 'cause the NCO in charge was drunk, etc., etc.

I haven't understood that other reason yet, you know, the one in the songs. Some of them are ugly though and some are fat. There have been fellas die who used to scrape barnacles off of barges, etc. So?

What can I say about a guy who's lying in the mud and stuff with his cetoplasm and cellulose torn and running out of small circles in his head? He'd rather be eating hot buttered popcorn down on one of Chicago's beaches—probably.

You've got the right idea, anyway.

SP4 M. B. Anderson, 25th Infantry Division, Vietnam

The day this letter appeared in the newspaper I read it over and over, finding myself in tears. I read it to a dozen people, copied it into a letter home. I kept looking at the lines "Some people here are dying for lighting a cigarette at night.... Some of them are ugly though and some of them are fat. There have been fellas die who used to scrape barnacles off barges."

I was surprised at first by my reaction, unsure why those lines kept bringing me to tears. Most of the time I saw the American military as "the enemy," "the other." Truth was, I sympathized with the National Liberation Front—the Vietcong. I believed that the Western technological mindset was fundamentally poisonous and would exterminate millions with ease. I believed that we were witnessing the death of the West, and I embraced an apocalyptic vision of the world not so far from that of the Unabomber of more recent times.

It is very hard for people who came of age after the war ended to understand how the Vietnam War became part of our skin and bones. Along with nuclear war, it became the

fabric of our nightmares. All around us we saw the newspapers printing lies. To many of us on the left, the government
seemed like an alien entity. American officials painted Ho
Chi Minh as a Stalinist; we saw him as someone who considered the American Declaration of Independence as a great
living document and had used it as a model for a future independent Vietnam. Our own country seemed to be this huge
technological giant that was attacking a group of peasants
who were fighting a civil war. I went on marches, but I didn't
believe they achieved very much. I was pessimistic and troubled about the future. At one and the same time, I saw the
American GI as innocent victim and sinister agent of the
Pentagon war machine.

And now I was reading this guy's letter over and over and
crying because I understood, in a way I had never understood
before, how young and innocent the American soldiers
were, and how truly alienated they were from our society—
just like me.

May 5th 1967

Dear M. B. Anderson,

I read your letter to the *Daily Californian*....

Yes, people are dropping out and "being beat" and the
war goes on. One gets angry at them, but then one is
struck down by the futility of it all. We are not enough.
We have no power.

For all our freedom, it is a freedom to be ignored. If
we lived in a dictatorship, we would be beaten, persecuted, put in prison. But we would have an effect. We
live in a democracy, but we count for nothing.

Thus, people give up. Frustrated in fighting the external world, they turn inward, into the personal, into the
hippie scene. I cannot be a part of that scene, but I also

don't know what to do. So, I go on a march, but that does
almost nothing ... and the next day *Time* magazine
comes out and tells me that the march was proof of the
"moral strength" of the nation, that it proved we were
fighting for freedom in Vietnam. The next week they escalate the war ...

Your letter was beautiful. I admire greatly that you
can be there, and feel the way you do, and still retain
your sanity.

Good luck to you.

Good luck to us all,

Margot Adler

It took almost a month for my letter to reach Marc Anderson in Vietnam. During this period I had a series of vivid
dreams filled with soldiers, spies, Chinese political advisers,
KGB agents, U.S. army generals whose bodies had the shape
of tanks, totalitarian labor camps where workers found
roses in mines and tried to avoid being crushed by machinery, regimented societies like those described in Orwell's
1984 or Zamiatin's book *WE*, and as always in those days,
World War III.

"I think it is very easy for a person to go insane over this
war," I wrote home. "One must put up numerous emotional
blockades to fight it. I think the U.S. is determined to win
and will drop a nuclear bomb on Hanoi, and that our forces
will invade the North. I find it difficult to read papers or
watch the news. I think we all feel imprisoned in help-
lessness. We must not think about it or we would lose our
minds. I wonder if a lot of Germans felt this way during
WW2. How can one condemn all the Germans unless we
condemn ourselves."

I was also obsessed with the hippie movement, agreeing

with their rejection of the consumer society, while hating their solution, dropping out. And yet I understood that seduction too. How easy to retreat into the personal in order to save one's sanity. Finally, a letter arrived.

May 26, 1967

Dear Miss Adler;

I received your letter this evening, covered with postal stamps redirecting it from most every place in the R.V.N.

You seem to have hit the nail right on the head, by the tone of your letter which is possibly typified by, "then comes the moment when one is struck by the futility of it all." I know exactly how you feel, as I fight "their" war and one with myself. It's quite obvious what dangers there are in permitting an idea of futility, when it comes to life, etc. You seem unduly let down though because of your results from demonstrations. I know you don't expect revolutionary legislation the next morning. But if your letter warms me, makes me smile inwardly when I close it, and will last for a minimum of weeks—what effect will reading 250,000 people demonstrate or express strong disapproval toward this thing have: I hunger for a discussion with you ... but I guess it'll have to wait....

Sincerely,

Marc Anderson

June 5, 1967

Dear Marc,

I've been thinking of how to answer your letter.... No, I don't expect revolutionary legislation the next morning, but unless the anti-war movement grows greatly (and I have grave doubts about that) nothing internal is going to stop the war.

Here at Berkeley, one can lose one's perspective. People here don't see the war that you see, the meaninglessness. And they don't want to see it. That's what I meant about "I admire that you feel the way you do and keep your sanity" for it would seem that if one had to fight one would desperately want to believe, almost have to believe that it was right. And the people here sending their sons also must want to believe.

It seems to me that Vietnam is only one manifestation of a society that is deeply sick. If we end the war in Vietnam, but nothing else, there will be many others. And yet I have no easy formulas. I often envy those people who have "found Christ" or are sure that the minute everyone drops acid the world will be saved. I don't have any easy answers. I call myself a radical, but I don't know what that means . . . not in a positive sense anyway.

There will probably be a lot of anti-war activity this summer. . . . Actually, it's always surprised me that it's been so calm. I am surprised that no one got desperate and blew up his local recruiting station. Not that that would do the slightest bit of good, but I'm surprised that no one has gotten desperate enough to do it. . . .

As yet there is no real organization of people opposing the war. The left-wing groups fight each other over meaningless details, and it sometimes seems as if they fight each other as much as they fight their real opposition. . . . Sometimes the radicals sit around for hours talking about "how to build a radical movement" or "awaken consciousness."

Off the subject of the war, the biggest event to help life along a bit is the new Beatles album, Sgt. Pepper's Lonely Hearts Club Band, which came out Friday. It is strange and beautiful, an ode to life. On Friday there were people standing in line outside the record store, waiting for hours....

Well, I have to stop and study for finals. Until later, Margot.

Knowing a soldier serving in Vietnam changed my attitude—not politically, but emotionally. I still felt the majority of the Vietnamese supported the National Liberation Front, and that they were more right than we, but the war now appeared in a different light. I now knew that there were intelligent, sensitive people fighting in the U.S. Army. There Marc was—perhaps against his will—and how could I continue to say as glibly as I had done, that I hoped the Vietcong would win? I realized how easily our ideals allow us to slide into sanctioning the death of innocents.

June 11, '67

Dear Margot:

I don't know why I found it so surprising that you seemed to understand this idea of the people over here rationalizing and forcing themselves to believe that this military method is correct. It would be extremely difficult to fight and kill in this way, while all the time feeling it is wrong. Severe enough, in fact, to drive one towards a breakdown or suicide. Simply—one cannot kill if he doesn't believe in it. Again, this is part of the two wars I spoke of. I once had doubts about the rightness of even self-defense, but I know it is too dangerous to introspect about that while I'm here. I, at one time, thought I knew, but since various occurrences I now must wonder, but most important, I must wait 'til

I'm in a non-war situation or it would surely cost my life
the very next time.

Do you recall an operation called Attleboro? Started
in early 1966. When things get really thick it is not the
case that the troops are fighting for their freedom and
for V.N.'s freedom, and all this other business. During
these fire fights, each individual soldier is fighting for
nothing but his life. During a pitch black night you are
assaulted by hard-core troops from maybe thirty to forty
feet away. Six to ten of them chained together, chained
to machine guns, running directly at you, screaming....
You don't really think I was thinking of anything Red,
White and Blue. For 72 straight hours the 1/27th and 2/
27th was in an intense fire fight, stood off 9 human-wave
assaults, fired 1/4 of a million dollars in ammunition
and defeated three regiments of suicide hard-core. No
one in their own mind can believe that slaughter like
that is right. The only thing that kept them going was
that they believed that if they pulled the trigger long
enough and hard enough it would sometime be over and
they would be a little closer to going home. To go home.
What a strange motivation that is. To kill for it. To sin
for it, like Jesus never conceived of sin....

Why don't you tell me what you do, who you are—really, what your major is, etc. and then we could continue
this business after a slight break....

Sincerely,
Marc

I told him about myself. I asked him how he came to be
in Vietnam. I described my life in Berkeley and what I was
studying. I told him I didn't do that much as an activist, that
it was "always the 'cadre' battling the 'doubter'" and that I

had never done that much rebelling: "At first I just accepted a lot of unconscious assumptions from my parents who are quite radical. As I reflected and realized the complexities in things it has become much harder to come to conclusions and to act. What is so difficult is to still act, amid doubt."

And I wrote that I was about to go to jail for three weeks because of my activities during the Free Speech Movement sit-in in 1964. I had decided to go to jail rather than pay a $250 fine and go on probation, because the terms of probation included a ban on certain kinds of demonstrations. I wrote that I was uncertain about my motivation, that I couldn't help feeling it would be an interesting educational experience "and yet there is this feeling that I am 'theirs' ... you must feel it in the army: that you can't leave or you will be court-martialed."

June 28th, Santa Rita

Dear Marc,

I haven't received a letter, perhaps we are crossing in the mail, or you are out in the field....

I went in last Wednesday. So today is day 8. I do not know how long I shall stay here, but the maximum is 25 days.

This is a very strange place, in many ways very un-jail like, or at least what I was led to believe jail would be like. Santa Rita is mostly for men. And there is room for only about 100 women. It seems like a cross between a children's summer camp, Women's Army Corp and girl's boarding school.

One is outfitted completely. The main dress is a blue uniform with a white peter pan collar and white cuffs, white shoes and socks. I live in a dorm with about 25–30 other girls and each has a cot and a stand by the bed. There are eight other FSMers, two others left and a few

more will be coming in. The rest of the people in this
dorm are in for forgery, theft, prostitution, and pushing
dope. To say the least, it is a completely new experience
to live with these people and to find out how surprisingly normal they are.

The women wardens treat the inmates like children—even the middle-aged inmates. Some of the
people here do act childish, but I wonder how I would
act if I had to stay inside for half a year. This idea of treating adults like children can be dangerous: when someone says she is sick the deputies will often believe the
person is shamming, and so they will not receive adequate medical treatment.

We, the FSMers, have generally received equal treatment, but the wardens don't seem to treat us as such children. I am not completely certain why. It is true we are
quieter, but I think the main reason is that we are mostly
white, upper middle class, college educated.

The regime is amazingly healthy. 9 hours sleep, three
quite reasonable meals, and quite a lot of spare time.
During week days we have six hours of work. To my continued amazement, I am spending my six hours ironing,
a job for which I am completely inept, but I am learning
slowly. You may remember Tom Lehrer's famous comment about the army: that it was so democratic, it was
also democratic in regard to ability. That seems to fit
this place, too. During free time, I can knit, read, and go
into a garden which is open and where one can play
Ping-Pong and badminton.

Freedom is so much more than the classic concept of
freedom from encroachments. Here, there are a hundred petty rules, things you can't do and must do.... But
yet, in this rather rigid atmosphere I and other FSMers
find ourselves strangely relaxed, not uptight, and men-

tally freer than at many a time. Also the other inmates are extraordinarily real. There is no phoniness.

I have quickly learned a new vocabulary—such words as wired (high), smack (heroin), crank or crystals (speed), tracks (needle marks), geeze (to shoot), running (living from crime), boost (theft—especially putting stuff between your legs). Anyway it is a side to life that might forever have remained a statistic had I not come here. I can only write two pages, so I will have to stop.

Margot

June 30, '67

Dear Margot:

I only have a few minutes. . . . We're sitting in the middle of a group of rice paddies now, waiting to move out on another operation. They said the mailman would be around in 15 minutes or so. I don't know how long it will last or how long I'll be out. . . . I don't understand exactly why, but I always feel like writing to someone just before an operation. I was going to explain to you that I know that feeling of being someone else's, of being imprisoned—all too well. I haven't time to expand on it now, but I thought you would realize not all experiences are good. I mean not all have a positive effect on one, so I don't understand why you'd volunteer to be jailed. I know two weeks is nothing, but . . .

As to "how I got here?" in next letter.

The sun is baking me now. Of course in a few hours it'll be night, pouring rain and I'll be shivering. I see they are gathering up their equipment. I better close. Gotta Run. Take care.

Sincerely,

Marc

Santa Rita Prison Farm and Rehabilitation Center is located in Pleasanton, California. During my stay, the prison held about sixty women. There were two dorms—one for those awaiting sentencing and one for women serving out their terms. Each had about forty beds. There were smaller dorms for drunks—mainly older women—and for women who worked in the kitchen and had to get up earlier than the rest of us. The walls were cream and green, a bit brighter than the common institutional green. The beds were green with green bedspreads, and the barred windows had curtains with a faded rose pattern.

We were each given a bed and a nightstand with two drawers. We were given three pairs of socks, three pairs of underpants, three bras, three blue uniforms, a pair of green shorts, a sleeveless cotton jersey, a pair of white shoes, a towel, a washcloth, a toothbrush, a small toothpaste, a comb, a bar of soap, a pair of slippers, a laundry bag, a denim jacket, and a nightgown. We had to keep all our belongings inside our night-stands; only an ashtray and Bible were permitted on top.

The prison operated on a strict reward-and-punishment system. A messy bed earned you one infraction; three infractions resulted in a pink slip which led to a punishment, like doing dishes, or losing a privilege, like attending a movie. Serious offenses, such as passing a note to the outside, were punished by solitary confinement in a windowless cell for at least ten days. There you received less food, had to wear a nightgown, could only read a Bible and had to ask the deputies' permission to turn on the light.

Every morning we were roused at 6:30 for a head count. The deputies would say, "Let's count, girls." Unlike the movies, there were no whistles. Breakfast was at 7:00 A.M., then there was another count. We would go to work at about 8:10

A.M., have a fifteen-minute coffee break at 9:30, go back to our dorm at 11:30, then another count, then lunch, then return to work until 3:30, then another count, then dinner, then at 6:00 we could watch the news in the recreation room, then another count, and then a final count at 9:30 P.M. and then bed.

Visiting day was Sunday, and the conditions were ludicrous. We stood in a large cage with our hands behind our backs, talking to friends who stood on the other side of the cage. But meals were no worse than those at school. When I put milk in my cereal, it felt like heavy cream; it took me a day to realize that I had been drinking skim milk for the last two years.

The women prisoners had created an entire culture of ingenious substitutes. Jewelry was forbidden and so women made their own out of the silver paper in cigarette packs. Tampons were forbidden, so women rolled their own by taking a sanitary napkin, cutting it in half, rolling it into a tampon shape, then placing it in the middle of the gauze-like outer lining and tying a knot. They had also created a substitute for eyebrow pencil from the charcoal residue of burnt matches.

Letters were limited to two a day, and each was limited to two pages. They were censored for curse words, which were cut out with a scissors. I'd sometimes put one curse word in to show people how the censorship worked. "This is a new experience for me," my father wrote. "I have never written to anyone in prison. I have never even seen a prison, except the prison part of certain mental hospitals, and I have been in army stockades during the war." He advised me to pay my fine and leave after a few days. My father believed that you could read about jail in a book and you "did not jump off a bridge for the experience of it." But, ever the Adlerian, he wrote that I should think of prison as a place where "cooperation is as necessary as it is in any other community, since the overriding issue in life is, always, to bring self-interest into accord with the common interest." He hoped I would use my time constructively.

My mother, writing on the evening of my first full day, asked if the reality was as "glamorous" as the fantasy. She told me not to see myself as a heroine, and that while "prison bars do not a cell make," I should feel free to pay my fine and get out if after "1, 2, 3 or any number of days you've had it and want again the freedom of directing your own day, at least outwardly."

My father's wife, Tanya, emphasized the practical. She wanted to know if I lived in a cell. Did I wear a uniform? Did I work in the laundry? She confessed that her knowledge of prisons came mainly from Bogart and Cagney. She was also the most perceptive. She wrote that she admired my courage for walking through the gate knowing that it would close behind me, but she was not sure what principle prompted my choice. "I have the sense that there is something involved that may be difficult to define or describe—more in the feeling life than in the cerebral life. Was there also a feeling of wanting to be identified with a group—and a rather unique group at that—involved here?"

The truth was that I was not quite sure why I had chosen to go to jail. Possibly, yet again, to explore and test myself, to see a side of life I had never seen, to meet and talk with people I would not have ordinarily met. I also wanted to spend some time with Bettina Aptheker and other Free Speech Movement women. And somewhere in all this confusion of motive there was the principle of the thing. I was taking a stand. But, thinking about it now, I wonder if I also wanted to enter jail in order to commune in some indefinable way with Marc, to be in my own version of the army, to experience my own loss of freedom.

I ironed uniforms for six hours a day—I who had lived

comfortably in a messy state and had probably ironed all of two shirts and five skirts in my entire life. It was boring work. Worse yet, I was so terrible at it that several women complained about creases in the uniforms I ironed. Fortunately, after two weeks my job was changed to gardening.

One day as the guards locked us into the ironing room I started thinking about the meaning of oppression. How different was I really, I wondered, than a secretary in an office? She couldn't run off to the ocean, or to her home, without permission. If she did she might get fired. Her door *seemed* open, but in reality she was just as locked in. Marc's place in the army as a draftee seemed another form of servitude. Few in the world were truly free.

Yet prison life was oddly free of anxiety. As a teenager I had joked that the only way I would lose weight was if someone locked me in a room and fed me bread and water. Well, that was happening now, and my fat was melting away. Prison made dieting simple; if I controlled my urges at meals, there was no way to go on binges. My life was completely controlled by others. I was sleeping nine hours a night. I was rested and relaxed. I secretly believed—although I would have been ashamed to tell anyone—that if I could just lose fifteen pounds in prison, that alone would justify the experience.

I now also understood why people returned to crime after having been in prison. Everything was peaceful and secure. Meals, a fixed job, sleep, clothes—all your physical wants were cared for. To return to a life of constant struggle, of being poor, would be a most difficult adjustment. "I suppose many of the people here are 'difficult' out in the world," I wrote, "but here one does not have to know the 'why' or 'wherefore,' and at times the truth is a surprise. Many of the problems that might come between us in the 'real world,' like

racial tensions, are mitigated here. Here we are all in this together."

But finally jail did begin to get to me. By the third week I
was going stir-crazy. It wasn't the rules—in general I found
them easy enough to follow without dwelling on them—but
every once in a while something would happen that made
me realize that *they* possessed you. A girl was put in solitary
for passing a note; another girl got gravely ill and the deputies refused to take her illness seriously until she needed to
be hospitalized. One woman was jailed for "welfare violation," for becoming pregnant while on probation. When she
arrived at the jail she told us her baby had been taken away.

I also had not heard from Marc in two weeks, and every
time I read a newspaper or heard news of the war I became
afraid that he had been killed. The war seemed very far away.
I began reading Tolstoy's *War and Peace*. There were so many
parallels—people leaving for the war because they craved
adventure, innocent youth rationalizing and spouting patriotic phrases, the unreality of war.

July 8, 67

Dear Margot;

I finally got your letter this morning. I'm sorry I
couldn't get one off sooner.... It seems to me I came
out to the field around the 28th, but I don't really know.
I also thought you had said you didn't go in 'til the first
... this is foggy to me because we burn our mail—it
wouldn't be wise to be captured with anything personal
on you.

Health treatment. The army considers one shamming
as long as they eat, so they'll hardly give adequate medical treatment. I've lost most of the hearing in my right
ear as the result of several throat infections that they

wouldn't treat.... It is all typified by a fellow who died of pneumonia here because "there was nothing wrong with him." ...

Short on Time. Will write in a few days.

Marc

July 17, 67

Dear Marc;

Perhaps the strangest feeling upon leaving Santa Rita was the insecurity of it. I was there for only 20 days, and yet, in that short time I understood the feeling of ambivalence toward leaving. Everyone said, "Aren't you glad to be out?" And I was, but.... Suddenly I had to face all the problems I had left outside. There was something frighteningly pleasant about the security in jail, the lack of tension, the absence of decisions.

Today as I walked on the main part of campus, to the tables manned by political and religious groups, I started talking to a student sitting behind one of the antiwar tables. In the course of the conversation, he made some glib comment on the fortunes of the war.... It was the kind of remark that two months ago would have passed me by without a thought ... not really a remark, but a tone. I felt like slugging him. All I did was mumble something about innocent people being trapped. So your letters have made the war more human. Most Berkeley students are personally isolated from the war—we know few people there, and that isolation allows us to make insensitive comments.

I guess I still would like to know how old you are, where you are from and what you were doing before and how you got there. I also wonder if you get information on antiwar activism within the military, like Cap-

tain Levy's trial, the Fort Hood Three, PFC. Patrick's
case, etc. Stay well and safe.

    Sincerely,

    Margot

July 26, 67

Dear Margot:

Your stay in the "brig" seemed to have duplicated (in
you) many of the emotions I've also felt. For example, "I
was glad to leave, but ..." You're right—there's a type of
security in having no responsibilities or problems (of the
civilian type) and lack of competition. It reopened a
whole panorama of thoughts I'm concerned with, especially now—as the end is beginning to approach—
readjusting to responsibility, decisions, etc.

    Your reasons were interesting. I suspect there was a
touch of stubborn idealism in not wanting to pay for
something you felt was "right." They didn't put you in
jail for expressing your dislike of something, but because of the means you chose.

    "About the Author." Am from Chicago. Born in 1946.
For 8 months prior to induction I was an ambulance
driver and was also a medical attendant. The job was 60
hours a week, but a lot of that time was spent hanging
around (when business was slack) so I used that time to
study and was a night student at a city school.

    How did I get over here? I was a high school student
when inducted. So I appealed. The draft board said that
since I had at one time dropped out and gone to California, that it was their policy to induct those who did not
go consecutive semesters—which indicated that they
had no intention of finishing. They did not see the point
when I explained, "Do you people think I would work

60 hours a week and attend night school if I wasn't in-
tending on finishing? So after I was in for seven or eight
months my brother finally completed research on how I
could still get out. So I filed for a "207 erroneous induction." It must have been valid cause it pissed them off
and a few days later I was on my way to Vietnam. That is
the American government in action! Two beautiful years
down the drain so these silly bastards can play their little games....

Thank you so much for letters. I devour everything
you have to say!

Marc

96 days!

July 26, 67

Dear Margot;

I'm in from [the] field. I don't know if that is good or
not. At least out there they don't harass us. After a short
while back here, I start heading for trouble and thinking
and being depressed, angry, bored, nervous, drunk, with-
drawn, apathetic, pathetic, wasted, horny, insomnia-ish,
lazy, bitter, paranoid, etc.

Casualty rates have dropped this past week. One guy
was shot four times in the face by someone in another
squad (accidentally) and someone from the 1st of the
8th artillery came to our club and commenced to tell
everyone how rough they had it. When asked why he
didn't join a "line company" there was, of course, no
answer. He continued, continued, until he drummed
up a fight. He and his friend were taken out back and
beaten. He was killed and his friend had to be evacuated to the States. Those were the only deaths
recently....

Will you get your B.A. in Berkeley? Do you like pop-
corn (my recent obsession)? I shall end this rambling.
  Sincerely,
  Marc

                                               July 26, '67
Dear Marc,
  Yesterday, news of the war was relegated to page
seven. The news is filled with violence in Detroit, New-
ark, Maryland, Toledo and East Harlem. I just read another of those "how could it happen here, how unjustified, we were making such progress" editorials, and it
makes me want to scream! So you may find the next paragraph outrageous and upsetting.
  It is terrible to see the leaders of this country continue in blindness. I feel they are bringing about their
own destruction. Now they become scared, self-
righteous, indignant and will pass anti-riot laws and
condemn "outside agitators," never grasping that even if
there were outside agitators nothing would have happened if things were not at the boiling point. I fear that
they will continue to hide from the fact that if they
don't do something about the ghettos—and not something token—Detroit will only be the beginning of a
real blood bath. They arrested more than 2,000 people. If
they arrest any more, where are they going to put them?
Perhaps in the detention camps that were built and remain empty, that were called for in the McCarren Act of
1950, in case of a National Emergency. But what is a National Emergency?
  The violence frightens me, but somewhere deep
down I feel "it serves them right" and yet I know that
that is a self-righteous attitude. When I really get pessi-

mistic I see a society that is crumbling, with every solution uncomfortable. Enough of that.

The story of your induction was really incredible! . . . Have you read *Catch 22*? I know you are pressed for time, but if you have any spare minutes, even if you don't finish it, it is probably *the* book to read while there—hilarious, cynical, etc. Also, would you like a subscription to the *Berkeley Barb*? Hundreds of subscriptions are going to soldiers in Vietnam, but it's a hippie-radical paper, so if it would cause you any trouble, I won't send it. It's not a gem of good journalism and its editor fully admits this. Its purpose is to provide people with news and information on anti-establishment groups and events.

Two nights ago, I went with some friends to the Haight Ashbury and we walked around watching everybody "do their thing." I had never spent an entire evening there. It is a very strange place. For all its fame as "love" street, there was an underlying atmosphere of anger and unhappiness. Few smiled. Perhaps if they were happy and at one with the world, they wouldn't be here, but still, everyone thinks of the hippies as the "love" generation, and so the reality made a deep impression. I went with some friends and one of them had a guitar and we played on the street and sang, and some guys with bongos and tambourines joined us. That part was fun. Many of the people we met were truly strange, such as the 80-year-old wino who accosted us and asked us to play an old Henry Byrd ballad, and the man in a cafe who read out loud one of the worst plays I have ever heard.

I saw a map with troop placements. They put down the 25th Infantry Division around Cu Chi, west of Saigon. Is that where you are? Also, are they making use of your ambulance experience? Probably not, I would guess. I am interested in everything you feel like and can talk about—daily routine, work, military life. Is it true that the ARVN [South Vietnamese] soldiers won't fight—that's what I read in the papers, and if the papers mention something like this, it is usually worse.

Your letter was very flattering, but I'm not really courageous, and I am not sure what courage is. A professor I once had said that courage is the ability to act in the face of doubt, and that those who had a philosophy of certainty had it easier. But when I am truly honest with myself I must admit that I have not had to really fight for my values. My parents have been fairly understanding, and both have very radical views, so my rebellion has been in the opposite direction, more conservative. Not rebelling has its good points—I haven't had to be angry or vindictive as many rebels are, but I also haven't really been tested.

Margot

July 30, 1967

Dear Margot;

I would rather not receive the *Barb*. I hope you understand this. Losing a security clearance is a big deal, especially after getting one. I hope you understand this. I think I know what you'll think about this, but most of my actions now are aimed several years from now. It is something like—you gotta play their game until you can make up your own rules or you'll never be in the position to do that. Rather simple, I know, but it is the essence.

Of course the army isn't utilizing whatever medical talent I have! Or it wouldn't be the army.

I am right outside Cu Chi.

There is always much change going on, but to say the ARVNs won't fight isn't quite true. But they feel, "Why should we? Let the GI do it. They're so eager and enthusiastic about this war!" It took me a long time to understand the attitude people develop from being at war for twenty or so years. It's no big thing. They don't understand our demands. "The war will still be here tomorrow. We're in no hurry to get out there." I know, tho, when they want to they can be tough merciless fighters.

Marc

August 1st, 67

Dear Marc,

Berkeley is beautiful now. 80 is unusual here in the summer and it almost never rains except in the winter. You asked if I would get my B.A. at Berkeley. I guess so. They say one is supposed to feel that the whole world is opening up as one approaches graduation, but I think I feel it is closing. I don't know what I am going to do or want to do and neither do the people around me. How can one feel there is anything to do when the country is crumbling, when every life you save, or person who is rescued from poverty, only delays the inevitable tidal wave a moment . . . and who knows whether that delay is good or bad? If the country felt creative and new, one could do almost anything—build bridges, paint houses, pick up garbage—and feel fulfilled. And yet a friend of mine said that she wanted to go to Europe and live, but now she knew that she couldn't because "how can you leave your closest friend when she is down and out?"

I love popcorn and will send some. What are the people around you like? Are there any guys you can talk to?

Margot

August 2, 67

Dear Margot;

It's a bad night. I am on a duty shift now (4 till midnight) and things are usually slow about this time. The other guy who works with me is presently holding down the fort. We rotate an hour on and an hour off. Gives me a chance to walk around. I am bored stiff and restless and I made a mistake and let myself start thinking about 80 days, comprehending how (relatively) short it is, and going through it day by day. And then after I lived it, I "wake up" and look at the radios, realize I am still here and even if I have been through it mentally, I still must live it physically, and I wonder how many times I will do it. Maybe the "shorter" I get the more I will go through it so that by the time I have a week left I'll have been thru it a thousand times.

We sometimes rap each other about re-enlisting. No one believes me when I maintain that I would not re-up if I were offered Commanding General of Ft. Ord, a position on the Joint Chiefs of Staff, for a million, etc. I really doubt there is ANYTHING I would re-up for (except if the army was abolished and similar things). Do you believe that? Can you imagine anyone turning down a million dollars for three more years?

Tomorrow I get a two-hour pass. Can you imagine them feeling generous giving two-hour passes? Anyway, I will trot off into Cu Chi.... The village is secure in the daytime so we don't have to carry weapons. It's enjoyable tho, as I find the Vietnamese very friendly and easy to get along with. And one can release certain tensions at nearly 90% of the shops for about $3.28. The people are quite affectionate and I suspect one can realize the difference *or* what a large difference there is between their free love and America's attempt at it, which really results in free sex. *I* don't know how one can make two hours last long, but I'll come back much before I am

ready. Sometimes you see small children mangled and
blind, begging for money and food. Begging here is (or
was) quite honorable and so parents twist up small children to make them more heart-rending. Pleasant
thoughts tonight ... I'm full of them.

Later that night.

You wonder why I am nuts? I'll account for the last
two hours. Read our newspaper (*Stars and Stripes*), read
some magazines. Then one of the local dudes in my pla-
toon came in carrying a small lizard, turned on this big
floor fan and threw the lizard into it a couple of times. I
had to seek cover to prevent being splattered on. Now
it's hanging by a string and they're trying to light it on
fire (groovy, huh?), while at the same time a young volunteer is spelling out various anatomy and concept questions he is tripping over in a book he is reading, *Modern
Sex Techniques*. Those who aren't participating in either
farce are near hysterics at the way the two events are
coinciding. Sometimes this place is straight out of Edgar
Allan Poe.

So here I sit, Sunday evening, in some miserable little
radio hooch, with miserable little people....

The frog is dead (it was a frog, not lizard). You know
of course, this doesn't end it. Now I've gotta sit thru the
wake, the procession, last rites and words as it returns to
the earth. Nothing small. Ralph (they've named the frog
'Ralph') gets the best, most elaborate ceremony. It seems
that he died for a cause ... etc. etc. Had enough? I think I
will go out for some air, and see which side of the perimeter has flares up tonight. I would enjoy *Catch 22*. Take
Care.

Sincerely,
Marc

August 2, '67

Dear Marc;

About sending the *Barb*: I understand your situation
fully—it is full of complexity. Does one go along until
one can influence things in a position of responsibility
and respectability or does one leave? I don't think there
is one answer, but I only hope that those who choose the
first way will remember and cling to those values they
started with. Reagan, after all, was once a student activist and very liberal. While we are on the subject, do they
censor mail? Can my letters cause trouble? Or clippings?
I wouldn't want to subvert you—ha!

Hope you got the popcorn, and hope it was still fresh.
I had so much fun doing it. It was 8 AM when everybody
here is asleep or slowly taking that first cup of coffee as
they stagger into the kitchen, only to see me making
bowl after bowl of popcorn and enjoying every moment
of their amazement. And you can imagine their weird
look after I told them I was sending it to Vietnam.

Today four French-African students came to visit us
and I tried to remember my once fairly good and now
almost nonexistent French. It's especially difficult to
talk in broken French and them in broken English when
you are discussing Franz Fanon, he's a writer and a
spokesman for nations fighting for revolution and independence. When I am in these discussions with Negro or Oriental friends I always end up asking them,
only $3/4$ joking, if they will protect me when the great
world-wide race war comes and guess who is going to
lose. There I go, being pessimistic again, but I really do
feel that the communism-capitalism split is not going
to be nearly as important as the non-white (75%) vs.
white (25%) split, or Asia, Africa and Latin America

vs. USA, Russia and a tottering western Europe.
Enough.

  Margot

August 6, 67

Dear Margot,

So you think my typical day would interest you, huh?
Watch!

05:30. Some dude wakes us for reveille. We fall out at
6:00 and wait fifteen minutes for the C.O. to come and
get his report (fifteen minutes of our breakfast time). At
6:45, after eating, getting washed, shaved, clean our
hooches, we fall out again for a supervised session of
walking around picking up cigarette butts and such.
Then an hour of supervised work on the vehicles in the
motor pool. After which we start filling sandbags, usually 'til 8 PM or so. I then take a shower, drop in bed and
toss around for a couple of hours, "looking forward" to
tomorrow and tomorrow and ... The only variation is
when we have a duty shift, or monitoring radio, or working a switchboard, or whatever. That's what the infantry
support units are like. Now you can see why I wish I was
still in the 1st of the 27th. Being in the field has obvious
disadvantages but ...

Sometimes I see myself heading for trouble and I've
never been able to figure out how I've missed serious
punishments thus far. I guess I'll just plod along like a ro-
bot and do this and do that all quietly (like that Russian
painting of those peasants hoeing a vast field).

Are there people here I can talk to? Yes, a few. Sometimes we may dip, very cautiously, into a few things. I
know, tho, that the "old timers" over here are much
more approachable than the guys back in the world. The

American indoctrination is apparently more thorough than I ever gave it credit for, but then, as you pointed out, these people must rationalize this method or they'd never be able to perform it because of its magnitude and ghastliness.

Several of my Negro friends seem to see the light more like it is. The whole thing (apple pie, mom, etc.) is really amazing. They never attempt to answer why 70% of Sweden is strongly against our position, even physically opposing it, and why 70% of the world's nations feel the same.

There are two distinct types of soldiers here. This is important, but rarely considered. There are about 450,000 troops here, but only 60 or so infantry battalions, which is about 37,000 people. All the rest never see the war and wouldn't even know it is going on if they didn't read the newspaper. They represent 9 out of 10 and their opinions are rarely altered by being here. So the point of view here, the morale, and everything else that is published is deceiving, unless people know that it only pertains to those non-infantry units or those who aren't in field duty (like this company I'm in now).

Sincerely,

Marc

August 9th, 1967

Dear Marc;

I just finished *Catch 22*. I was physically and mentally drained afterwards and the book kept floating through my thoughts all night. I know you will identify very much with Yossarian. I sense you have been going through many of the same feelings. When you get to the end, I have a question: Is Yossarian's decision our only answer and hope? Is Sweden and all its physical and symbolic equivalents the only way out? Is there no way to fight either within or without the system?

Hope you received the popcorn.

Berkeley's a pretty odd place. We get to see all kinds of unusual things. Several months ago I saw several films from North Vietnam, and one by the NLF. One thing they showed was many young women fighting in the NLF. Well, it struck me at the time that that might present some unusual problems. I realize that when you're shot at you don't care who is doing it, but afterwards when some are killed or captured ... does that create any special problems for the soldiers?

Later.... That story of the frog really got to me ... the concern with death ... the needless brutality. You hear and read these things about guys after they have shot and killed a VC, standing over him, pumping bullet after bullet into him. I'm amazed that you can retain your humanity.

I am enclosing a newspaper, *The Bond*, not to be confused with the *Barb*. I figure if I enclose it in a letter it will be all right. It is expressly for those in the service. The article on the riots is mediocre, and the one on the workers rising up is nonsense....

Take care,
Sincerely,
Margot

                                              August 9, '67

Dear Margot;
I made it into the village on the 7th. I don't understand exactly why, but it always depresses me. I guess it is some nonexistent thing I see in their eyes. They are

quite fascinating though, especially the children. Back on earth I wasn't particularly fond of kids, but these are really something. Tiny little kids, both boys and girls, barely waist high, out running around hustling money with various products (trinkets) and services (shining boots) to sell. They are very independent and competitive and refreshingly unspoiled. The little girls with their long dark hair and big brown eyes, padding around in their bare feet, observing EVERYTHING that's going on, asking, "Hey GI—you give baby-son chewing gum?" really melt even the hardest hearts. A lot of them can speak enough English to converse a few minutes, at an earlier age than ours are even in school. I guess necessity does that. These people are being tread upon and some of them are fighting back, either diplomatically or unmercifully. Unleashing nearly half a million GIs on a foreign people, 12,000 miles from home and in a combat zone isn't quite the ideal condition for good or effective relations. Most of these guys have only one thing in mind (i.e. going home) and many other things become oblivious. I suppose it is understandable but hard to witness.

So there is going to be a world race riot, huh? When it does come about, however, it won't be the 75% running across a huge field toward the 25% so that three jump on each white. I mean it won't be hand to hand combat, will it? If it is anything else, do you really think we'll lose?

Marc

August 14, 1967

Dear Marc;

The village sounds fascinating and the unspoiled kids adorable, until we spoil them—as I guess we are doing.

What you say about their free love and our attempts at it
seems true. Ours probably comes from desperation and
a lack of real feeling. Around Berkeley there is a lot of
free sex. Last year, there were lots of nude parties and
many organizations grew up, like the Sexual Freedom
League. I always had a very "straight" attitude toward
them. I couldn't really understand who was limiting
their freedom once they had left their parents and community, with the exception of certain laws concerning
abortion. But mainly, I didn't see any love. I agreed with
them that our society has made us the victim of a lot of
stupid hang-ups, but their actions seemed to be an unsuccessful attempt to get rid of them.

Last night my father and his wife came to San Francisco. After walking around Chinatown, we got into a
long discussion on the hippies.

My father said: 1. the hippies are "pathetic." They are
unhappy and depressed and sad. The call of love is a cry
for help, some solace in a world of hypocrisy, a world
seemingly devoid of hope. They retreat into and glorify
the personal, but it is a small world.

2. They are anti-social—because they have given up on
society and leave her when she is down and out. Like
many utopians they would create their own society, but
if history teaches anything, they will fail. Through drugs
and mysticism they "discover the wonders of their
mind" and go on a glorious ego trip, whereupon they ex-
claim, "it's all within yourself." They forget the world,
and the trillion influences that created the mind.

3. They are useless, because they do not create much
except folk rock. They excuse themselves by saying they
are making their lives a work of art. But that is only for
them. They leave nothing tangible for the outside world.
In the end, ... they are stagnant, boring.

4. They are uncourageous because they lack the courage to do the one thing that takes real courage—to fail. They give up immediately. At their young age, they are sadly so old.

His points relate to some feelings I have had about the students I am encountering this summer. My friends and I have noticed that our studies seem intellectually disappointing. But it is we who are creating this situation by saying things like, "first I must find myself." And then when we are engaged in this search we wonder why this place seems dull! We want college to reverberate the world, yet we reverberate only ourselves. We magically hope this "finding ourselves" will just happen and there will be no more frustration. We never learn that frustrations never end and that one has to learn to live with them and survive them.

You, unlike many of the people here, do not seem to have that attitude, nor do the couple of other vets I've met here.

I've got to ask this: what can you buy for $3.28 at most of the shops? I have two very different ideas, one of which is drugs, hashish, etc. and the other is ... Your letters are great, as always.

Sincerely,

Margot

Half of August

Dear Margot:

I got your letter of the ninth today, and hope that you understand how much I enjoy each word of every page. Thank you!

This may seem more of a coincidence than is possible, but I do identify with Yossarian. In some aspects I am even more extreme than he, but even I find it amazing

how close we seem on a majority of his feelings and in
the way he expresses them. I don't have too much time,
but lately I've been falling asleep with the book on my
stomach at night so I've managed about 200 pages. From
what you've said I guess the ending is Yossarian's decision to spend the remainder of his life in Sweden. This is
really the most coincidental part, as I've been pondering
doing the same for a long, long time. Getting several
years of my education here (from the GI bill) and then
transferring to somewhere in Sweden and taking up citi-
zenship. I know factually that I could be immensely
happy in any one of several countries other than the U.S.

But I have another alternative, and that is my desire of
an M.D. degree, as I see that field as similar to a math major or some other far removed from the world of politics, society, congress, cops and the rest of the crap
which is sometimes just too far off, and moving too fast
in the wrong direction. So, I would just go about my
business, living comfortably and worrying about patients—or whatever. And in a way it is the same type of
solution. It will depend on my temperament after it has
had time to readjust. I feel that it would be foolish to decide my future while I'm here—if I did I would certainly strive to be a military criminal lawyer. Savvy?

About women and repercussions after a fire fight. During a fire fight it is very rare that one sees who or what
he is shooting at. Secondly, it is very rare to run across females so one just assumes they are males. I have only witnessed four events which involved females. On two occasions they were captured and the other two they were
shot. I don't know exactly what became of the two that
were captured. One was a VC pay officer so I doubt she
was mistreated, but there is no telling what became of

the other. One of the two who were shot was quite young and I suspect she was forced or persuaded to join them against her will. The other was just a female— quite dead, lying beneath the surface of the water in a canal. Someone went down into the water to check her for booby-traps, documents, weapons or whatever intelligence they might get. Apparently she was hit on the left side of her head with a tight shot group, as it all collapsed and ran down her shoulder and chest when the guy grabbed her hair and lifted her to the bank. I personally did not feel any emotion. (And on occasion I have wondered why. Maybe I did, but apparently it was not enough to note.) I suspect the guy who shot her felt bad. The ones who were drafted and are still sane have very normal reflexes. I know that females just seem to lend themselves to sympathy easier. Basically the same as back in the world. The emotion never went to the point of tears or anything similar AT THAT TIME. I once saw a little girl run over by a two-and-a-half-ton truck (killed) and the convoy didn't even stop. I'm sure a solatium payment was made and most likely in the amount of $35.00. There was no emotion there either.

People in the support command refer to the 1/27 and the 2/27 as "line animals," unfortunately much of it is justified. Here it gets much too complex and lengthy and I'd just as soon not get into it. Again pertaining to "Ralph" the frog, and repeatedly shooting a dead person (for a dead man is NOT a dead VC—he is just dead). There is no such thing as a dead VC or a dead American. Dead is a descriptive term. It describes a state of being (or not being, a state of existence). When screams in the night last several hours (years, actually) and then you find him the next morning (castrated, dismembered, or whatever and you know he felt every second of it), one doesn't have much sympathy for whomever they find that day. Things are done (on both sides) which even the papers don't go into. Here is when my immorality slaps me in the face. I see how little I am a long time afterward, but I'd duplicate what has been done on occasions, and enjoy it enough to really put my heart into it. Then when I realize what I am I go into a daze for days....

When I leave here I will have been here very near 365 days, give or take two days. I spent 246 days on the line.

I guess I have said enough, and probably too much on certain things, so I shall quit. I got the popcorn. It only lasted an hour or so. EVERYONE enjoyed it. They all thank you, and say you are wonderful, great cook, beautiful, can probably sew too, and one wants to marry you!?!?!?!? Honest. Thank you. (That sounds terrible—it is just not enough. It's about 1/10th.) Will write shortly.

Sincerely,

Marc

August 18th, 1967

Dear Marc;

I know that you will dispute the word, but your letter was beautiful. I've thought many of the same things about living in another country and about medicine. It always seemed to be one of those fields where you are not doing any harm ... and in this time that is saying a lot. But I am very ambivalent about going to live in a country that is removed from all these problems. It's part of that paradox of how we long for utopia and work for it, but could not survive in it.

I once was in St. Johns, in the Virgin Islands. It's the closest I've ever been to paradise. A native of there asked me if I wouldn't want to live there. He spoke of many girls who had moved there and married and achieved a happiness they had believed impossible. I thought about it, and I knew that I could not live there, even for a few years. And I was disturbed because I realized that I was the product of a turbulent society and the terrible truth was that I thrived on it. There was a part of me that loved world crisis, just as I loved to be in hurricanes although I knew they were destructive. I often feel guilty about this feeling.

A teacher I once had was discussing John Stuart Mill's "greatest good for the greatest number" and asked us, "Is your goal in life really happiness? How could it be? If it was you would never have come to this university!" And there is a truth in that, because one becomes ever more disturbed, unsure, and troubled. And so I had to say that it was not happiness I was searching for, but something more like richness and fullness in life. And that is why I do not know if I could live in Sweden, where everything is calm and the only problem is an unexplained unhappiness which results in so many suicides.

I thought a lot about the difficult things you said—all day. How complex it is, and how we are all both so innocent and so guilty. And that it makes no great difference that you are there and I am here, for I am equally responsible. And the guy who gets out with a note from a psychiatrist, or who pretends he is a homosexual, or who goes to Canada, is also responsible. And anyone who pays taxes is responsible. And those who refuse to read newspapers because they are too depressing. So all of us share it, and perhaps we share it just as much if we leave the country. I never can condemn the German people for World War 2 without also condemning myself.

And then we come back to our old question: do you declare yourself immediately, or do you wait? The argument for waiting seems very strong. But wait until when? When is the point that you turn? Gaining influence can take a lifetime. And so people never declare themselves. If you were now miraculously back at the induction center but somehow you knew everything that would happen, that you would go through, what would you do? Would you go through it and say that all your actions were planned with the future in mind, or would you go to Sweden or Canada, or feign psychosis, or go to jail?

I'm glad you got the popcorn and *Catch* 22. So someone wants to marry me—huh? Well, I'm not a good cook, only steaks and pancakes, and I don't sew at all.

It's 3:30 A.M., and I have a 7:00 A.M. shift cutting vegetables. Sorry for such a serious letter.

Sincerely,

Margot

Crossing the Divide

CHAPTER 9

A S MARC and I continued to write, our letters became longer and more frequent. But there was much that was left unsaid—on both sides. Although we were learning about the way we each looked at the world, we remained strangers to each other. One of the things I left unsaid, because I was afraid it would scare him away, was how powerfully I was attracted to him because, like me, he was struggling with the question of enlistment—the tension between the pull toward commitment to a group and a goal, and the contrary pull toward individual freedom. Even so, I almost blew it.

Marc hated the war. He was inducted into the army against his will, yet much of his upbringing, and his sense of morality, led him to accept it rather than run to Canada or go to jail. I was trying to decide whether to enlist in what he would certainly consider the enemy army—revolutionary communism. We lived in such different worlds that it never occurred to me that sending a copy of the *Bond*, a Trotskyist newspaper for servicemen, might imperil our relationship.

August 15, 1967

Dear Margot:

I do regret having to write this letter, as our correspondence has grown into one of personal friendship—

at least from my side, and I am afraid this will or may curtail it. I got that masterpiece, the *Bond* today. My question is: do you believe much of what it says and condone its opinion? This is the type of literature that would cause a normal anti-war person to enlist.

The first article I read was "Is this your last leave?" I need not pick it apart sentence by sentence. Basically all the information is incorrect and/or intentionally misleading. It is direct and straight propaganda. It appears in a "Serviceman's Publication" which should make it obvious to you. Is that where your appeals are directed? You know they are helpless, and that for the most effect one appeals to the civilian public—THOSE WHO DECIDE, not us. I could not fight my way through the entire mess, and only managed a few stories and patches of the rest.

You pride yourselves so much in individualism, that it is cool, and groovy, and in (with the outs) and the way to be if you don't want to be called a conformist. Well as it actually is, you people are even more sheep than those you call sheep. Because you are intelligent enough to question our system you are easily grabbed up by those who are openly opposing it. You all think Communism is all so cool, right? What would you do if they said, "All right, if you all are making so much noise for Communism, tomorrow we will change and operate exactly as they do in Red China." It would scare you to death. I can't believe that deep inside you want it to change. Even a seven-year-old girl can understand something so simple as—you never miss anything until you have done without it, or you do not appreciate what you do have until you experience the other. See you don't and you never will because you are just too stupid.... If you had stayed in jail for a year or two, I doubt very much that

you would think they (the authors) were so groovy. You
know pretty much what I think about the red-white-
and-blue business, so don't assume I've been secretly deceiving you and really like apple pie and Mom, and that
stuff. I shall patiently await your answer to the question
at the top of this letter. You have been a helpful friend
and companion and I've told you several times how
much I enjoy our correspondence. I hope we do not
have to terminate it, but I hope you understand my
position and respect my stand. I do not hesitate to be
counted by either side, and often I must draw the
line....

(Cut on dotted line and throw the above away. I had
to say something.)

-- --

Same Night
My confession for the night must be that I doubt that
the *Bond* was solely responsible for that release. A few of
my friends found it and started reading it just thinking
it was another military newspaper. They soon discovered
otherwise and also wound up equally upset. They are for
the most part the older of the crowd so I don't know for
sure if they'll get enraged and cause trouble or just leave
it at the great argument we just finished. Again, you have
not really anything to lose, I hope they don't turn it into
anything big, if they do you may be involved, as they
know who sent the popcorn, and that it came from
Berkeley, so tapping my mail won't be too hard. Let's
drop that and wait and see if anything else comes
from it.

I just gotta know more about you ... so why don't you
ramble extensively in the next few letters, send me a pic-

ture, tell me the things that make you mad, that make
you sad, that make you feel a stranger, like a nut, if you
really want me to stop off for a few days or whatever. I
can't help but feel that I'd be imposing. Oh by the way,
I've heard that some of your peaceniks are doing in lone
GIs who happen through Berkeley. Is there any truth to
this, I'd just as soon not have a dozen troops accompany
me (as I'm sure they'd be all too eager). It sounds pretty
disgusting to get involved with some of your 19 and 20
year old hoodlums who yell hypocrites at everyone.

What a rotten letter this is, huh? Will make it
up soon.

Sincerely,

Marc

                                    August 18, 67

Dear Margot:

Guess I'm in a better mood—finally, huh? I do not
fully understand your attitudes toward my attitudes, so
how freely can I express myself. I'm hopeful that you
sorta suspected, at the outset, that our correspondence
might be somewhat unusual. Anyway, what this all is,
is—I'm sorry about that ill-directed, unjustified venting!
Got your letter from the 14th. 69 days!!!

Is pouring out. This tin roof sounds like marbles are
falling on it from a few hundred feet.

You hit the nail right on the head by saying our free
love is a result of desperation and lacks real feeling. I'm
afraid I agree considerably with your father on the hippies. The most interesting and severe point, I felt, was
his relating they are uncourageous.

Is "straight" the same as conventional? Bring me out
of my ignorance.

I think my attitude towards the VN war has always been the same. I have become more embittered—strictly from being in the Army, regardless of where. The important change has been in my emotions. Where I didn't have much depth in one area—I do now. Example: I used to not be able to hate. If someone was obnoxious I would have absolutely no emotion. (This isn't easy to tell you, as it certainly isn't a virtue.) Now I know what a powerful motivation hate can be. It has depth far beyond anything else I have felt. I have never loved as intensely as I can (maybe do) hate—bitterly, passionately, driving, destroying, loathing. I have also found that pity has an immense capacity.

About people who "re-up": I can easily see how it happens. Your friends are in a friendly social environment (college), their minds continue to gain in keenness, while yours deteriorates. They don't understand mental scares. It is two separate worlds. My brother is the sole surviving correspondent of everyone I knew. They have their own lives and a year is a long, long time for young, red-blooded, fun-loving horny females to wait.

Drugs are much cheaper than $3.28. For some, it is a few moments of home ... a pseudo love. ... It reassures others that it is still there and worth staying alive for (that, itself, will carry many home). It is, as you said ... "the other."

Marc

August 19th, '67

Dear Marc:

Finished my shift of cutting carrots and lettuce and opening cans. Mailed off the letter of the 18th, lay down in bed, couldn't sleep. 11:30 went down for the mail and got your letter. I don't know what to say. God it sounds lame to say, "I am sorry." I am sitting here ... well, that doesn't matter ... just not knowing what to write, worried that I got you and maybe even me into trouble.... I realized that that article, "Is this your last leave" was inaccurate from some of the things you had said previously. I don't think it was sinister. I am very upset ... and sorry and sitting here like a stupid idiot crying ... and I hope you do not want to end our writing. I am glad you wrote that continuation. I really would like you to stop off and I can't even conceive how it could be an imposition. I told you a lot of people here are isolated from the human side of the war, well, that is the kind of thing I meant. This is the kind of discussion that may have to wait at least until I find the right words.

I don't have a picture ... maybe I'll go into one of those four for a quarter places. I am 5'6", have almost jet-black straight hair about shoulder length, very thick, almost oriental. I have green-brown eyes. I guess they are called hazel.... I am not even in a mood to begin to think about what makes me mad, sad, feel like a stranger ... no, that is not quite right ... I know what makes me feel sad ... it is now. Boy, is this a rotten reply to your letter. Take Care, you mustn't think that I meant to hurt or cause you trouble in any way ... please.

Sincerely,
Margot

August 20, '67

Dear Marc;

I finally got a little sleep, about nine hours to make up for having only three the night before. I know that I didn't answer your question. I am not really ready to do

so today, because I am not ready to face reading your letter another time yet.... But I can begin to tell you some
of the things I've been thinking.

First, although I never want to go through another Saturday like yesterday, perhaps it had to happen. It taught
me a lot about what happens to people—even myself—
in isolation. You see, it was, above all, tactless, to send
the paper, but what is more important, I did not think
that at the time. What I am only beginning to realize is
that we have expressed so many similar feelings, and I
do think we see much in a similar, impressionistic way,
but I forgot that circumstance has placed us in two so entirely different settings, two entirely different worlds
that we forget sometimes that some of the things in our
own world, that are so ordinary, so taken for granted,
are perhaps a shock in another world, a world that jars
with our own.

My reaction to the paper was that it was crude. I never
have liked a certain type of blatant political left language which certain groups use, where phrases are
tossed around such as, "fascism," "imperialism," etc. (I
better go looking for the paper—found it.) I agree that
servicemen overseas can do nothing, that they are helpless, and even the paper admits this on the first page, bottom. Actually the language which sounds like communist propaganda is mostly used by very radical, socialist
groups that hate the Communist Party and the government in Russia. These groups accuse the Communist
Party of being reformist liberals who supported Johnson
in 1964, but they are not part of any unified communist movement. They are often the most violent anti-
Communists. There are many such groups, almost all
small and sectarian. Each group spends more time

fighting the other groups and defending its particular type of ideological purity than doing anything else. But one has to live here, and breathe it, to understand it. I forgot that to someone in another world, it really sounds organized and insidious. In rereading the "last leave" article I realize now that it must have been hard to take.

Now I have to face your letter and see if there is anything else I've left out. Oh yes, the bit about direct propaganda. What exactly is propaganda? I'm sure these guys, whatever their many faults, are not sitting around some office with a handbook with which they measure their articles by ... sorry about this. They are almost assuredly sitting around some loft with a budget that never quite makes it, and writing what they sincerely feel to be true. I am not saying this excuses them their misinformation, but this stuff is not organized intentional propaganda. The U.S. and Russia can afford to do that kind of thing. These people can't. The easy way out is to accuse the ones you are fighting of being aware hypocrites. Most people, no matter what side they are on, believe what they are doing is right. I'm not sure the word propaganda has any meaning at all. As far as living in China, of course I wouldn't like it, but there are many reasons for that, and that too is not quite so simple.

You once said that there were a lot of things that would have to wait until you were in a non-war situation. Perhaps this is one of those things. Anyway it was terribly thoughtless of me. I hope you can forgive me and understand that it was not intentional to make you furious and upset.

"What makes me sad, mad, a stranger?" I guess people who are internally dead make me saddest of all. I get mad at people who are cliquey, or secretive. I get nuts only with people who show no feelings openly, who never cry or get angry and are always calm and sweet.

Please forgive me if it is possible. I hope you are not in trouble.

Sincerely as always,

Margot

P.S. I guess the one who wants to marry me, and the ones who think I am wonderful have changed their mind—huh?

August 21, '67

Dear Margot:

All kinds of bad things happening.... You may have heard of an operation called Junction City? Second Brigade and its battalions are going back to the same area within two or so weeks. When they briefed us, I naturally started smoking two cigarettes, quivering and such (bad memories from the 1/27th). Today the NCO said I might not have to go, cause I am getting short and everyone else has six to eight months left. Oh, Christ, I shall take up praying. I don't want to go into War Zone C— with 66 days left! Sob! Yech! Ugh! No-ooo! Maybe I'll be on R & R when they leave and they'll forget about me. Is late. This is incoherent.

August 24, '67

Dearest Margot:

Received your letter of the 21st today, and I see even more clearly now than I did after I wrote it how really ignorant I am of Berkeley and its ways. You're right— we're in two separate worlds, conditioned to respond to stimuli in (apparently) opposite ways....

No one has changed their minds about you. The guy who wanted to marry you—still does. "A girl who'd take

all the trouble to send POPCORN can't be that far off!" He
insists you wear black leotards with a man's white shirt,
no shoes, and walk about with a peanut butter sandwich
in one hand and a 900 page philosophy book in the
other. Long straight dark hair. He's positive, no doubt in
his mind....

I look forward to our meeting more and more as each
day passes.

Sincerely (poor word, now),
Marc

August 26, '67

Dear Marc;

I have three attempts at writing you a letter on my
desk.

Your letter of several days ago was great, made my day,
as I was feeling guilty and horrible about having sent the
Bond, and I was bothered by the feeling that somewhere
deep in my subconscious I wanted to provoke you. God,
I hope that is not true. In the end I guess I am glad you
sent the letter. When I first got it I was very upset and
one of my closest friends asked me what was wrong and
I said something like, "I've just gone and blown a friendship because I am thoughtless and cruel." And I explained what I had done, and my friend said, "but you
know, he could have not sent the letter at all—and sending the letter meant he trusted you might understand,
trusted you with the full strength of his anger."

Nothing terribly exciting to tell about, except attended four panels on Black Power, Riot and Revolution.
The most interesting thing about these panels was the
change in the audience reaction over the four evenings.
The audience felt hatred from the panelists. Most of us

kept asking the same question over and over: Don't you
think white radicals share common goals with you?
Can't we work together on some things like the war?
Doesn't advocacy of racial separation deny you the benefit of human interaction and richness? Can't you accept
me as a human being?

The panelists gave answers that really disturbed the
audience. To question 1: Why should we trust you? they
said. Years of experience have taught us that radicals
will be liberals in ten years, and why shouldn't you be?
You have much to lose. To question 2, they said that our
goals (even in regard to the war) are different. The audience believed one has to change a society that creates
such wars, but the panelists said, "We don't feel a part of
this society, don't care about it, don't want black people
fighting for it were it engaged in the holiest of crusades."
To question 3, the panelists said integration was not a
universal vision, it was ours not theirs, and the audience
was hurt because the panelists denied the sacredness of
that vision and had the power to deny it to them. To the
last, they said, "If you love us, so what?"

"Straight" does mean conventional, but it is broader. It
is opposed to the word "hippie." "Straight" means someone who is straight-laced, who doesn't turn on (not only
in terms of drugs, but to life as well). It also means someone who is caught up in the American success ethic, the
9–5 job. To look "straight" is to be clean shaven, suit and
tie, to have very short hair, especially a crew cut.

What you said about the changes in your emotions
was fascinating. I think being able to hate is often a good
thing. It is better than feeling nothing consciously and
having it all inside, festering, or turning it (as I often do)
into self-hatred. I do understand how friendships cool,

girls find other guys, but I can't understand how people could stop writing to you—if for nothing else, just out of curiosity, especially if your letters to me are typical.

I think I can get a glimpse of what you meant when you said your mind was deteriorating. I know that even by the third week at Santa Rita all these fifteen to seventeen radicals, a few of them truly brilliant, were sitting around discussing knitting and the next meal. If it's any reassurance—your mind seems fine.

Take Care,
Margot

August 26, 1967

Dearest Margot:

I reread yours of the 18th. I really marvel at how "eye to eye" we are.

You asked what I would do, were I at the induction center, and knew my future. The answer amazes me and I've always known it. Sometimes I forget about it or push it away, but—it's yes. I remarked to a friend once, "They won't be able to hold a non-existent military record against me. As a matter of fact I will use my presence in Vietnam to sharpen the ax I hope to swing." I knew all along I would end up here. I don't know how I knew—I just WOULD be here.

Those who copped out are a loss. They can never have the necessary influence now. "They were groovy" going to Canada—huh? No, they let us down, you and me, not our government. We could have used them. This you may not believe, but I was thinking of the future when I knew I'd end up here.

Be good. Take Care,
Yours,
Marc

August 27, 1967

Dearest Margot:

60 days,

The enclosed is one of many "short-timer" letters floating around. They could be better, but are amusing.

ISSUED IN SOLEMN WARNING

Dear _____

Very soon, _____ will once again be in your midst, de-Americanized, demoralized, and dehydrated, but ready once more to take his place as a human being, to engage in life, liberty and a somewhat delayed pursuit of happiness.

We forward in the interest of all concerned some "Dos" and "Don'ts" that should be strictly observed.

1. Prepare yourself for the initial shock of that first meeting because the man stepping off that airplane may bear a striking physical resemblance to the man you waved good-bye to long ago. He will appear out of place, nervous, and probably look at everyone with suspicion. You may, if you are carrying a handbag or pack, have to empty the contents of same on the ground for routine inspection. Avoid crowds and if you should celebrate the home-coming with a drink or two, don't question him if he prefers to sit at the table in the rear of the bar with his back to the wall.

2. His eating habits may be somewhat changed. He will probably want his steak well done and maybe shove milk aside and ask for a beer. Incidentally, the word "rice" should be avoided for quite some time and at no time during his first year back home should you suggest eating in a Chinese restaurant.

3. Do not serve iced tea at any time!!!

4. He may spend much time in the bathroom flushing the toilet. Think nothing of it; he just wants to watch it work! Also, he may desire to take many baths in boiling water. Check his water before he gets in it.

5. A loud clap of thunder may have one of two effects on him. He may dive under the bed and yell VC; or,

if he recognized the sound he may grumble "those &%$&%$&%$ monsoons are back again."

6. Keep in mind that beneath this tanned and rugged exterior there beats a heart of pure gold. Treasure this, for it is about the only thing of value he has left. Treat him with kindness, tolerance, and an occasional fifth of good whiskey, and you will soon be able to rehabilitate this hollow shell of the man you once knew.

August 28, 1967

Dear Marc:

THEY BETTER NOT SEND YOU INTO WAR ZONE C ON THIS JUNCTION CITY BUSINESS (much good it does to say that). Actually the army might make me a cadre yet, force me to do some meaningless act, like blow up a draft board.

Thank you so much for the picture.

No, I don't wear black leotards (too warm), although I did in New York. No white man's shirt, although I do have a blue work shirt that would do. I wear dresses, not jeans or slacks usually. Generally I do not go barefoot, last time I did was June, but I do wear sandals, I do love peanut butter, and the dark straight hair which is only beginning to be longish is, as I said, quite true. So is the philosophy book, at times, at least when I am taking political theory courses.

I had a strange dream the other night, where somehow I was in "Nam" (that's what a lot of GIs call it, isn't it?). It was all very vague. In one dream you were out in the field and all you had to eat was lettuce. It was pretty bad lettuce, too. There was some fighting, but mostly just sounds of shots in the distance.

I also had a crazy dream the night before last where I almost joined the WACS. I have never been able to get over this obnoxious ad I saw in *Seventeen*, it went something like this: "Meet Corinna" (and there is this beautiful off-beat girl in slacks feeding her horse). "She is a lieutenant in the Women's Army Corps." And then it goes on to say how much she loves her work and how her favorite book is *The Prophet* by Kahlil Gibran—which is certainly the most un-military book on earth. How she cooks, is engaged to be married, is full of ten million feminine virtues and joined the army because she wanted to do something for her country.

The idea of having to go out on another operation with only sixty days sounds so frighteningly Yossarianish it is incredible. I remain your humble servant from Berkeley, who plans a coup d'etat if you are sent into the field!

Margot

August 29/31, 1967

Dearest Margot:

It's monsooning out! Bad. Cold? Ugh! It must be all the way down to 75 degrees. I can't help thinking of those poor line dogs out there ... miserable, freezing. Jesus it can be cold. Lying in a foot of water all night, in an L.P. (listening part), not moving, barely breathing. . . . The brigade is (all of a sudden) NICE.

I may be more out of touch than I realize concerning Black Power, and can only gauge how much it has grown in ten months. I remember my first impression of Black Power was the Negro was saying, "O.K., you don't like us—well we won't like you. We're gonna invent Black Power." The only answer I thought was justified was #3, their thoughts on the war. I would feel much the same thing probably.

I don't like Black Power for the power sake. I can not

recall any power which has ever triumphed after they lost sight of the value of one innocent life. Has there ever been a war to end wars? Can we beat democracy into anyone's head? I doubt might (will ever) make right. Pretty soon Black Power will piss people off and it will only cost the Negroes ten years to another generation (25 years).

Thank you for LONG letter. Was lying in my bunk ... empty, now I'm all right. Take care. 56.

Yours,

Marc

September 1, 1967

Dearest Margot:

Got word today we go into War Zone C on the 8th. My R & R was canceled. On September 8th, I will be in the 40's. They can't do this to me. Jesus, I'd hate to get "zapped" in this miserable outfit. In 1/27th at least there would have been dignity. The guy who took my place there as an R.T.O. was hit twice on his first time out. I hear he only got about ten feet from the chopper. I'll never know how I made it ... guess I kept turning side-ways at the right time ... enough.

The GIs here don't call it "Nam" but you wouldn't want to hear what they DO call it.

Will write long one tomorrow.

Yours,

Marc

September 3rd, 1967

Dearest Marc;

I was planning to write on the plane to New York, but the airport in San Francisco was so depressing that I couldn't think of anything but how awful it was. It was midnight and there were scores of soldiers—most either

going to or coming from Vietnam. I sat in the same row
with a guy who had just returned from Cu Chi the day
before. At the airport there were also a number of hippies and the place was swinging. One guy had a guitar
and another a recorder and there was a jam session of
sorts going on. The hostility (mostly covert and unspoken) between the soldiers and the hippies was depress-
ingly noticeable. The hippies were generally only concerned with sitting around and "doing their thing," but
one guy managed to get into an argument with a drunk
sergeant who was on his way to Vietnam. It was *wrong* because the guy was going, but it was *understandable* because
five months ago, I might have been capable of starting
that same argument. The other groups of soldiers just
gave the hippies stares and shouted "send them to Vietnam ..." The whole thing made me feel low all around.

When I got your letter of the 26th, I was disturbed by
your comments about your induction. I guess I couldn't
understand how going through all of this would give
you an edge in the game, in "swinging your ax." It is true
they (who is *they*?) won't hold a non-existent military record against you, but don't worry, when *they* want to hold
something against you, they'll find it. I truly believe this
staying "clean until ..." is a great trap and rationalization. I wish it were otherwise, it would make it a lot easier. When I really face it, I don't think that marches, articles, are going to end the war. I often feel that the peace
movement—this is not original—provides an acceptable
outlet for discontent and therefore is a stabilizing force
in this society. But, don't kid yourself, the minute you or
I or anyone has some kind of effect, the government is
going to change its tactics towards us and take away our
freedoms.

I do feel that you have probably learned an awful lot

from being there, that it has deepened you emotionally, but I can't understand some of your feelings. Yes, the guys who went to Canada are copping out, but that seems true no matter what you do. If you go to jail you are giving them two or three years of your life. If you go to Vietnam you are giving them two years and accepting their war. If you keep your deferment, somebody else goes. The one who cops out least seems to be the full time resistance worker. I guess I do not understand what you mean by the ax you hope to swing and when you plan to swing it. What position of influence are you seeking? I also don't really understand your attitude toward the war, except that the army is hideous. Anyway, maybe I am all wrong in thinking that induction argument is a rationalization, but even if it is, God knows you could use a few! I am always amazed how honest you are with yourself, how you have managed to stay sane and not rationalize everything. How you have retained your humanity, even gained in it!

The enclosure was clever. Are you going to have to go on that operation? What exactly happens on an operation? I am still quite foggy about all that. Please forgive me for not writing,

Margot

September 5, 1967
Gayhead, Martha's Vineyard

Dearest Marc;

I'm sitting on a porch overlooking the ocean at the house of some of my mother's closest friends.

About Black Power. It's true that Black Power frightens people who do not understand what it means. It doesn't mean Black control over whites. They would say that this is a society of White Power and that the only way they can get ahead is to do what every immigrant group in America has done—get a degree of economic and political power that is *theirs*.

I agree that power corrupts and that revolutions often bring about their own corruption, that the value of life and humanity is lost. It is one of the most bitter truths. But without power, one is also lost. Perhaps revolutionaries go beyond logic. There is going to be horror and innocents are going to be killed no matter what happens, whether there is a violent conflagration or if nothing happens. Enough of this. I will write again soon,

yours,

Margot

September 6th, 1967

Dearest Marc;

I'm lying in bed in faded pink pajamas. It is very quiet out. One can hear all kinds of wonderful sounds if one listens carefully. First, there are the crickets and the bell in the buoy somewhere out in the harbor that constantly rings, but very faintly. If one continues to listen one can eventually make out the sound of tiny waves breaking on the shore.

I started to read an article on the war by Jonathan Schell. What exactly did you mean by "at least in the 1/27th there would have been dignity." That the people were better, or knew more what they were doing?

I realize you will have little time to write out in the field, but tell me anything you can, since I am ignorant of even the most commonplace things, the mud and rain and heat and cold and food, scenery, etc. Even the most trivial things will be interesting!!!

Please take care!!! I am thinking of you often!!!
Yours,
Margot

September 7, 1967

Dearest Margot:

Your letter and card were dropped off this evening.
The official date of the operation is the 11th now, with a
slight possibility we may not go at all.

About operations: for all units except infantry battalions, operations are as follows. The unit packs up all necessary equipment and convoys to designated location,
which an Infantry element has already secured, and they
(inf.) set up and maintain the perimeter. The unit then
performs its functions. Brigade Headquarters is the
brains, central headquarters for the 1/27th, 2/27th, etc.
The second brigade remains in the perimeter. The reason we even leave Cu Chi is so communications will
reach the infantry Bn's who are further out. Savvy? See,
it's just like moving Cu Chi base camp to a temporary
new place. The only thing I, or anyone in the Brigade,
has to worry about are mortar attacks. So you see? You
have nothing to worry about. The chance of me catching
a sniper round or mortar round are so rare that only I
worry about it, and really only since I'm "short" (too
short, 49!!)

The ones who "hump" or go out and search and destroy are the 1&2—27's. They worry.

I've done my share of that, and I'll do enough worrying for both of us—yet.

Please answer following: My induction was a rationalization because of ?? (What?)

SCENE

18 year old, summer of '64, still going to high school. That means I didn't graduate in June. One beautiful day after I picked up a friend and we were on our way to 1st class we decided to drive to the country and go to a rifle range, knowing that the cost of being caught would be expulsion. We were caught. When I got home around noon, my father said, "Get your books—take them to school. Mr. Miller (the truant officer) wants to talk to you." I did. We talked. He waited for a plea of clemency, which never came. Actually, it was pleasantly short. "You know I must expel you," he said. "Yes, I know." All very calm, with no animosity. After long pause, he told me to turn in my books, which I did, and quietly left. It's funny, but I can't remember whether or not I went back. I think I did, and then quit sometime in the next semester. I was far from a success, academically, and was wasting time—in a sense. So I changed jobs, went to L.A., got lost—bad, came back. I had to hitch-hike ... $7.80 for the whole trip. I could get into a pool game every now and then and in Oklahoma City, I picked up $25 dollars which carried me back.

I saw a lot, I realized a lot. I could be pretty happy as an I.B.M. puncher at 160/wk in Chicago with some little girl I'd find and an apartment near the lake.

To get back: I got a job driving an ambulance 60/ hours a week, and went to night high school. Got my induction notice. Fought it! I was three weeks short of graduating (which meant a lot to me). I intentionally quit fighting it. I thought I'd get it over with. I suspect secretly inside I wasn't yet awakened and was still looking for something ... change ...

I did weigh what I was doing and if I could use it to my advantage. I don't mind hippies being hippies, just like homosexuals can be as homosexual as they want, but I act in such a way that I (try) not to infringe on anyone and at no one's expense. Are you telling me that NONE drop out because they are afraid of how futile their efforts may end up or because they may end up in something they don't like? Things aren't the way they like 'em, right? So they drop out. Real courageous! Well, things weren't as I liked 'em in civilian life, or when I spent many nights lying in a foot of cold mud and water, fighting mosquitoes, hungry, alone, scared half out of my wits (that any second my head would explode). Tough huh? Well, I couldn't very well stand up and say, "You people aren't like me, you don't think like me ... I quit, I don't want to play anymore." Hard? No, that's the EASY way out. And I couldn't do it in civilian life. It is the same identical thing. Only when the hippies stand up they are standing on my toes. (None of what I say here is right to say for me, sorry. I know it.) But let's reverse the situation, after you comprehend what it's like to not mind dying. How many of them would stand up for me? I read where they laugh at us, laugh at our dead, call us suckers, send VC blood, and then tell you that these very same dead people aren't worth living with, or for. There isn't much else one can do—than give his life, hoping his cause is right and not in vain, yet never knowing— and then be spit on when you come home? These "line dogs" aren't morons. Their IQs are same as mine and yours. I know a few who I believed were 140 and up. They wonder if they are right or if the hippies are right, and I doubt it is much fun to die and not know.

This is a rotten letter and some day I'm not gonna let

you get me into them, cause then I upset you and spend three letters apologizing.

49—hard to believe. In fact—I don't ... not 'til I'm on the plane. Save me!

Yours,

Marc

September 7th, 1967

Dearest Marc:

I was rereading some of your letters today and I kept on being struck by your tolerance and flexibility toward almost everything. That has always been a quality I have striven to achieve: to understand the complexities in things and to have compassion in a multitude of directions and avoid rigidities.

I'm not sure where you are. I gather it's toward the Cambodian border.

Can you understand non-religious people being superstitious? So, although I am an agnostic, I find myself knocking on wood, crossing my fingers, even praying once in a while ... sort of on the theory that if he's up there why not play safe. TAKE CARE,

yours,

Margot

September 9th, 1967

Dearest Margot:

Your shells arrived intact this evening. The green one is possibly worn glass? The postcard reminds me of the badlands of Montana. It is inviting.

Tonight I'm feeling better. I've been constantly vomiting since the 7th ... was bit by a scorpion and that has made me pretty ill. Guess I'm over it now—or will be in the morning.

I gotta cut this short tonight. They broke our backs
sandbagging today.
Marc

September 10th, 1967

Dearest Marc;
I went back to visit a rocky beach I remember from
my childhood. When I was six I didn't appreciate this
beach, as I preferred sandy beaches where one could dig
and build sand castles. Here one comes upon land that
looks pretty close to what a Scottish moor is supposed to
look like, gaunt, stark, powerful. The beach is rugged
and deserted, with big boulders and there are no people
or habitations in sight. It must have looked almost exactly like this a thousand years ago. The gray sky, the
wind which blew the tall grass and the occasional drops
of rain completed the scene. These are the places that I
find awe-inspiring. The place feels strong; you feel like
an intruder, you feel that this place will be like this always, unless man builds a parking lot on it. Perhaps that
is what I find so exciting in hurricanes—the sheer
power of nature and how little we are in comparison,
and how terrifying, but incredibly wonderful that is.
I send my thoughts,
Margot

September 12th, 1967

Dearest Marc;
You want to hear something absurd and funny? ... a
few nights ago I had several very clear dreams and there
was this one in which you were out in the field, and you
were in the mud and absolutely freezing, and you had
had only a few winks of sleep and you woke up sore and

stiff, and what you wanted most of all was a BACKRUB! but I couldn't send it through the mail!

Boy, the truant officers around Illinois must be tough! In my school, senior year was a blast. I guess I would have given them the plea they wanted, but I admire your guts.

Could you really be happy as an IBM puncher? I'd go out of my mind with boredom after a year, and I bet you would too.

On the hippies again: when I said I don't think they are a waste, I meant it all depends on what they eventually do. I'm willing to let a person sit around for a few years to "find themselves"—even if they don't, as long as they are productive in the end.

The hippies are doing some good things. The "diggers" have a free store and a free food place and bakery. If you help distribute the food or do something else good for the community then you have a right to the free food. But many just "take." There is also a free bus service that goes from Berkeley to the Haight twice a day. Some hippies do have jobs as mailmen, *Barb* sellers, some own shops, are musicians, writers, but the unhealthy ethos infects everything and has spoiled what in part was good.

No, I cannot comprehend what it is like to not mind dying. I fight against the acceptance of death—even the knowledge of its inevitability—with every inch of my being. I am unwilling to accept the moderate portion of things life will bring.

Now, this part gets difficult. I've skirted around the edges often, but it is hard to tell you. To start out easy: the hippies are not the people giving blood to the VC, North Vietnam, etc. The hippies wouldn't get up enough energy to do that. Most of the hippies are apolitical. They may wear a peace button, throw flowers, even go on a march if it's a bright and sunny day, but they are not the ones who are doing anything about the war. I am sure that not many, and then only the unthinking, callous and ignorant, laugh at the GIs or the deaths.

About giving blood to the VC—this is usually done through the International Red Cross. Sometimes they divide the blood equally between North and South, sometimes not. I do not think this is in the same category as laughing at the GIs. And here is where it gets very difficult to talk about.

I am beginning to feel, No, I *know* one can feel two different ways about something like the Vietnam War: politically and humanly—both at the same time, and one can believe in both—however impossible that may seem. I previously looked at the war almost completely politically. Oh, I was agonized by it, by the deaths, but deep down I looked at it politically. I had read a lot of analyses, documents, knew something about its causes, and had taken a very militant position. I don't think I need or should go very deep into this. I guess understatement is enough. I can elaborate verbally later—it sounds better verbally anyway.

I even had agonizing dreams on the war, but still it was more in terms of what this war made us, what we were doing, not the lives lost. It was remote—the lives. I didn't know anybody who was there. I did hear hypocritical speeches every day by representatives of our government and I saw pictures of burned kids—that I could get upset about.

Then a funny thing happened. I read your letter and for the first time, when I looked at some TV footage of the GIs fighting, it was different, not serial number stuff, and this personalization of the war increased.

When I said you expressed yourself poetically, I meant it. And just imagine what finding a poet and wonderful person in the US army did to my world view!!! So there was some change and conflict, and a broadening of outlook, and now the war is much more real and I guess I've got a better, more human outlook and attitude. But I still haven't changed a lot of my basic political views. I've got to place them both side by side until they harmonize.

One thing you may find hard to comprehend is why people do things like giving blood to the VC. (By the way, I've never done so, but that is just a quirk of circumstance.) Please believe me when I say that farthest from their mind is any wish to do harm to the GIs. There is a feeling of such tremendous guilt and shame at being an American, and supporting (through taxes) an unjust war, a civil war, in which America should never have involved itself. People feel guilty about the bombings of the North, the villages bombed by mistake, children, etc. They feel that there is no adequate care for them, that this will do something to counter it.

The argument against doing this—that it's hurting the GIs—well, I guess any help, even the saving of non-soldiers but supporters of the other side *is* hurting the GIs. But the government also says that stopping the bombing, peace demonstrations, protests, all of these things are aiding the enemy and hurting the GIs and maybe it is. And they even say that now that we're in, we're in, and we've got to go further in with our air support or else we're letting you down. But I still do believe that the only way to end the war is to END IT, that is by ending U.S. involvement. The horror of it all is that no matter what we do, innocents are getting killed—GIs, kids, etc. I have no idea if you will understand all this, but I have great faith that you will, and that you will understand that we are all so torn, never quite knowing (as you said) if we are right, or more right than wrong. Oh, I'm beginning to get incoherent—it's nearly three a.m. I hope I haven't been overly vague. I guess I meant to be a bit vague....

9 AM I guess what I was trying to say was that one can have two views which are contradictory—that one's feelings about people on the barricades may conflict with one's logical analysis, that where one stands politically may conflict with where one stands personally. Please, please do not get too upset over this. Somehow I know you won't—and that you won't still amazes me. Anyway, take care,

yours,

Margot

P.S. You have reassured me about the operation. I'm not as worried as I was. Margot

Returning Home

NINETEEN SIXTY-SEVEN was the year of the first really massive antiwar demonstrations. It was the year that activists adopted the slogan "The streets belong to the people" and the year that draft cards were burned by the thousands. It was also in 1967 that activism and street theater merged: Jerry Rubin appeared before the House Committee on Un-American Activities dressed in the uniform of an American Revolutionary soldier, and the Yippies threw five-dollar bills onto the trading floor of the New York Stock Exchange, causing a frenzy and stopping the ticker tape. Father Philip Berrigan and three others poured blood over military draft records in Baltimore. The year began with the First Human Be-In, when twenty thousand hippies came to Golden Gate Park in San Francisco.

Despite still being something of a left-wing nun, I was there at the be-in that January, distributing copies of the *Berkeley Tribe*, an alternative newspaper, and listening to music. As I looked up at the podium, where Allen Ginsberg was chanting his poetry, I saw the black-jacketed Hell's Angels standing on top of the speakers, arms folded, silent and impassive, exuding an arrogance and macho that no one acknowledged at the time, any more than we admitted that the warrior stance and stead-fast gaze of the Black Panthers were macho. In theory, the Hell's Angels were guarding the sound system from those who re-garded the hippie fest as dangerous anarchy. Cups of fruit juice laced with acid (LSD) were offered everywhere, and it felt as if everyone except me was experiencing some partially drug-induced feeling of community, although I am sure that hun-dreds of the rainbow-hued, perhaps even thousands, were, like myself, simply *passing*.

By 1966, in Berkeley it was normal for students to smoke mar-ijuana on weekends, even in our co-op, which was relatively staid by Berkeley standards. At the same time, I remained terri-fied of LSD and secretly believed that I would go crazy if I took it, that my deeply flawed true self would surface and reveal it-self to all. I also remembered that my oh-so-liberated mother had once told me that there were certain limits to freedom, that she was still the keeper of my health and she would have me hospitalized if she ever discovered that I was taking acid. Outwardly I argued and raged at her; inwardly I shared her fears. Perhaps it was because I had watched my mother "go crazy" and attempt suicide, and thought that if so strong a pres-ence could so easily succumb, I was certainly at least as vul-nerable.

But since some of the "grass" I smoked in college had clearly been laced with stronger stuff, I had a few genuine psychedelic experiences even without knowingly ingesting LSD. One night, returning to my room stoned on grass, I gazed at a pic-ture of Karl Marx and watched the image change into Ho Chi Minh, and then into Santa Claus. I looked into a mirror and saw myself transformed into a skeleton.

I was as intrigued with drugs as many of my peers, but my caution and determination never to lose control shielded me from much careless experimentation. Marijuana did seem to enhance all the senses, especially smell. One night, after a few tokes at a co-op pajama party, I noticed scents as pathways, as I imagine wild animals do. And as I lounged around in my pajamas with my friends, I suddenly was aware of a zigzag scent leading from my nose to my friend Zana's armpit.

Although I was terrified of LSD, I resolved that I would have the courage to take it by the time I was twenty-five. I actually wrote this down as a New Year's resolution several years in a row. But I was determined to wait until "set" and "setting" were perfect, and since they never were, I soon amended the resolution to say that I would try LSD by the time I was *thirty*. In fact, I waited until I was thirty-four. And when I tried it the experience was benign.

But that lay far in the future. In Berkeley in 1967 I found the hippies self-indulgent and decadent, and yet I envied them their freedom. They were the other choice. And they were everywhere—so ubiquitous and persistent! They kept peeking through the letters Marc and I wrote, joining us in our dialogue, calling out to us, perhaps even mocking us: Look at us! Relax! Don't take yourselves so seriously! We're here, the other option—the one you're not even considering.

September 29th, 1967

Dearest Margot:

Only a few minutes. Have gotten all your cards and letters. They're keeping me going. I don't know how you time it, but the popcorn arrived when I needed it the most.

The Battalions have been hit hard lately. I'm at my old job again ... "attached to 1/27th" for portions of this operation ... they needed someone with experience to carry the old man's radio. Assholes! That is just why I shouldn't

have to. I think I told you the fellow who took my place
was hit the first time out. Last night 1/27th had 22
W.I.A's, 3 K.I.A's. Every time these simple *!@*!@ing lifers go near the Cambodian border they get burnt. The
VC have been dug in there for twenty years. The first
K.I.A. last night had 47 days (or so). Yech. I don't know
why I am telling you this. I haven't written 'cause I've
been too pissed off to write you a letter like you deserve
... so what do I do when I do have time!

Gotta go. Thank you for mail. I'll write whenever possible. Yours,

Marc 28! (Good grief—my heart is fluttering!)

October 2nd, Monday

Dearest Marc;

Back in Berkeley—tired. Walking around from office
to office, picking up forms, going to classes, not sure of
which, what and how. Looked in the mailbox ... but I
should give it a couple more days before I start officially
worrying. I keep on telling myself there are three or
four good reasons why there is no mail: you are out on
that operation, the mail was really slow during the last
operation, maybe they hold up letters until the whole
thing is over, you weren't sure of my address ... but sub-
jectively I fantasize all kinds of other reasons: something
happened—the worst—but then, wouldn't my letters
come back? But maybe they wouldn't.

Berkeley seems more populous than ever. I have never
seen so many people. I saw the lines at the bookstore and
ran.

I'm feeling rather empty, voidish, wondering how you
are, what you're thinking, what twenty days left feels
like.

October 3rd, 1967

Yay! a letter and everything is all right (except that bit about the 1/27th), but almost everything.

Hey, did you read about the guy who wrote on the back of an envelope that he wanted to puke on the President and the FBI investigated him as posing a threat to LBJ, because "if enough people puked on the President, it could kill him." No kidding. Button of the week: Come back, Truman, all is forgiven!

Things are happening fast here. There is a big teach-in scheduled and Stop the Draft Week. Everyone seems to be on edge, except my roommate who just got off the phone talking about a cooking recipe. She has no position on the war at all, and thinks that "well, maybe wars are natural" ... God, am I intolerant! Will continue this later.

Margot

October 9th, 67

Dearest Margot:

Thanks for so much mail.

Saw a show tonight at our club. Two beautiful girls, dancing, band. Naturally the troops were animals. I'm getting so goddamn sick of GIs—eating with, sleeping practically on top of 'em, shower etc. Ten minutes of privacy is impossible—and I used to hold it sacred—before....

What does it feel like to be short? It doesn't. I don't sincerely believe I'm leaving yet. Not 'til the plane is a few hours away. I also don't believe (realize) I'm getting out. I'll be in for ever. Not 'till death—couldn't be so lucky, FOREVER. I've been in the army all of my life! And I'll always be in. I don't know what I'd do were they to

extend me. I'd secretly kill lifers. That's right. I'd be a
lifer killer. Then I'd mutilate the bodies and mail 'em to
the Joint Chiefs of Staff. I'd also get in cahoots with the
VC. These miserable rats crawl out of the swamps in
Louisiana and think the Army (tenement) living is
pretty groovy.

Nice letter, huh? Should I call you from Oakland—or
wait 'til I get to Berkeley? Climbing the walls tonight—
for some unknown reason. Will muster everything I can
to try to write a decent letter tomorrow night. Be good.
Take Care,

Love,

Marc

October 9th, 1967

Dearest Marc;

This letter is going to be a kind of Berkeley equivalent
to your GI's letter to wife or girlfriend that you sent me
a long time ago:

I didn't realize until last week the need for such a letter. I was talking with a friend who had spent a year in
France. She had been reading French newspapers and
her attitude about the war was very informed, but she
looked at the war as someone who hadn't been here. Her
view was very hard. I found myself very restrained, talking very softly, painting grays. Then we went to her
friend's house and sat around with some other people
who were discussing the draft, and I kept on imagining
that you were in the room, as you might be soon and
how I imagined you might react to some of the things
that were being said.

Coming to Berkeley is going to be a shock—interesting, exciting, perhaps sunny, mild, beautiful as well, but a

shock. Not only because suddenly the whole atmosphere is going to be militantly against the war, but October 16th is going to be Stop the Draft Week, with massive protests to try and stop the Oakland Induction Center from functioning. There will probably be arrests. October 16th is also the day that a group of people have decided to turn in their draft cards and refuse to cooperate in ANY WAY with the selective service system. They are going to send back all mail directed at them, and are willing to face arrest. This group is probably not going to be enormous, but it is nationwide. These guys are pretty militant and because they are willing to give up their deferments I admire them, but people who have decided to put everything at stake aren't always tolerant of others.

I said to one of these guys in the group RESISTANCE, "Look, I just heard you say some eloquent and sensitive things, but don't you see that many of the soldiers are trapped?" And he became very quiet and said, "Yes, I know ... but you see, we handed out a statement to people saying that they would refuse deferments and would refuse to go, and two thousand people signed it, gave their names and addresses. Later, when we went to each and every one, hardly anyone would go through with it. So we get cynical and elitist. We have to see it this way ... we are, so to speak, your Viet Cong, your hard core, your cadres."

No one knows what is going to happen during Stop the Draft Week, but tensions will be high, and some of the attitudes will be hard. Today, at a rally for Stop the Draft Week, Don Duncan, military editor for *Ramparts* spoke. He was with the special forces and was seven years in Vietnam. He said some pretty strong stuff: that one has to make a conscious effort when one gets out, that anyone who thinks that the army hasn't changed his thinking at all in subtle ways, won't be able to see that it always does a little. You might have found him hard to take. Then you are going to come across open and active support for the NLF and that may be hard. It's easy to label them as communists, but most of them are not. There are also a couple of Negro guys who sell the little red book of Mao's quotations straight from Peking. I guess if you survived a year in Vietnam, you can survive a while at Berkeley.

Love,
Margot

The meeting of the group Resistance affected me greatly, and I only told part of it to Marc.

It was very different from any political meeting I had ever attended. They spoke very softly, slowly, and personally. No slogans. They were disgusted with the left groups in Berkeley and their concern with theory and strategy. They had determined to free themselves from the oppression of the selective service system. They said that those who took drugs or starved in order to flunk the physical were still "theirs." What they said made sense to me, for I knew that the draft forced men to stay in school and to choose certain fields while in college, thus achieving through "democratic" means what was policy in totalitarian countries.

It was all so moving. The men said that they had decided to start with the totality of their own lives and to act in a personal way against the machines of the state. And their first act was to refuse to cooperate with conscription.

But then the resisters said a most disturbing thing. It was this: Every man has thought at least for a moment, even if only when drunk or high, about refusing to cooperate.

Berkeley was a scary place, they said, because everyone would agree with what they said but few would really commit themselves.

I found this subtle elitism hard to handle. Here they were saying, in effect, that all the guys who aren't with us have made their choice. All I could think of was Marc, who seemed no more worthy of condemnation than myself. We were both so innocent and so guilty.

October 16th, 1967

Dearest Margot;

If I am not out of Cu Chi (and at Long Binh) on the 26th I'll know for sure that I'm not really in the Army. I'm dead! And actually I'm in Hell ... for eternity! Destined to keep going home in two weeks. I'll just keep going home, and going home and going home ... in two weeks. Ayyyyy!

Got your letter of the 9th. You devoted a large portion of it to readjustment, which the only thing I am sure of is that there will be one....

In truth, I must say the topics taking up 98% of my thoughts are things like toilets that flush, hot and cold running water, sheets, milk, a back rub (where I can find one), food—as much and as often as I want. (I lost 30 pounds carrying the radio in 1/27th.) Females to see when I choose to look. As you notice, most of my dreams are of the basics, the "small" things. I'd want to just lay on a bed, in some motel—and watch TV, order pizzas (every hour), have a few Vodka gimlets or Black Russians. Go to the movies, and possibly between popcorn runs I could watch some of it. Take a bath! Good grief—you think! What a simpleton! Anyway, there will be a reasonable amount of time allotted to such things.

I believe you know I'll leave country on 27th—11 days. Not much else. Am smoking near two packs/day now. Shamming and all now that I'm clearing post.

Yours,
Marc

October 18th, 1967

Dearest Marc;

ugugugugugugugugug! You probably read some stories in the news that may have had some vague relationship to what happened in Oakland this morning. I wasn't there, but I have read a number of stories and got reports from many people I know who were there. It was pretty rough. Several of the CBS newsmen got beaten up and therefore they were pretty accurate about what the police did. One guy had a rib broken, and I guess newsmen protect their own. There was tear gas. Tomorrow should be more of the same. I think I will bury my head in my studies and forget about the world.

Before I forget: phone 5492713. It is going to be strange crashing illusions. I am desperately trying to be as pessimistic as possible, to play everything down, to not have any illusions. But I know I have many. I live so much of my life in fantasy, perhaps because reality is so much harder.

I want to meet you so very much and yet I am so very afraid—because maybe communication will be harder and at least with letters there is the illusion of it being easy, and illusions are at least better than nothing, they provide a way of not facing the abyss.

Please don't get upset ... I am planning to go to the

Oakland Induction Center tomorrow. Thinking muchly
of you,

Margot

October 20th, 67

Dearest Marc;

I think I write more mental notes to you than real
ones, and they change in mood as the hours pass, and it
is only by chance which one actually gets written.

I distinctly remember the tone of various mental letters today, the one at 5:30 a.m., at 8 a.m., 5:30 p.m. and
now, and all are so different. I don't mean to say that I
am constantly composing letters, not whole ones ... just
pieces. Maybe I even compose them in my sleep!

Whatever you heard on the news this week—forget it.
I was just listening to the news and they called the demonstration in Oakland the most violent and riotous of the
past week. I admit that it was probably hard for the newsmen who were running around to understand what was
going on, and why the demonstrators were so elated, why
they considered it such a victory, even though not much
happened. I'm not even sure I can put it into words.

4:00 A.M.: I awake and dress. All is quiet. Beautiful
night. A few people appear sporadically, cars pick them
up, beat-up V.W.'s, a sports car, station wagons. The streets
look empty. No one waits for more than a minute, there
are always rides, a slow steady stream. Carol, a girl from
England, and I get into a V.W. truck, too many people get
in and the car won't move, so we get out and into another
car. We drive through deserted streets—the radio is
tuned to an early morning program where a patriotic organization is interviewing the Oakland police.

5:00 A.M.: LaFayette Park. It's depressing. There is a

sickening feeling that it is going to be bad. Sheep to the slaughter. Some group is handing out a leaflet saying that there has been no provision for peaceful pickets. I see a few familiar faces. I feel there are only a few people, I feel despair.

Blank sheets are handed around to write your name and address on, who to contact for bail. I don't plan to get arrested but I fill in the sheet: provision for the unknown and unplanned, for who knows what will happen? About 10% of the people have brought motorcycle helmets for protection, or improvised versions. A few have invented shields, anything from foam rubber to wood and cardboard with slogans on them: "patriots against the war," "Che Lives." A large jar of Vaseline is passed around—protection against mace, which the police used on Tuesday. Supposedly the Vaseline causes the gas to bead and drop off. The Vaseline is greasy. There is a pile of hastily made peanut butter sandwiches lying on a bench. Carol and I share one. It tastes incredibly good. Anything would.

Monitors for the demonstration are telling us the plans. It will be different this time, they say. No sit-ins, no blocking, instead there will be many mobile, flexible groups who can move quickly, and when the police move in, we will move the other way, split, reform, and go in another direction, come back ... it all seems to be a peaceful version of guerrilla tactics. But at 5:15 A.M. it is still dark and nothing will dispel the sickening feeling of despair. There are now more people, but that doesn't seem to matter.

It is getting lighter, but it is still quite dark. I am walking around with a certain "Frank," who was a student in a class I was taking last year. He's the one with the "Che

Lives" shield. I think I am following the shield, not
Frank. It seems a symbol of safety in the face of the unknown. At the corner, near a parking lot where all the
police seem to be assembled, is a large and not so flexible crowd. We decide to leave this group of people in favor of a more flexible group. Various groups are circling
various intersections. It's impossible to get any feeling as
to size, number, area, mood. We get into a circle of
people that seems to contain the best and worst of the
lot: the worst being the black Maoists, who seem to be
everywhere, wrecking things. They call themselves the
"real" communist party; they follow Peking, and almost
all of them seem to be black. I always get the feeling
when I see groups like these that they are really FBI
agents who want to screw up the works. Across the
street is what some people are calling "a peaceful picket"
but everything seems rather peaceful at the moment. In
fact, there aren't the "violent" and the "non-violent," as
the press would have you believe, only the mobile and
non-mobile.

Later, I walk around, and hear a police chief say there
is an unlawful assembly here, there is a plea for dispersal.
It is now light and suddenly I begin to recognize loads of
people, people I haven't seen in months: my professor of
political science, ex-jailmates, suddenly many more
people than before. Sunlight is dispelling fear. I walk another block to a coffee stand and buy coffee and two terribly gooey and fattening donuts. I walk around, meeting people, walking on again.

It's 7:30 a.m. and I am at a main intersection. The
whole atmosphere has changed. The intersections seem
blocked. Several people have donated their cars and put
them in the intersection and let the air out of their tires.

A couple of cars *not voluntarily* donated are also in the middle. Besides the moving circles of people in the intersection, and the cars, there are cement benches, and garbage pails. Some cars are trying to get through, most are let through after a short argument. Incidents that could have happened, don't. There are several pro-war people standing around with signs, even walking through the crowds. There is no heckling by either side.

9:00 A.M.: Everyone is relaxed. There are news reports that they have called out the national guard, but it never actually happens. What happens is hard to describe, different people see different things. But where I am there is this weird feeling of hope, so absent this year. The police move, but there is no panic. The call of the day is "don't panic, hang loose, be flexible." And suddenly there is this feeling that we aren't a hodgepodge of very separate groups fighting each other, and the strangest feeling comes when we look at the intersections, not one, but six or seven, and realize that it is almost 10 AM and the buses have not come, or tried to, that the intersections have held, and no one has been hurt.

On the news I heard that one or two people were beaten and I saw one guy arrested, but everyone—the police, the demonstrators—seemed restrained. The police sent for reinforcements and finally there were enough police to do what they needed to do and they simultaneously moved in all directions. There were walls of police and the people moved back slowly, no riot, just slow walking. There were finally enough law officers to form lines at each block so that people couldn't come back to areas they had been pushed away from, and finally, at about eleven, the two buses carrying employees of the Induction Center came through. Soon after, there were five buses of inductees. When I saw the 6:00 p.m. news, they showed the guys getting out of the buses. A couple of them were with us—you could tell by the *V* sign for victory, which is a standard sign in radical movements. After that, dispersal was quick. I gather that within an hour everything was back to normal.

I guess you are wondering why it was considered a victory. What was accomplished, after all? They got 10,000 people. They shut down the center for four hours, shut down much of downtown Oakland as well, and it was pretty peaceful. That's all.

I think the elation came because 1. The day contrasted with the previous four days of despair and the fear of the early morning. 2. A feeling that the demonstrators were taking the initiative, not the police. 3. There was a calmness and rationality and unity to the movement, militant but not hysterical. 4. That the threatened split between the militants and the peaceful picketers never happened. 5. While there was no victory as the press and public understand it, there was a whole new sense of tactics, and there was the sense of a valuable lesson, a step in some process of growth.

I started this letter at 7, now it is the next morning. I came home, flopped down on the bed and was *out* until five PM, clothes and all....

October 22nd, 67

Dearest Margot:

Finding difficulty holding pen, so in a short while I won't be able to read this.

Got yours of the 19th today. Regret very much that this Oakland stuff is pissing me off. The reason is nothing but selfish—admittedly, but while I'm there I'd be

awfully goddamn mad if the functioning was interrupted enough to cause me to stay in there an extra day
… or 6 hours … 3! These next few days will be miserable,
exhausting; processing here (5 days), processing Long
Binh (2 days), Travis, Oakland and the nights sleepless.
That has already begun. When I get to US of A. only one
thing will be on my mind—Getting out as soon as possible. It is weak to take such an attitude, but if I am delayed, I won't be in any mood for harassment when I do
walk out. Understand? I hope so. It is like making a long
journey and then being locked out at the end. Savvy?

I know well what you mean about our communication. I don't expect anything insurmountable, tho. I've
found your letters very stimulating, unique, etc. I've
been in awe (periodically) at how closely we do think.
They have often been worn, much more so than you
think or will ever know.

Unfortunately I didn't write sooner. I feel I know you
intimately—and have for a long time. I realize these past
few months have flown by for you (vacations, etc.), but I
have the advantage here.

"… creating illusions" Already in for a letdown huh?
Don't take it so seriously. I suspect we'll both be (unnec-
essarily) working to "enjoy" each other (as it will turn
out). I hope I don't have to visit you in Jail. I have this
"thing" about Federal Institutions! Thanks for letters.
FIVE DAYS!!! It's not real!

Yours
Marc

                          Undated but clearly late October, 1967
Dearest Marc:
Can't wait to meet you! Even if you end up hating me.

And we sit across from each other at a table and don't know what in God's name to say to each other. Don't worry, I'll let you be alone, flush toilets, sleep, take baths, watch TV, order pizza, and I'll even do the hardest thing of all (for me), stay off the political. Sometimes I find it hardest to talk about the simplest and most vital things.

Pinch yourself! It's really true! It is really honestly over and you're almost on the plane!! All and Everything,

Margot

I sat around waiting. When Marc arrived in San Francisco, he sacked out for almost a day, then waited until the guys he was with had left. When he called, he had a deep and resonant voice. There were no awful pauses, perhaps because I kept asking questions like "Did you have your pizza yet?" It turned out he had been living on thirty-one dollars a month in the army so he could send money home to pay for the Triumph he had been dreaming about during the whole year. He was waiting for his money order.

On Tuesday I hopped on a bus after my 11 A.M. class to go to San Francisco. I must have been half out of my mind because I left my sweater on the bus. He was staying in a cheap motel in North Beach. I no longer remember its name. There wasn't even a mirror in the hallway to make sure I looked okay. I went to his door, thought "Here goes," and knocked. First shock: he was six-foot-three! With his short, sandy hair and his army uniform, he looked very straight but nice. We went for coffee, walked to Fisherman's Wharf, went back to his motel room and ordered pizza. We were friendly, polite, strangers to each other. The beings whose souls and hearts had cried out to each other remained silent. He kept the TV on, but we didn't watch it much. We drove around in his new

Triumph a bit, until we came to a motel on San Pablo. Then we drove to Berkeley, and, somewhat in a daze, I picked up my nightgown and a toothbrush and a comb and we drove toward the motel.

I was not sure what I was going to do. I was twenty-one years old and I had not had a single joyful sexual experience. My sexual encounters with three different men had ranged from disastrous and unfinished to mediocre but endurable. I was convinced that I was flawed, that he would flee the minute he truly saw who I was. I was also madly in love with this soldier who had written these outpourings from the heart, these cries from hell. I knew that this obsessed correspondence had been the first real passion and love of my life, and here I was facing someone who seemed like a stranger, as I must have seemed to him.

I also knew that I could not be dishonest with him. If I shrank from his caresses and kisses, and said nothing, I would hate myself forever. I had always been repulsed by guys coming on strong and fast, kissing passionately before I knew anything about them, and I knew that I would always regret it if that happened with Marc.

When we reached the motel the oblique language of the letters continued in life; he said nothing direct, just, "You'll have all the privacy you want." And then I realized I'd forgotten to take my birth control pills, which I had begun taking the year before despite few opportunities to put them to the test. Perhaps my forgetting to take them was some inner voice expressing my fears that sex would sully this meeting, or perhaps it was an even deeper desire to throw myself into the maelstrom and lose, for one minute, my iron sense of control. I had just finished my period and so my chances of getting pregnant were low. But I didn't know how low, and abortion was still illegal. I was well aware of the old joke about being "a little bit pregnant."

The motel room was stark and simple. I was wearing jeans and a turtleneck, and suddenly I felt myself getting tired, always my most effective way of dealing with sexual insecurity. I lay down on the bed fully clothed. He lay down beside me and we talked. And he started very slowly, caressing my shoulders, and I waited for that familiar moment when I would feel funny inside—the memories of all the times in my life that young men had started "making out," so gently for the first few moments, but then too quickly pressing forward. I remembered how many times I had stopped them, and how frustrated they had become when I didn't want to go the distance. They were always so hasty, these young men, always two or three steps ahead of me, intensely pushing forward while I was so very slowly opening toward discovery and intimacy.

There, in that motel room, I waited, wondering how I would feel, but never once did he push me. For an hour or so we lay there in our clothes and then, at the very moment that his fingers began to slip off my turtleneck, I felt some of those old, ambivalent fears and feelings, so I said that I was unsure.

He said that he wouldn't try to persuade me to do anything I didn't want to do, and that I could go just as far as I wanted, and I felt reassured. He seemed to know every right word and gesture to make me feel secure. I couldn't believe, given his experiences, that he could be so incredibly gentle in every word and move. He had "been around," as they say; I remembered the passages where he described paying three dollars to find a bit of comfort and home in the local village, and his hands and his body seemed very sure. But it wasn't just that. He actually knew how to enter the timeless stream and to allow the world to dissolve, whereas I was always the tense and analytical one, never willing to simply slide into the feeling side of life. At one point he simply said, "Can't you see that you don't see the forest for the trees?" And it was true; I was always stopping because of some small thing or another, whereas he, despite the fears and shocks he had received, was able to be fully in this moment. And mysteriously, the moment when I was ready to say "no further" never came.

The next morning we got up and went out to eat pancakes, and later wandered around Sausalito, but in the daylight everything seemed more formal and restrained. The war came between us. The only time Marc was relaxed was when he was in his car or in a closed room. He really did prefer to sit in a public place with his back to the wall. He was uncomfortable with the slow meandering that was a staple of my life. He liked his steaks "well done!" whereas I liked them bloody. On the docks of Sausalito he tasted fish-and-chips for the first time, and he wasn't sure that he liked it. So we went back to the motel, watched TV, and went to bed.

Sex was different that second night. He seemed more remote and I was not as reassured. The next morning he told me he had five dollars left and he needed to go to Southern California, where he had some relatives and he could get some more money. He dropped me off at a breakfast given by some radicals I knew, and left.

After the breakfast, I walked home through the middle of Oakland, getting more and more depressed. Then I got angry at myself, realizing that I was now going to spend the next three weeks worrying if I had gotten pregnant. I started feeling anger at Marc for being so wonderfully reassuring. I got more and more anxious until I finally went to the student clinic; after hearing all the relevant data, a counselor told me that my chance of getting pregnant was only between one and five percent—somewhat reassuring.

Then I started replaying the last few days over and over, analyzing everything. In some ways I felt I knew less about

Marc now than I had known before. Was he always strained around people? After all, his letters had stressed, over and over, his devotion to privacy. Or was he experiencing the effects of the War? Or just the shock of being back? Now that he was gone I felt empty, yearning for him. I knew that if he had said to me on the last day "Come with me to Chicago," I, who had always been so carefully controlled, would have thrown up my life and left Berkeley a year before graduating. But nothing was said. I did receive a short note: "I found it very natural to express affection with you."

November 11, 1967

Dearest Marc:

Question: Are you bored? Depressed? Smoking more now and enjoying it less? Staring out the window? Lethargic? Horny? Having that sinking feeling in the pit of your stomach that you are supposed to be happy ... and wondering why you are not? Are you thinking, "I'm out of the army, what more could I want?" And yet wanting more? Wondering if there isn't something wrong with you?

Well ... Cheer Up! Because, it is a known fact that after WW2, GIs came home and after the first elation spent months on their front porches staring out the window, not wanting to do anything, or go anywhere, feeling low and not understanding why.... So, if you are in a similar situation, you can rejoice in the not very consoling fact that you are NORMAL. Thanks, you say.

You are probably driving somewhere across the great expanse. This letter will probably get to Chicago after you arrive. It's infuriating! I have composed three long mental letters and they all flowed easily and this one isn't doing that.

I guess I am wondering who you are, and in a funny

way knowing less than I knew before. And I guess I am angry at myself for a lot of things, especially for doing and saying the things I told myself I was not going to do and say. I KNEW that you'd feel strained in Berkeley, and even wrote you a letter about it, and yet I wouldn't accept it. I know some people who lived in Mexico for many years, and when they returned to the United States they could no longer make small talk on the phone. I knew all this, and it didn't do me a bit of good. Still, way deep down, I wanted you to feel completely at home in Berkeley, with my friends, meandering around, and although I knew it was impossible, I wouldn't let it go, kept pushing things. Now there is nothing I am sure of except warmth, gentleness and kindness.

And yet for all that, Friday happened. Everything that happened was the exact opposite of what usually happens with me. Previously I've always run, doubted my ability to respond. So to feel the exact opposite … how beautiful. I don't want to put more of this on paper, it makes it small … and it wasn't.

I don't understand why Friday was beautiful and Saturday not, why Friday was mutual and Saturday seemed selfish.

I'm full of a lot of self-doubt now, wondering if you will want to write now … maybe now that you are back, it isn't necessary to you, maybe only a chore. Please be honest about that, although it scares me a little. Anyway, take care, hang loose, welcome home and if you are anything less than miserable and confused, you are doing well. I still don't know who you are and what you are. Remind me that I'm not supposed to and neither are you. I remain,

yours,
Margot

Soon after writing this letter, I dreamt that I was in Vietnam: It is hot and humid and so very green. I am standing up to my calves in water, in a group of rice paddies. I hear the whirrrrr of a helicopter overhead. I look up as it flies over me. Out of the window drops a letter. It floats down and zigzags in the air and I try to catch it, but it eludes my grasp and drops into the water. I pick it up and notice the address: it's from Marc. I open the letter, but the water has blurred all the ink and the writing is now illegible. I wake up and immediately think, That's it; Marc is out of Vietnam, but in some odd way I am still there, and it is I who now need his letters the way he once needed mine.

Marc entered school and then dropped out. He sold encyclopedias for a while to earn a living. We wrote, but the letters were brief and mostly unrevealing. Years later I found out that after a rough patch he had pulled his life together and was making his living as an environmental organizer. More than ten years after his return from Vietnam, he came to New York. We sat in my living room and I took out the letters. He had not seen them since Vietnam. I had been so obsessed with our correspondence that I kept carbons.

The two piles of letters lay before him, a pile of mine and a pile of his. He glanced aimlessly through the pile of my letters, not really looking at them at all, simply letting his fingers flip through the pages. Then I picked up one of his, one of the letters that still chills me. "Listen," I said, "do you remember writing this?"

When things get thick it is not the case ... that the troops are fighting for their freedom or Vietnam's freedom ... during these fire fights, each individual soldier is fighting for nothing but his life. During a pitch black night you are assaulted by hard-core troops from maybe 30–40 feet away.... For 72 straight hours ... [we] stood off 9 human wave assaults, fired $1/4$th of a million dollars in ammunition and defeated three regiments of suicide hard-core. No one in their own mind can believe that slaughter like that is right. The only thing that kept them going was that they believed if they pulled the trigger long enough and hard enough it would sometime be over and they would be a little closer to going home. To go home, what a strange motivation that is. . . .

And Marc said "Stop!" and pulled the letter away from me. "I thought I had it all blacked out."

On Unbecoming a Cadre

I N T H E spring of 1968 I was only months away from graduating from Berkeley without any idea about what I was going
to do in the future. Until then I had had only one real job—
selling housewares in a department store—and my confusion
about career had rarely bothered me. Jobs were plentiful, and
unlike the pressured students who enter college today, many
of us simply assumed we would find the right career in due
time. But I had begun to notice that compared to the budding
astronomers and engineers I knew, my career goals were desperately vague.

My family had certain convictions about which professions
were honorable; the others were seldom mentioned. It was honorable to be a doctor, an artist, a writer, a musician, a teacher—
to help people or to give a new vision to the world, preferably
of a world more sane, more just, and closer to the socialist ideal.
Later, in the 1980s, I would find it utterly incomprehensible that
students were flocking to business schools in droves. I had
never seen my father or mother read the financial pages of the
newspaper. In my world, business was never considered an
option.

The family held another unspoken assumption: Whatever

one did for a living, the underlying goal should be to change the world, to make it more human, to turn the world upside down if necessary until, in the words of a Brecht song, the hungry have their soup. Although I have since been influenced by Thomas Kuhn's *The Structure of Scientific Revolutions*, and have come to understand revolution as a shift in consciousness as well as in politics and economics, I still agree with my parents that a life not devoted to transforming the world is a life wasted. God forbid you should just have a job!

In the end I chose journalism almost by chance. One morning during my senior year at Berkeley, I turned on a radio station and listened to a news director read George Orwell's essay "Politics and the English Language." He talked about the Vietnam War and how the war's defenders were turning our language into Orwellian Newspeak; that it was important to call things by their real names and to describe them fairly. Such a simple and powerful idea. A year later I was living in New York, writing newscasts for WBAI-FM (one of the radical Pacifica radio stations) and getting a master's degree in journalism from Columbia University. I was also watching my mother die. Her lung cancer had been diagnosed as terminal, and her doctors had said she had a year to live. And since none of this had been told to her, I carried a harsh secret, one that was particularly burdensome for a daughter who had hardly ever kept a secret from her mother and believed in truth with a capital *T.*

At the same time, along with a friend at the journalism school, I was making plans to join the Venceremos Brigade, a group of American radicals who were going to work in Cuba for two months. We managed to get a professor to approve our journey as an honors project. I went in part for the adventure— even to travel to Cuba was illegal—but I also went to experience what a new revolutionary society would be like from the inside, what being a cadre in such a society would feel like, even for a limited time. And also, in the same way that young people travel to Israel to experience the kibbutz, I wanted to live in community with others and to share a life of common purpose.

Several of my mother's friends urged me not to go to Cuba. My mother was ambivalent. The cancer had left her much diminished. With radiation treatment, she was improving for the moment, but she was fragile and her fighting spirit was gone. Only Roz, a neighbor who lived two floors below and who was famous for holding fabulous parties for artists and intellectuals (the parties for Alger Hiss that I remember took place in her home), took the contrary position.

"I urged you to go," Roz said. "We all knew that if she was well she would have wanted you to go. I said, 'Look, if she gets worse, we'll send you a telegram, and Castro will send you home!' And then after you went I felt so guilty, because I had told you that Castro would send you home, and I made it all up." Rozzie behaves just like my mother did—she believes she can always go to the top.

The purpose of the Venceremos Brigade was to help Cuba with its ambitious, ultimately unsuccessful campaign to harvest ten million tons of sugar, Cuba's most important export crop. Organized by a group of American radicals and supported by the Cuban government, ours was the first of many groups of Americans who would go to Cuba to harvest sugar, pick oranges, construct houses, and help support the Cuban revolution. Then, as now, America waged economic war against Cuba, which had been crippled by the American trade embargo. Cuban cars were old and lacked spare parts, and Cuba was forced to sell most of its sugar to the Soviet Union. By helping in the sugar harvest we were defying the American embargo.

In those days, just traveling to Cuba was risky. The U.S. gov-

ernment had imposed a travel ban, and was stamping all passports with the words "not valid for travel to Cuba." (The dean
of the Columbia School of Journalism said that my friend June
and I could obtain special journalism visas from the State Department, but we both decided that we didn't want to be
different from the rest of the group.) One could only go to
Cuba from Mexico or Canada. In Mexico a government official
(was he CIA? we wondered) stamped each of our passports with
the word "Cuba" on the page facing the travel prohibition, thus
branding us as violators of American law.

We were a diverse group, this first Venceremos Brigade.
There were Quakers committed to total nonviolence as well
as at least a dozen Weathermen, who viewed their sojourn in
Cuba as part of an effort to recruit members for the coming
violent struggle back home. The Cubans viewed our vast internal political differences as irrelevant; just by coming to Cuba
we were breaking the economic blockade and showing sympathy to their revolution. Some of the Weathermen, however,
acted like missionaries, turning every conversation to the
question of our political salvation.

Our plane landed at Havana's José Martí airport late at night
on December 5. Five or six hours later, after debarking, processing, and a four-hour bus ride, we arrived at our camp ex-
hausted but exhilarated. Most of us had little need for sleep;
our group's median age was nineteen. So after breakfast at 4:30
A.M., we joined the Cuban revolutionaries in celebrating our
arrival with music and dancing. This created an impression of
our Cuban companions that stuck: they work hard, but they
can still dance; they are so full of energy they often can do
without sleep. An incident some weeks later reinforced my impression. After a bus ride of several hours, we arrived at our
destination for a meeting. But in Cuba, events did not always
happen on time. As we waited, a communist official sat by the

roadside, a few feet from our bus. He started to bang out rhythms with a spoon and a fork and a pot. In minutes others had joined him, and an impromptu, homemade orchestra played for about an hour, until the meeting finally took place.

Our camp was in Aguacate, a hilly area. Tall green stalks of cane stretched into the distance in every direction, relieved only by occasional lines of even taller palm trees. Conditions were fairly primitive. We lived in gray-brown canvas tents with double-decker bunk beds. The days were hot, with temperatures in the eighties. The nights were bitterly cold, occasionally near freezing, and we often slept fully dressed in work pants, socks, and anywhere from one to four sweatshirts. I draped my winter coat over my one thin blanket.

Every morning we got up before dawn, took a cold shower, and ate a light breakfast of *café con leche* and a roll. We collected our machetes and large clay water jugs, and went out to the fields. We wore boots, straw hats, work gloves, and protective eye covering. When it rained the fields turned into a red-brown ooze and we returned caked with mud. When it was dry, passing tractors would kick up clouds of red dust. We worked in the cane fields until a mid-morning snack, called a *merienda*, then worked until lunch, took a long afternoon lunch break in the heat of the day, and worked until sunset. Dinner, like lunch, consisted of rice, beans, soup, potatoes, yucca, and occasionally some fish or meat, along with tiny cups of sweetened coffee. In the evenings there was time to relax and for films and concerts by local musicians. Many Cuban artists had contributed work to the camp, and paintings and posters were everywhere.

We were taught how to cut and pile the cane. The top part of the stalk was left behind for local farmers to feed to cattle. The rest of the stalk was cut into several pieces. We stacked the cane in piles of 750 to 1,000 lbs. A tractor with a forklift would

then load the piles into trucks that would transport them to
the nearest sugar mill. At first the men cut and the women
piled, but after a feminist rebellion we could choose either
task. I did both, but often I piled the cane, along with many of
the other women.

But before we began our first day of work, we were taken to
a factory to watch the cane being processed into sugar, molas-
ses, and other by-products. We watched it change from juice
to powder and we came to understand the all-too-important
place of sugar in the Cuban economy. We saw how the sugar
was packaged, transported, and sold for hard currency and
goods. We came to know the price of sugar in various international markets, how much money each ton of sugar would
bring, and what products Cuba would buy with this money. We
viewed charts that showed us how our own brigade's efforts fit
in with the national campaign, and when we put all the details
together we understood not only the process, but also the con-
sequences of our daily activity—something few workers anywhere ever get to do.

Aguacate was cold at night, but by midday, working in the
fields, we were drenched in sweat. One very hot afternoon I
was gathering and stacking stalks of cane and I began to get
into a repetitive rhythm, up and down, bending, picking up,
bending, picking up. I fell into a light trance, singing to myself.
Then came a moment when I picked up a stalk of cane and
gazed at it, and in that instant, in my mind's eye I could see the
whole process at once: from my hand on the stalk to the growing pile, to the machines that lifted up the piles and put them
on trucks. I saw the cane carried to the factory and cleaned. I
saw the juice boiling in vats, and the juice turned into syrup
and granules. I saw the sugar poured into large sacks and the
sacks lifted onto railroad carts, just as I had seen in the factory.

Then, as images continued to flow by, I saw the bags of sugar arrive in Europe and the Soviet Union. I saw them exchanged for machinery and currency. Looking at a single stalk of cane in my hand, I understood how each motion I made fit into the larger whole. In an instant I understood Marx's notion of alienation and labor—how for most workers, unlike the artisans of pre-industrial societies, the product was divorced from the process of creation, and the work became meaningless and bureaucratic. In none of the jobs I had held in my own country— starting with my first job in Bloomingdale's three years earlier—had I ever understood how my own daily work related to any larger purpose. I suddenly knew that under the right circumstances I could shovel shit for a living and feel deeply connected. And that without such a connection, I could create a painting, build a skyscraper, or even fly a rocketship to the moon and still feel dissatisfied.

Several evenings before this magical instant, we were watching a film, *Hanoi, Martes 13* (Hanoi, Tuesday the 13th). In one scene, Vietnamese women, in groups of three, were constructing bomb shelters in the streets of Hanoi. The women carted bags of cement and mixed it in crude containers. The image stayed with me. In Cuba, Vietnam was never far from my thoughts, or from those of the Cuban revolutionaries; they saw Cuba, like Vietnam, as waging a war (albeit an economic one) against American imperialism. There were posters all over Cuba that emphasized this close association: a Cuban peasant standing in a cane field and above him, in a cartoon bubble showing his thoughts, a Vietnamese woman in a rice field, with a rifle slung over her shoulder; at the bottom of the poster was a simple phrase, *Como en Vietnam*—as in Vietnam.

One sunny day we even cut cane with a group of visiting Vietnamese soldiers—some from North Vietnam and some from the National Liberation Front (Vietcong) from the South. It was then two years after Marc had returned from Vietnam, and many nights after my dreams of illegible letters dropped from helicopters flying over rice paddies, and I had suddenly crossed the great divide between military enemies. I was standing, momentarily, on the other side.

Many of the Americans present cheered the Vietnamese wildly, some of them shouting with the Cubans: "One, two, three; many Vietnams," a slogan that meant that revolution should be spread throughout the world. I couldn't join them, but I understood their outburst. We all felt such guilt over the Vietnam War that many of us would do almost anything to assuage it. The Vietnamese soldiers were silent and reserved, and most spoke neither Spanish nor English.

At another time, on a dark and chilly night, our group visited a new Cuban town. We slowly trod a rocky path, our way lit by what seemed to be a thousand torches made from the stalks of cane. The torches spread out until they became diamonds of stars stretching out into the blackness. The town was Ben Tre— not Ben Tre, the provincial capital in Vietnam that was destroyed during the Tet Offensive, but Ben Tre, a tiny village of forty-two houses newly constructed by the Cubans for workers who labored in a cattle insemination plant. At the entrance to the village stood a statue of a Vietnamese peasant leading a goat.

During this visit we were shown a play and four short films about the Vietnamese, including one of Vietnamese children studying in the trenches and another of Vietnamese women practicing guerrilla warfare in the water. We toured a new store, a barbershop, and a beauty parlor. Then we walked into the new day-care center. It hadn't yet opened, but the teachers proudly showed us around. On the walls were pictures of children playing—Vietnamese children. Given this constant juxtaposition of cultures, and how strongly the Cubans were identifying themselves with Vietnam, what happened next was strange but perhaps not totally inexplicable.

It was another hot afternoon. I was working with two other women, piling cane again, getting into a rhythmic, trancelike state. I was thinking about those women mixing cement on the streets of Hanoi. My work of stacking the cane in piles did not seem so very different from theirs. It seemed almost natural to switch places with the women in the film. And for one timeless moment I did. As I sweated under the blistering sun, the cane fields disappeared and I was suddenly standing in the streets of Hanoi, the cane in my arms transformed into bags of cement. I was no longer myself. I was no longer in Cuba. I was a Vietnamese woman. *Como en Vietnam.*

I wrote in my journal, "To spend time in Cuba is to spend time in this odd, cosmopolitan crossroads that links Cuba, North Vietnam, rebel South Vietnam and much of Latin America." In Cuba, Vietnam seemed more tangible than it had in the United States. The Vietnamese working in the rice paddies seemed like brothers and sisters working under the same hot sun. They seemed like heroes and heroines who never got tired or stopped fighting. They seemed larger than life, people to look up to and emulate. The sugar harvest felt like a great war.

For example, a Cuban might claim that harvesting ten million tons of sugar (in fact, only seven million tons were harvested in 1970) would deal the United States a stunning defeat. In the United States such a statement sounded utterly preposterous, even insane. But in Cuba in 1969, I and others believed that the United States could be defeated by a successful harvest, just as it could be defeated by Vietnam. Each harvested stalk of cane felt like a blow against the great technological power that was trying to bring Cuba down. Cutting cane was empowering, and many of us who went to Cuba had not been feeling very powerful, for all our revolutionary talk and bravado. The Vietnam War was continuing to escalate, and nothing activists had been doing seemed to help. This feeling of empowerment, real or not, seemed to us like food and drink given to a starving person.

In the cane fields, among the cadres, it was easy to miss the other side of the Cuban revolution. And we of this first brigade were incurable romantics. Every morning I would read the official Cuban newspaper, *Granma*. When I had scanned the English-language version of this paper in the United States, it had seemed pure propaganda, filled with unctuous statements by party officials. But in Cuba *Granma* made sense. This was partly because the daily Spanish-language version of the paper actually contained real news, unlike the weekly English edition, which seemed to contain only official speeches welcoming various friendly delegations from socialist countries. But that was not the only reason.

I later noticed something curious. When I first returned from Cuba, the *New York Times* seemed like propaganda—I could pick out biased statements in almost every article. But within three weeks the *Times* seemed "normal" again, and several months later, picking up a copy of *Granma*, I was quickly aware of its flaws. Was I brainwashed in Cuba? No, but I had succumbed to a more subtle and universal truth: it is hard to dissent from the society you live in, particularly when you do it alone, without group support.

In the 1960s, revolutionaries formed collectives for precisely this purpose—to gather strength from one another so they could more easily act as dissenters within their own culture. But the collectives felt harsh to individualists and loners like myself, and they often emphasized "struggle" and the tearing down of individual self-esteem. Like many women, I had too little self-esteem to begin with and tended the little I had with care, so I refused to enter such groups. Later, in the seventies, the feminist and self-help movements developed more gentle ways to nurture dissent from mainstream views, through consciousness-raising and support groups. But even these groups were only partially successful. And later, as a journalist, I found I was constantly fighting against myself as I succumbed, again and again, to the official reality maps of the *New York Times* and the *Washington Post*, and even—gods help us—my current employer, National Public Radio. It is a relief not to fight, to accept the received truth, to fit in, to be normal, to unconsciously do what so many journalists do—narrow the definition of news until it is a thin band of the officially "newsworthy," and usually least interesting, parts of reality.

Some have suggested that people like me supported the Cuban revolution because while we were there we were limited in our sources of information. Objectively that was not true. Most of us had portable radios that could bring in half a dozen Miami stations with ease; and in fact the Cubans had a richer picture of North America than we did of Cuba, and they were familiar with the latest rock songs. But our sources actually *were* limited because we limited them ourselves. We preferred, by far, Radio Havana and Prensa Latina, with its wealth of news about Latin America and Africa. We found that most Cubans laughed at the Russians and focused most of their attention on their own continent. We found ourselves doing the same. One day when there was an electronic glitch and the news over Radio Havana was cut, an American *brigadista* (member of the Venceremos Brigade) said with a naïveté that seems poignant in the late 1990s, "Damn it, I know the people of the world are winning. I want to know how."

Many years later, when a thousand people were murdered in Jonestown, I found myself growing angry as one commentator after another talked about the poor demented souls that went to the shores of Guyana and gave themselves over to a cult. I found the smug sense of superiority of the news commentators offensive, because I knew a truth in my soul—I could have

been there, in Jonestown. What's more, I understood that almost any sensitive, searching person could have died there. Although I was turned off by gurus, includng Jim Jones, I understood immediately that many of those who joined his society
were seeking the same thing I had sought—and briefly
found—in Cuba: a revolutionary sense of community and purpose. One might argue that the Venceremos Brigade was just
another kind of cult, with Castro as its guru. The comparison
does not hold in most aspects; Castro did not live with us, he
made no demands, no one other than ourselves expressly censored our information. But the same passion was there. The
sense that life and work and purpose were integrated at every
moment gave us a powerful feeling of connection with each
other and with our daily work, and it also made us feel that we
were actors in world historical events. If the United States had
invaded Cuba during my time there, I, who had only shot a rifle
twice at a summer camp shooting range, might have willingly
and without much ambivalence laid down my life to defend
the Cuban revolution.

All that said, our Cuban socialist utopia was far from bliss.
There were painful political and cultural divisions, particularly along gender lines. As a result, although I was working
vigorously in the fields seven hours a day and eating mostly
rice and beans, I gained twenty-five pounds and was continuing to eat myself into hugeness. On some unconscious level
I knew that I needed to be a larger person to survive here,
that my mind would only be taken seriously if I was big
and ugly.

On the surface Cuban machismo was very much under
wraps at the camp. Apparently, the Cuban government had
even given a directive to the Cuban cadres to downplay sex
and gender issues. But that didn't mean that sexism was ab-

sent; I noticed that the prettiest women in our group were not taken seriously by the Cuban men. For example, one of the smartest and most educated of the women could easily have posed for a Playboy centerfold. She could outtalk me on Marxist theory any day of the week, and she couldn't get anyone to listen to her. I also noticed that relationships only went in certain directions: North American men and women went together, and Cuban men went out with American women. The Cuban women kept themselves apart. And so did I.

Crawling into my bunk after an exhausting day, I would often hear the sounds of lovemaking ten feet away. I found it hard to bear. It made me feel sad inside, tense and lonely. The noises were even harder on my friend June, who found sharing a tent with twenty women and the casualness about undressing and nudity difficult in themselves. A nudist at heart, I had trouble only with the sex, and that was because each night it forced to the surface my own feelings about the lack of love in my own life. These were feelings I would have preferred to remain hidden as I entered the world of dreams.

My friend and I asked for a meeting to discuss the issue of sex in the tent. We were in the minority. Later, several women who disagreed with our position decided to have dinner with us. They told us we were not being good revolutionaries, that it was "uncommunist" to be possessive of one person, and that we should understand the need to "smash monogamy." They told us that U.S. culture made us hate our bodies. As much as I agreed with this last point—my own body, getting larger every day, fast approaching two hundred pounds, filled me with revulsion—I didn't want to be told what to think. When I pointed out that the Cuban women seemed to be abstaining from sex, they said that the Cubans were in a different "cultural situation," meaning, I realized moments later, that the Cubans hadn't reached the exalted stage of liberation that the Americans had achieved.

We compromised. Henceforth, the men who slept in our tent would leave in the morning before the women dressed, and women who wanted to make love with the men could go to the men's tents. June and I found ourselves becoming closer to the Cuban women, whose prudish attitudes seemed for the moment closer to our own. One of the lessons of Cuba for me was that our "cultural revolution" was not the only path.

The political diversity of our group also caused problems. The Cubans (all of them *militantes*, young communists) seemed to have a level of unity beyond our comprehension. They looked at us with puzzlement when we spent ten days fighting over how to write a letter of support to the Black Panther Party after one of their leaders, Fred Hampton, was murdered in cold blood. The Weathermen held several stormy meetings to explain their ideas to the rest of us—college students, high school dropouts, Black Panthers, Young Lords, pacifists, GI organizers, and the many unaffiliated people like myself. At the one meeting I attended, people shouted and screamed at each other until 1 A.M.

Soon after this meeting, the Cubans showed us the film *Lord of the Flies*. In Cuba, *Lord of the Flies* seemed to be a completely different film than the one I had seen in the United States. The story I remembered was disturbing, about lost boys who become increasingly violent, disorganized, and irrational—a treatise on savagery and the frail hold of civilization over human nature. In Cuba, the identical film became a critique of our disunity and lack of discipline. The lost boys in the film engaged in silly actions; they let the fire go out, they hunted at night when you could not see, and, just like us poor Americans, they took meaningless votes (does the beast exist?). In Cuba, the movie seemed to be about us, the crazy, arguing North Americans.

The Cubans refused to hold political meetings of any kind, preferring to talk casually to us in groups of twos and threes, relaxing, sitting around a meal. But while the atmosphere at the camp was comfortable, I felt a pressure building up inside, as if the voice of Rayna Prome was urging me, once again, to devote my life to revolution. Everyone seemed to be responding to a similar inner urgency. Some expressed a new optimism, others spoke of a sudden need for seriousness, still others pushed themselves ruthlessly forward to become activists.

But this time, three years after I said no to the Communist Party in Berkeley, I did not have to confront anyone directly. My trip to Cuba ended abruptly. At lunchtime on the day before Christmas I was called to the central office, a small, white, wooden building with a few tables and chairs and one archaic typewriter. Boris, second in command at the camp, entered, sat down beside me, and took my hand; he reached with his other hand into his pocket for a crumpled piece of paper. The words were written in pencil and smudged—pens were scarce. "We have received a cable from our UN mission in New York," he said. "It says your father is very ill."

I looked at the crumpled paper and read, "*Su padre está muy gravo. Dos a diez dias a morir.*" Two to ten days to die. I began to cry, but I was also bewildered, since it was my mother who was ill. I wondered if I would be an orphan or if it was my mother who had taken a turn for the worse.

Boris held my hand and very gently told me that the biweekly flight to Spain had been delayed and would not leave until the next morning. This was a common occurrence in Cuba, but for all I knew the Cuban authorities might have delayed the plane until I was notified. "If you want to leave," Boris told me, "we will try and get you a seat on the plane." He told me to pack my bags and be ready.

I was numb as I walked back to my tent. I decided to go immediately, but June told me many years later that I seemed strangely ambivalent about leaving. During my time in Cuba I had lived in a strange state of denial over my mother's illness and my duty as a daughter. I knew that my mother, had she been healthy, would have told me to seize such an opportunity, but I also remembered that in her state of weakness and mental deterioration, she had expressed distress at my going. Mostly I denied my inner turmoil and the world of sickness and lies I had left behind.

As I walked to my tent, numb yet strangely aware, as one always is in those moments of crisis when everything around you slows down, I heard an announcement over the loudspeaker that there would be a general meeting in the recreation hall. It was the announcement that everyone had been waiting for. Fidel Castro would come to the camp the next day and spend four hours in the cane fields with us, then he would meet with us and answer questions. I stood apart as the room went wild. Everyone was clapping and shouting "Fidel! Fidel! Fidel!"

I walked back to my tent. It was empty. I reached behind the double-decker cots and wooden lockers and pulled my suitcase out onto the gravel floor. A small field mouse scurried past. I started throwing my clothes into the suitcase, not even bothering to fold them. Occasionally people entered the tent and I began to cry again. A young woman named Gay came in. She reached into her locker and drew out a checkbook. "If you can come back, I'll start a collection—I'll start a campaign tomorrow so that you can return." She tore off a check and signed her name. It was blank. "Take it," she insisted. "Just in case you need it." I knew she went to a fashionable women's college, but I had never even talked with her; I didn't even know her last name until I looked at the bottom of the check.

As I continued to pack, I realized that I had no use for most of my things. They seemed unnecessary and I started to give them away. Angela entered, a dark and striking Cuban woman who had an air of sadness about her, a loss somewhere. She was accompanied by Naida, a chocolate-brown woman whose face was sculpted but soft. I reached into my locker and found my two silk scarves. I gave one to each woman. This puzzled me, because I had always been a fairly possessive person and these were the most beautiful things I had brought to Cuba. Then I started divesting myself of everything. I gave away books and notebooks and pens, and mosquito repellent, and rubber bands and socks, both dirty and clean. I emptied the batteries from my tape recorder and gave those away too. Never had I felt so entirely unattached to material possessions.

When night came I couldn't sleep. I wandered around the camp, drinking *guarapo*, a sweet drink from the cane plant. Finally I eased myself up to my top bunk and lay there fully dressed. At 2:00 A.M. there was a scratch on the tent door. I jumped down from the bed and walked into the cold air. Two Cuban men were standing in the dark. They asked me what I was taking, other than clothes. Only two books and my brigade sweatshirt. They told me, "You must understand that when you go from Cuba to the United States, you become a diplomatic question. We want to avoid problems."

I was driven to the airport in an old yellow taxi with black checkers, like the old New York City cabs. We drove through miles of dirt roads bordered by cane fields, until we came to Havana and the José Martí Airport. It was Christmas morning. The airport was crowded. There were girls and boys in their Sunday best and workers in work clothes, grandmothers with large baskets on their laps and little children clinging to their moms. There were people flying to other provinces and exiles flying to Spain. Everyone waited patiently— the Cubans stood on so many lines that there was even a song that went something like "In Cuba, we line up for our food, but we don't live off others."

I had five hundred dollars in cash, but when I was handed my tickets the Cubans refused to take my money. The seats on the Cuban plane were small and the vomit bags were labeled in Russian. If safety instructions were given, I did not hear them, and people were smoking during takeoff. The food was incredibly good and so was the beer. The silverware came from other airlines—Avianca, Air Canada, Swiss Air, Iraq Airlines. But if you didn't look too closely, the knives and forks and spoons seemed to match—perhaps a metaphor for the whole country.

We arrived in Spain, where I boarded an Iberia jet for New York. Since it was Christmas Day, the plane was practically empty. The flight attendants were dressed in royal red, with matching caps and shoes. They carried trays of red roses with stems wrapped in silver foil. There were two roses for each passenger; by the end of the journey they had withered and died. There were maps to be read once and thrown away, disposable slippers, and postcards of the jet that would never be sent. I was assaulted by European abundance and wealth. I picked up my crumpled copy of *Granma* and started to read about the harvest. The entire paper was six pages long. I thought of a photographer I had met in Cuba who told me, "Often my pictures will not get into the newspaper because, with the shortages, there is simply not enough space." It was like traveling from Belzoni to Little Rock all over again. I had come out of one world into another all too quickly. Everything—the plane, the other passengers—seemed decadent to me.

The air was cold and damp and the skies were filled with sleet when I arrived in New York on Christmas night. I noticed the tall gray buildings on the way from Kennedy airport and the large posters with advertisements for cigarettes and Coca-Cola. The public propaganda that had surrounded me in Cuba exhorted me to *do* more, or to *be* more. This private form of propaganda seemed even more insistent, but I felt less included in the message.

My father was well, but my mother had worsened. The cancer had spread to her liver. Six weeks later she was dead. At home in New York, I moved about in a state of shock created by the combination of family illness, constant hospital visits, and the clash of cultures. When not at the hospital or back at Columbia, I retreated into my home, finding it difficult to walk outside. Advertisements were an almost bodily assault. It took a week for me to be able to go out easily, to read newspapers or look at television. Going into grocery stores took longer; I was shocked by the quantity of goods and I found that money felt foreign in my hands; I had not handled any in four weeks. I felt like an alien in my own culture and I wondered what place there was for me here. I wanted to hold on to the feeling that anything was possible, that the will of the people was greater than any technology. So when my father handed me an essay from the *Monthly Review* that suggested that moral incentives would not carry the Cuban revolution much further, I felt a flush of anger—although after I read it, a tiny seed of doubt began to flower.

During my first week back in New York I was mugged a block from my home. A group of six children—the oldest no more than eleven, but brandishing a tiny knife—demanded my purse. I had lived in New York City for most of my life, but I had never before been robbed. A week later my boots were stolen. I do not think these events were coincidental. Rather, it had taken only a month for my New York armoring to disappear. Gone was the brash swagger as I walked the streets, always seeming to be going only as far as the next doorway. Now I no longer belonged; I looked like an alien and therefore like prey. But slowly I returned to myself. Within weeks, my eyes were darting quickly, never resting too long on one spot, and I walked with confidence. I was also, once again, a citizen of the United States. I read the *New York Times* without dissecting every paragraph and I chose among twenty different shampoos happily, without comment. But I still vowed to return to Cuba.

Two years later I did return, with a group of some twenty radical journalists. On this one-month trip we planned to attend seminars on journalism in Cuba, tour the island, and spend a week exploring a Cuban media institution. Since I was working in radio, I would go to Radio Havana.

During those two years, my belief that I *should* be some kind of socialist revolutionary had not changed. But what I was actually *doing* was reading about nature and feeling a fear for the plight of the earth.

After a year at the Columbia School of Journalism and six months reporting on the New York Black Panther bomb conspiracy trial, I had taken a job running Pacifica Radio's Washington bureau. "Bureau" was something of a euphemism—it employed just one and a half people. I quickly memorized the names of a hundred senators and countless representatives, worked intensely, and ate constantly. I became even heavier than I had been in Cuba. I was way over my head in the strange land of Richard Nixon's Washington. On the outside I tried to look reasonably "straight" and presentable; I spoke softly and politely. On the inside I was raging. I was working in a tiny office in the National Press Building that Pacifica Radio shared with Seymour Hersh, the journalist who had recently uncovered the Mylai massacre in Vietnam. He told me that he couldn't imagine what I was doing in Washington, and said that I was clearly the type of reporter who would ask insipid questions at a White House press conference. I wondered if he was right. I ate even more.

I worked long hours and did an adequate but far from brilliant job. I reined myself in tighter than a drum, became an armored maiden struggling to be accepted in the world of Washington journalism but seldom daring to be creative.

The strange, unspoken sexual tension in the Washington of the Nixon years did nothing to make my job easier. One day I went for drinks with a young man who decided to give me a bit of advice. "You must understand the sexual mores of Washington," he told me. "Notice the skirt length." I looked and saw that the young women who staffed the congressional offices had skirts that were even shorter than the standard miniskirt of that era. "Thousands of girls come up here from the South," he said, "to staff the offices of Congress and the FBI. The ratio of men to women here is four to one. The women sort of function like Playboy bunnies." I no longer remember this man's name, or even what he looked like, but I remember that I tensed inside and vowed that I would be taken seriously no matter what the psychic cost.

Perhaps the moment that best symbolized for me my year in Washington was Tricia Nixon's wedding. For anyone who grew up after the Vietnam War, the feelings that Richard Nixon arouses in many members of my generation must seem incomprehensible. Even before Watergate we considered him a war criminal and a mass murderer. This was, after

all, the man who rained down bombs on Vietnamese peasants, mounted lethal incursions into Cambodia, called war
protesters criminals, and, in our view, by delaying the American troop withdrawal until after his 1972 reelection, was responsible for the death of many GIs and Vietnamese.

It had been raining in the Rose Garden, but the rain had
stopped. President Nixon came out of the White House to
engage in some light banter with the reporters, no words of
war or body counts today, just an ordinary father joking
about giving the bride away. As I stood there, outwardly polite, engaging in inconsequential talk like everyone else, my
hand accidentally and ever so lightly brushed against Nixon's
collar. For an instant I fantasized that I was a guerrilla fighter
sent to bring him to justice.

But instead I went on a reporters' tour of the White House,
one that emphasized the flower arrangements and the huge
wedding cake, which stood at least eight feet high. It was a
storybook cake of white flowers, frills, and spun-sugar love-
birds. As a compulsive binger, I quickly noticed that it was
my favorite kind of cake—one where the icing was dominant. As I stood there I had this incredible desire to dare one
revolutionary act—to just let myself fall into the middle of
the cake, and make a snow angel of icing. Or, if not that, to
at least dip my finger in the frosting, creating a long, thin
line. But instead I stood there, a model visitor. At the crucial
moment I was unwilling to do the outrageous.

In that noxious atmosphere of Nixon's Washington, a
world I so despised that I left it nine months after I arrived,
there was one bright spiritual flame—the ecology movement. A hundred activist groups were emerging, publishing
newsletters and staging actions. My personal ecological hero
was a person from Chicago calling himself (or herself) the
Fox of Kane County, one of the very first eco-saboteurs. The

Fox had a trademark: depositing excrement and garbage in the offices of polluting corporations. I loved the Fox so much that I had a rubber stamp made with the words "Support the Fox of Kane County," and I stamped this motto on all my personal letters. I knew in my heart that this eco-saboteur would have had no doubts about whether or not to fall into Tricia Nixon's wedding cake.

I had already read Thoreau, Rachel Carson, Marston Bates, and John Muir. To these I added Loren Eiseley, René Dubos, and *The Environmental Handbook*. One day I found John McPhee's *Encounters with the Archdruid* and Arnold Toynbee's essay "The Religious Background of the Present Environmental Crisis."*

As I wandered in and out of congressional hearings on the death of the seas and the contamination of the air, I noticed that my response to the nature writers was ecstatic, even religious. It went beyond politics. The idea that everything is tied to everything else in the universe seemed so true. The words of these writers touch on the deepest questions of meaning—who we are as human creatures and what our relationship should be to the cosmos, to the cycles of life, and to each other.

The idea of ecology as *religion* made sense to me. I read Toynbee's essay over and over. Toynbee argues that monotheism contributed to the environmental crisis by portraying God as "up there" and "apart" and we human beings as "below," that the biblical injunction to "subdue the earth and multiply" gave humans "license to exploit the earth." Older Pagan and animistic religions had a different notion of the sacred, said Toynbee, one that saw the whole world as vital and alive, and human beings as just one part of that sacred

* Arnold Toynbee, "The Religious Background of the Present Environmental Crisis," *International Journal of Environmental Studies* 3 (1972).

pattern. Toynbee's words pointed me to a journey toward the old religions of the earth.

As I searched for "an ecological religion," I began to dream of buildings crumbling. I wondered if these buildings symbolized the structure of Marxism I had relied on for many years to hold my moral world in place. From an ecological point of view, Marx was flawed—limited by his belief that human beings must conquer nature. As the buildings crumbled during my nights, during the days I wondered if I was a traitor to Marxism and the left by beginning to embrace ecology and, even worse, religion. But secretly I began to believe it was all of a piece. What, after all, had Marx meant when he wrote, "Criticism of religon disillusions man not so he is forced to wear his chains without the comfort of illusions, but so he may break the chains and pluck the living flowers"?* Couldn't the "living flowers" be a spirituality grounded in the real and material world, divorced from churches and official religion but tied to the living, sacred earth?

As I began to think about religious questions, I began to be at odds with much of the American left. For most of the left, religion was anathema and ecology was only a concern of white, wealthy liberals, a diversion from the important battles between workers and capitalists, or between black and white. Similarly, the Cuba to which I returned in 1971 was a poor country that believed in development at almost any price and rarely considered its cost to future generations.

1971 was an odd time to be in Cuba. American intellectuals were worried about Cuba's treatment of artists and writers,

* The most beautiful translation of this passage by Karl Marx is in Christopher Caudwell, *Further Studies in a Dying Culture* (London: Bodley Head, 1949), 75–76. For a more accessible version, see Karl Marx, *Selected Writings in Sociology and Social Philosophy*, trans. T. B. Bottomore (New York: McGraw-Hill, 1964), 27.

and about its persecution of homosexuals. In the United States the radical movement was in complete disarray. President Nixon had ordered the bombing of North Vietnam, yet there was little public reaction since large numbers of ground troops had been ordered home and the bombing seemed remote and abstract.

And this time I wasn't whisked out to the countryside for a stint cutting cane with gentle and earnest cadres. In Havana I saw a more complex world. I got pinched and jostled by Cuban men, which had never happened in the camp of the cane cutters. The Cuban attitude toward gays seemed very Catholic: gays are "anti-life" because they do not procreate. I began to wonder about other things. During a visit to a model mental hospital I wondered how many of the patients were being forced to take psychotropic drugs against their will.

But for most of the people I met, the Cuban revolution still worked. What I began to understand was that there were two Cubas—the Cuba of the revolution and the Cuba outside it. If you were for the revolution, everything worked. No matter what your job, or how hard the effort, there was an electricity in the air, a sense of community and shared goals. Sleep was often unnecessary, music and dancing could happen anywhere. But if you were outside of the revolution, like the two gay men I met on the plane going back, nothing worked. You noticed the shortages, and daily life seemed an interminable battle. Both Cubas existed side by side, often within a hundred steps of each other.

I spent a lot of time thinking about those powerful feelings of integration I had felt in Cuba during my first trip. How much of it was due to being in a socialist country? Or was it just that I was in a small country, doing a concrete task, with no machines between me and that task? Was the free-

dom I felt the freedom from possessions? Would a Cuban feel
an equal and opposing freedom in the United States—the
freedom from scarcity? Were we all oppressed by different
kinds of limitations, experiencing new types of freedoms
and new kinds of limits whenever we were transplanted into
a new environment?

In Cuba I met Arnoldo Coro, an engineer and an editor
on the paper *Juventud Technica.* For him, he said, the last twelve
years had been the equivalent of twenty-five for any normal
human being. Out of his graduating class of over two hundred young engineers, more than a hundred had left for the
United States after the revolution. For an engineer, to stay
after such an exodus meant doing literally everything. He
had run factories and sugarcane plants. He had been called
in to solve a thousand emergencies all over the country. "I
have grown more as an engineer than anyone could who
left," he said. For him the revolution was a blessing. But at
the same time, Coro was not a *militante.* When asked why, his
answer was simple: "If you are a member of the party and you
are asked to get on a motorcycle at a hundred and fifty miles
an hour, you do it. I want to know exactly what I am doing
and why! And I don't want to be in endless meetings." Coro
managed to support the revolution and yet live pretty much
the life he chose. He taught me some of the practical skills
of living in scarcity, like how to recycle a marker by re-
newing both the ink and the felt tip.

One day our Cuban hosts took us to an agricultural plant
where students were both working and studying. When
asked what they wanted to do with their lives, they said they
hoped to be doctors and teachers, but they added, always,
"Whatever the revolution needs, that's where I'll go." I
looked at these kids and wondered if they meant it. If they
didn't mean it, then they were living a lie, and if they did

mean it, then they were a different order of being than myself, so much less alienated and better integrated into their
society. As I pondered these questions I also found myself,
once again, using words like "honor," "duty," "educating ourselves." Cuba made you look at your work and your life
with seriousness.

The second week of our stay was devoted to lectures and
seminars. One of these—a lecture—would change me forever. The speaker was Angel Guerra, formerly the editor of
Cuba's youth newspaper, *Juventud Rebelde*, and then the editor
of a glossy monthly. He was a riveting speaker and he held
the audience spellbound. Even today, more than twenty years
later, I remember parts of the speech by heart because as he
spoke he laid my life out on the table and dismissed it. He
held up a mirror to my face, and, looking at myself, I knew I
would never be the revolutionary journalist he was calling
to action.

These people who sit in the cafes of Paris, people like Sartre,
who try and tell us how to run the Cuban revolution, you
know, they have never been very good Communists....

Are we to print Sartre's books? Are we to publish the Theater of the Absurd? Our newspaper often only has six pages,
because there is no paper. We need paper for our children's
textbooks. Those are our priorities....

Are we to publish books which lead to ideas of defeat and
demoralization, when we must build a Spartan youth, that
will be willing and able to face the military might of the
United States?...

A revolutionary journalist is first a revolutionary, second a
revolutionary, third a revolutionary, and finally a journalist.

As I listened to these words, I found tears coursing down
my face. I was breathing hard. I wondered if perhaps Camus
had felt like this during the Algerian revolution—with one

foot in France and the other in Algeria. For I knew, surely and instantly, that part of me would always want to sit in the cafes of Paris pondering the Theater of the Absurd or its equivalent, and that this pondering was and always would be a large part of who I was.

But, oddly, as I was listening I felt that I not only understood Guerra's position completely, but accepted it as the necessary attitude of a Cuban fighting for his country's life. I could see that in a world of such scarcity, freedom of the press was not absolute—other priorities might come first. I could even see myself through Guerra's eyes, as someone steeped in bourgeois traditions, making decisions based on an upper-middle-class sense of abundance that was totally absent in Cuba. I had the choice to be a revolutionary or to sit in that cafe.

And I also saw, really for the first time, that I would always be a person who debates these choices, who revels in the many layers of reality, who loves the way that almost every verity has many opposing truths, how the oddest oppositions can be synthesized and connected in new ways. And I understood that these differences are good, not something to get beyond, to overcome, to dissolve, to mend, in some battle to gain the one truth, the one religion, the one political system. That in fact, one of the great tasks is to help human beings feel comfortable in the complex and glorious chaos of this world, to help promote choices that aid potential, that promote autonomy, freedom, and cooperation, that allow people to feel whole despite doubt, to act fully and freely despite the uncertainty of being alive in this world.

Yes, part of the work I wanted to do involved fighting a war on poverty and exploitation and systems of caste and class. But the battles I would wage would be my own, under my own authority, not those of any party, or vanguard, or purveyor of expert opinion. For what I had done with the Communist Party in Berkeley, and had just done yet again with the revolutionaries in Cuba, was the most natural thing in the world. I had stepped up to the abyss, looked down, and stepped back again, rejecting all answers that did not come from skin and bones and my always ambivalent, continually doubting, heretic's heart.

Heretic's Heart

I'M RIDING on a bus through East Germany. It's 1973 and my revolutionary days are behind me, but somehow I have agreed to join a delegation of socialists and peace activists for a tour of the GDR. The bus is traveling between Potsdam and Dresden, and as I look out the window am I thinking about these historic cities and their fate in World War II? Or about communism? Not at all. I am debating about whether or not I am going to join a Witches' coven.

"You must be kidding," I think in my mother's tone of voice, although I then realize she would never condemn such a move. I remember the books on her shelves, *Zen and the Art of Archery* and *The Way of Zen* by Alan Watts. And I think to myself, "Once I almost joined the Communist Party, and once I thought the only honorable profession was to be a full-time revolutionary. Perhaps Marx was right, history first appears as tragedy, and then as farce. Here I am standing at the precipice once again, but this time I am asking: Shall I become a Witch?"

And then it hits me: if it doesn't work out, I could always leave! Why did such a simple thought never occur to me during my two other attempts to leap over the edge? Perhaps because in my family tradition Witches didn't even exist, so becoming a Witch couldn't have seemed like an act of commitment. Becoming a communist and ensuring yourself a large FBI file was far more serious, although the truth is that today both Wicca and communism can get you fired from a job, or give the other side in a divorce the ammunition it needs to win a custody battle.

My religious and political confusion had permeated my working life. I'd become sick of journalism, of reporting what the columnist Russell Baker dismissed as "olds": coups, tornadoes, disasters, crimes, political upheavals, wars. Like Baker, I sought "news": archeological finds, scientific discoveries, things we might actually care about in a hundred years or more. I desperately searched for the longer view, the more eternal. And I began to find it, through radio in the early morning hours—the most magical time of day.

It is 5 A.M. at the radio station. I am sitting in almost total darkness watching the dials in my solitary rocketship. It is easiest to invoke the dream state in this darkness that mimics the starry night, where instead of the points of light from planets and stars, the lights are the buttons and dials of this radio studio where I sit alone, the captain and engineer of this ship that makes a two-hour journey every morning. My rocket is named *Hour of the Wolf,* and just like the *Enterprise,* its mission is to explore new worlds. And in sadder, more reflective moments, I think that despite the moon landing and the hopes it raised, this is the closest I will get to the other planets in my lifetime.

The early hours of the morning, when most people are asleep and few are listening, and those that are awake may still be half in dream and reverie, allow conversations that would never even begin later in the day. During these hours people are willing to reveal their deepest hopes and fears in a state of innocence. The radio can allow imagination and fantasy to soar, perhaps by encouraging the same intimacy— imagined or real—that Marc and I created in those letters that crossed from Berkeley to Vietnam and back. The thing about radio, as Tony Schwartz, the public relations genius, once said, is that "people were born without ear lids." Unlike television pictures, sound flows all around us, and the flood of images that come to us from those sounds is, in large part, our own creation.

Today we live in a world of strident talk shows, where received opinions on the state of the world are trumpeted back and forth, and anyone who might dare to unfurl a hope is quickly put down. But at WBAI-FM in the early 1970s, a period of wild and wonderful experimentation in free-form radio was taking place. Pioneers like Bob Fass, Steve Post, Larry Josephson, Liza Cowan, and others could open the phone lines and just let people talk, never screening a single call.

I've been given this two-hour slot because no one else is using it. I don't yet have the chutzpah to ask for anything better, but here I am free to try my hand, while I live on an unemployment check of thirty-two dollars a week. If the show's a success, WBAI will hire me back.

At five in the morning there is nothing that cannot be changed. Mostly there are questions and feelings and yearnings. Anything can happen. A story is read on the air, an interview is conducted. The phone lines are opened and anyone can turn the world upside down or at least change the ship's course.

A cab driver begins a show by calling in to talk about the day that passed. A science fiction story prompts a discussion on utopian and dystopian ideas. A woman reads a document called "The Asexual Manifesto" on the air, and calls from the solitary and celibate follow for days. I tell about my experiences with group sex, and another week of intimate conversation begins. Or I close my eyes and speak into the ether about my ambivalence about having children—my fear that I will be trapped in a system that I have always avoided; that my need to be accepted will triumph over my need for freedom; that I will be transformed into a Stepford wife; that having been an only child, I haven't learned how to take care of a child. The letters pour in; I read them on the air and the talk continues. Women call up with babies wailing in the background; some talk of the unexpected wonder of their children, the joy of participating in life and community, while others dare to ponder if they have made a huge mistake.

Over the course of three weeks, a friend and I read *Ecotopia*, Ernst Callenbach's underground classic, aloud over the air.

How many people are listening? Certainly thousands, certainly not hundreds of thousands, but the depth and intimacy of response is larger than one can calculate. I still have boxes of letters, multi-paged, single-spaced outpourings. Now, in the 1990s, several million people may listen to one of my reports on *All Things Considered* and I might not receive a single response. But in the 1970s, on that 5:00 A.M. show, it was possible to create a community of seekers.

I play with the occult; I invite palmists and astrologers to enter my spaceship. I remain a skeptic, although an astrologer tells me I will write a book before I am forty, and I do, and a palmist tells me my parents separated around age eleven, which they did. Psychics and healers enter my dark and starry studio. So do psychologists and anthropologists. The guests range from the brilliant to the appalling. Those on the edge of science come into my rocket ship—the creators of holograms, people who talk to plants, those who say they can photograph auras. I watch the psychic Yuri Geller read my mind as he sits beside me. Is he a fraud? Or does he augment his genuine talent by sometimes cheating? I'm suspicious of all systems, refuse all gurus, but believe that, at bottom, we are so much more than we think. I believe that Australian aborigines can smell water, so why shouldn't a psychic occasionally be able to read my mind? I do believe that all religious and magical systems contain a kernel of some ancient knowledge, usually encoded in an unacceptably authoritarian system.

The old Marxist inside me warns that all this religion stuff is an opiate, an oppressor. Sometimes it is. But I also know that religion means to "re-link" and that meditation and ritual allow me to enter timelessness and to encounter the real mysteries of birth, life, death, and regeneration. A teacher of "Mind Dynamics" tells me that "the little child who got napalmed in Vietnam *didn't have to be there if she didn't want to.*" "Boy," I rage, "these occult philosophies do let the anxious middle class feel secure with their privilege." I am desperate to understand the divide: where is spirituality liberating, where is it oppressive?

Science fiction provides a structure for my wanderings, and the writers troop into my cabin—Peter Beagle, Ursula Le Guin, Joanna Russ, Norman Spinrad, Samuel Delany, Robert Anton Wilson, and countless others. In the late twentieth century, theirs is the only literature of ideas we have. Dismissed as "genre fiction" while the literati spend hours reading books that do nothing more than chronicle failing relationships, science fiction explores everything from telepathy to politics. Nothing is taken for granted. Society, love, and work, even gender, are remade. There are anarchist and capitalist utopias, and worlds in which human beings travel faster than the speed of light, sport wings, and experiment with their own genetic engineering. There is always further, as the old sixties slogan said.

Feminism, from politics to sexuality, is also part of my world, and ecology and green politics and critiques of technology that say, Hold on!—you can't remake everything without destroying the earth! Theodore Roszak and Murray Bookchin make their appearance.

Amidst this explosion of variety in the early morning hours, is there any order? Very few things seem evil, except apathy. That which aids potential is good, that which limits it is evil. Creative order is good, as is creative disorder, as Robert Anton Wilson once said. Destructive order and destructive disorder are bad.

It is 1996. I am walking on South Road, in Chilmark, back on Martha's Vineyard. I pass the Abel's Hill cemetery, where so many Mayhews, Flanderses, Pooles, Tiltons, Larsens, Nortons—the old names of this island community—are buried. Lillian Hellman is buried here too, her small, thin black stone difficult to find, surrounded by shells. Most people come here to see the grave of John Belushi, and to participate in a ritual as poignant in its own way as the letters and flowers left at the Vietnam Wall. On the top of the rough boulder that marks his grave is a constantly changing altar created by people meditating on their addictions. This morning's collection is small: a beer bottle, two pennies (a potent symbol for our culture's greatest addiction), a cigarette butt, a piece of candy (ah, my own addiction), a wild rose (attended by visiting yellow jackets), some rocks, a clam shell. In the past, I've seen pills, rolling papers, a coke spoon.

The human tendency to connect to others, to ancestors, and to the cosmos through simple ritual, despite the stigma in our secular culture, amazes me. People create ceremony everywhere they go. Sometimes the occasions are obvious: the birthday parties, Thanksgiving dinners, and religious celebrations. Others are more surprising—just watch the thousands who hold up cigarette lighters in darkened rock concert cathedrals. Or, in New York City, on the night before Thanksgiving, when thousands gather in the streets to watch while the floats for the Macy's parade are pumped up with helium. As at some great Latin American festival, tiny children sit on their parents' shoulders or are held up to watch in awe as Superman or Spiderman or Snoopy begin to form from oblivion, a giant hand, a foot, a head, appearing as once did the gods of old. We can mourn that our cartoon gods seem lightweights in comparison to those of the Greeks, but people make do; they create gods from what they are given. And, as writer Patricia Monaghan once said, "Our culture doesn't encounter the mysteries very well—we do birth, death, even marriage very badly."

As I sit by this graveyard I think about how ritual allows us to enter a different realm, the timeless one.

The Old Left was so afraid of the irrational. Although many of my parents' friends stood reverent as they watched artists paint, or listened to a symphony or a poem, most were afraid to enter the artistic, dream realm themselves, and it is no wonder. My parents and their generation understood the misuse of religion, the self-delusion that leads to witchhunts. Dogmatists, many of them, they were also afraid they would be taken over, subsumed, overwhelmed, because in their world, everything is either/or. There is mysticism or rationality, good or evil, male or female, light or dark, Christian or Pagan. I've come to realize those choices never made sense to me.

I've been reading this manuscript to my father, who is past ninety, as he lies in a hospital bed fighting pneumonia. He has always been such a militant atheist and foe of mysticism that I can't think of any way to talk to him about death. I desperately want him to have a better death than my mother, who died in such confusion and pain. My father, who is still planning his lectures and seeing patients, tells me he wants to see the millennium, and, knowing him, I think he just might, but even that is just a few years away, the blink of an eye. I also know that if he wants to fight death every step of the way, that's his perfect right. But how can we talk about the mystery of wind, sea, fire, earth, the things we return to? Nothing in his culture will allow him to think about this ultimate mystery—or am I wrong, does he think constantly about the end, though he refuses to talk about it?

At one moment, his glasses off, his fever high, he hallucinates a beautiful painting in front of him, a man and a woman sitting together. His face lights up, as if he were a small child seeing his first rainbow. Eventually, when he puts on his glasses, the painting dissolves. But, clearly, it is beauty that is the most easily available mystery in our secular society—unlike religious ecstasy, it seems to come with few strings attached. But both reveal that the world is more than our daily experience.

Back on the Vineyard, on a sunny July afternoon, my four-and-a-half-year-old son is walking on the beach with a butterfly, a painted lady, on his finger. It had been lying on the shore, sand coating its wings, unable to fly. My son walks, keeping the butterfly on his finger. Later he carefully moves it to a towel. Several of his friends handle the butterfly with equal care. Finally, half an hour later, someone helps him to remove the sand, and the butterfly slowly moves its wings and flutters away.

The next day he reaches toward a small white moth and it allows him to pick it up. Is it concidence? My skeptic's mind says yes. Or is it mystery? Have the community of moths and butterflies communicated to each other that this young human is trying to be their friend? I want to open my mind to non-ordinary reality but keep the skeptic—a faithful friend who has so often protected me from self-delusion—by my side.

In our either/or obsessive world, people go from one totalistic belief to another, from one cult to another, from one religious or ideological war to another. Skepticism and mystery are sworn enemies. You are either a socialist or a capitalist, although the truth of the world is mostly mixed economies. You are either a skeptic or a believer, instead of having spiritual faith but being at home with constant doubt. This mentality works something like addiction—it's all or nothing. Either you think LSD will save the world, or you think everyone who takes it will lose his or her mind. But many people really can have a glass of wine without becoming alcoholics.

The world of the Old Left had great truths, but its principal failing was that it could not bridge these divisions. It was too afraid of the irrational and its pull, and it did not really understand the human need for the juice and mystery of ecstatic experience; it did not realize that one can enter the flow of the mysterious, the non-ordinary reality known to all artists, poets, and indigenous peoples without losing one's intellectual integrity; that one can dance round a bonfire until dawn and still make one's living as a scientist or a computer programmer; that one can work to end poverty and exploitation but still embrace song and dance and dream. Like shamans of old, we can attempt to maintain our balance as we walk in different worlds.

In my own life, I still begin each project with the question, What can I do to turn the world upside down, to question assumptions, to undermine received wisdom?

I have set aside the need for perfection. My relationship to my body and to food is healthier, but I accept that there will always be occasional binges. If I maintain the balance seventy-five percent of the time, I have finally come to understand, that is success.

My own evolution over the last twenty-five years, to embrace the earth traditions, the Pagan traditions, was partly a way to make my peace with the dreamer and doubter, this person who loved multiplicity, who would never be pleased with a single reality, truth, or map.

Though not for everyone, the earth traditions allow me a life of balance, and allow me to remain optimistic; they allow me the grace of perceiving the cup as always half full, never half empty. These traditions say that all is holy, the body, the mind, the imagination, birth, sex, death—and that the stuff of the sacred is all around us, right here, right now, in the material world. You don't have to die to get the good stuff— which doesn't mean that other worlds besides the material do not exist.

I know now that the mysteries are everywhere. It is not necessary to read a holy book, or hear a divine revelation; the mysteries are in seed and scarlet leaf, and in the *doing* which has very little to do with *believing*.

I am singing again, as I did as a child, and collecting rounds and chants. I have realized that chant and song is my pathway to the stars, and that I have a talent to bring others to share in ecstatic song, so that those who have been told they can't sing can throw caution to the wind and come into their own voice, to sing, to shout, to ululate, to listen, to explore, to experiment, to harmonize.

We sit in a circle and my friend Eclipse is drumming— the deep, sonorous sounds of the Jimbe, her arms strong and muscled from such continuous work. Others join with drums and bells and rattles. I am leading a circle of song. Then comes the lingering tone of a deep bell; then silence, candlelight, and sage. "It is time to remember," says Eclipse. And the women, and sometimes men as well, let imagination, fantasy, (or is it memory?) take them (forward? back?) to a magical place, and their voices call out to one another in the darkness:

"Bare feet on cool stone floors." "A canopy of stars." "A waterfall." "The sounds of crickets." "A procession of dancers with urns on their heads and snakes coiled around their arms." The voices continue to create a place for ceremony.

And then the chants—most of them from the various contemporary communities of women, Pagans, Witches, but also a sprinkling of songs from the East, and from indigenous people, all of them simple, so that it is easy to soar, to call and respond, to break into parts, to occasionally add drumming and dancing, and to learn, once again, what earth-based peoples have always known: that to sing something over and over for a very long time (long for us, that is, we who often grow uncomfortable when something lasts for more than fifteen minutes) stops the intolerable busyness of our culture, so that we can return to that eternal stream the ancients knew when they performed their ecstatic rites.

From coast to coast, the sons and daughters of immigrants are singing and drumming—in small groups and large, under trees, in churches, in living rooms. The sons and daughters of slaves are singing also. They are also reading, researching, writing, creating, rooting around in the ashes for something more. They know that their ancestors had rich traditions that were thrown away or destroyed by others. They also know some of these traditions were oppressive.

Their work may seem silly to outsiders, but they have taken on a huge task—to create anew what was lost, a vibrant culture, filled with songs, ceremonies, dances, lullabies, myths. To create such a culture—one that is rich yet at home with notions of individual freedom and modern life—what a Herculean task!

But a possible one. And as the last flames flicker out and the last tone dissipates, each person returns to their ordinary life with some small remnant of the incredibly subversive notion that the world and we can be transformed and reborn, that "we are as gods and might as well get good at it."*

Almost all initiatory journeys return to the beginning, and, as in the famous poem, the wanderer knows the place for the first time. The journey of this barefoot minstrel starts in the place where nature and music and mystery abound, and where talents and dreams flourish. Then, as in all such journeys, there is the exposure to fears and trials, and teachers both good and bad; there is the great toll that society and culture always extracts, the long time when dreams and talents and desires are submerged, and the ensuing struggle for freedom and values. At the end of my own journey there is a return to ritual and song.

I think back to that old school picture—the ten-year-old girl with the fake lute and the pageboy haircut, singing about a falcon's escape and yearning to be a minstrel, wishing to be like Constance Clume, giving courage to the troops as they prepare to fight for freedom. And I finally know to be true what I never believed before: that there really are minstrels in the world, perhaps millions. How lucky to finally claim my heritage as one of them.

---

* *Whole Earth Catalog* (Menlo Park, Calif.: Portola Institute, 1969), 367.

Acknowledgments

Thanks to the City and Country School for keeping me sane during the 1950s, and for fostering creativity and independence. To my teachers there, especially Gay Slaton, Mary Card, and Ruth Rafael. To all twenty members of the class of 1960.

To my friends and teachers at the University of California at Berkeley, especially Zana McCarty Miller, Kathleen Pullen, Sheldon Wolin, and Jack Schaar.

To my mother, Freyda, for writing those letters and giving me a zest for life.

To Marc Anderson, without whose scream from the abyss in 1967 this book would never have been written.

To the New York Public Library—both the Frederick Lewis Allen Room and the Wertheim Study—for providing a quiet place for research and writing.

To Wendy Strothman, the former director of Beacon Press, for reading the letters and seeing a larger book.

To Susan Worst, my editor at Beacon, for gently and skillfully making it a leaner and better book. To Chris Kochansky, for adept copyediting.

To the many friends who read the manuscript and gave

important advice, especially Ken Barcus, Kathleen Cameron, June Erlick, Lee Felsenstein, Alison Harlow, Bernie Hirschorn, Dena Levitt, Eclipse Neilson, Arnie Sacher, Caryl Wheeler, Willa Zakin, and my husband John Gliedman. Often, although perhaps not often enough, I was wise enough to incorporate the suggestions they offered. All mistakes remain my responsibility.

To *Star Trek: Deep Space Nine* and *Star Trek: The Next Generation* for allowing me to escape into a better future.

To my husband, John, and my son, Alexander, for allowing me to live in a surprisingly wonderful present.

INDEX